CU00686575

Leaks, Whistleblowing and the Public Interest

To Constanze

Leaks, Whistleblowing and the Public Interest

The Law of Unauthorised Disclosures

Ashley Savage

University of Liverpool, UK

Edward Elgar
PUBLISHING

Cheltenham, UK • Northampton, MA, USA

© Ashley Savage 2016

All rights reserved. No part of this publication may be reproduced, stored in a retrieval system or transmitted in any form or by any means, electronic, mechanical or photocopying, recording, or otherwise without the prior permission of the publisher.

Published by
Edward Elgar Publishing Limited
The Lypiatts
15 Lansdown Road
Cheltenham
Glos GL50 2JA
UK

Edward Elgar Publishing, Inc.
William Pratt House
9 Dewey Court
Northampton
Massachusetts 01060
USA

A catalogue record for this book
is available from the British Library

Library of Congress Control Number: 2016935782

This book is available electronically in the **Elgar**online
Law subject collection
DOI 10.4337/9781783474905

ISBN 978 1 78347 489 9 (cased)
ISBN 978 1 78347 490 5 (eBook)

Typeset by Columns Design XML Ltd, Reading
Printed and bound by CPI Group (UK) Ltd, Croydon, CR0 4YY

Contents

Preface

I first became interested in the topic of unauthorised disclosures by public servants after reading about Clive Ponting, the civil servant who leaked information alleging that the government had covered up the circumstances surrounding the sinking of the Argentinean cruiser, *General Belgrano*, during the Falklands conflict. He was acquitted of breaching the former Official Secrets Act 1911, section 2. The Act which replaced section 2, the Official Secrets Act 1989, is still in force today, however the momentum for unauthorised leaking and the methods used to disseminate the material are changing. In the new age of leaking, how can whistleblowers raise concerns in the public interest without breaching the law? What is the public interest and who should determine it? Are the accountability mechanisms in place adequate to provide an alternative to unauthorised disclosures? This book based, in part, on my Ph.D thesis, aims to answer these questions.

I have a number of people to thank. I wish to acknowledge the fantastic support I received from Edward Elgar, in particular, John-Paul McDonald and Elizabeth Clack, during the preparation of this manuscript. Thanks are due to Professor Brian Martin, Professor David Lewis and the anonymous reviewers who provided feedback and some excellent suggestions for structuring the work. Completion of the book would not have been possible without the support of Dr Richard Hyde, University of Nottingham, who read drafts, provided detailed feedback and continuously acted as a sounding board to discuss ideas. My thanks are also due to Professor Tim Wilson, Northumbria University, who read drafts and provided reflections, and to research assistants Sean Mennim and Mary McCloskey. During completion of the Ph.D at the University of Durham I was extremely fortunate to benefit from the considerable expertise of Professor Ian Leigh. I could not have wished for a better supervisor.

My final thanks are due to Mum for empowering me with the confidence to reach my goals and to Dad and Wendy for their support. Any mistakes in this text remain the fault of the author.

Table of cases

European Court of Justice

New Zealand

United Kingdom

United States

Republic of Ireland

Table of legislation

1. Introduction

The unauthorised disclosures by Chelsea Manning and Edward Snowden represent a significant turning point, indicative of a future whereby large quantities of official information can be leaked and where not only the disclosures but the discloser may traverse geographical and jurisdictional boundaries.[1] Despite this, the act of making an unauthorised disclosure or 'leak' of official information is not a new phenomenon. The United Kingdom has witnessed several high profile instances of leaking in the last 30 years.[2] The difference between then and now is that anonymous posting of brown envelopes containing photocopied documents to journalists has been replaced with memory sticks and online outlets to facilitate disclosure. As a consequence, the volume of leaked documents and an increased preparedness of outlets such as Wikileaks to publish documents in their pure un-redacted form has left governments and the organisations tasked with state security struggling to keep up.

The Manning and Snowden leaks provide a unique and unparalleled insight into the work of the Armed Forces, diplomatic services and intelligence services, respectively. The leaks also highlight the lack of transparency and oversight of these activities. Post 11 September 2001, there has been a marked increase in data collection and retention. Intelligence gathering and sharing has become increasingly reliant on a network of global partners.[3] Whilst such collaborative efforts act as a powerful defence against acts of terror, the actions present considerable

---

[1] For general reading on the background to the leaks see in particular Luke Harding, *The Snowden Files: The Inside Story of the World's Most Wanted Man* (Guardian Books, 2014); Glenn Greenwald, *No Place to Hide: Edward Snowden and the Surveillance State* (Hamish Hamilton, 2014).

[2] For coverage of unauthorised disclosures using traditional methods see further Nicholas Jones, *Trading Information* (Politicos, 2006), and Harold Chapman Pincher, *Chapman Pincher: Dangerous to Know* (Biteback Publishing, 2014).

[3] See generally, James Igoe Walsh, *The International Politics of Intelligence Sharing* (Columbia University Press, 2010) and Hans Born, Ian Leigh and Aidan Wills, *International Intelligence Cooperation and Accountability* (Routledge, 2011).

challenges to the well-established rights to privacy and freedom of expression.[4] The threat of terrorism, at least from the perspective of the United Kingdom, can no longer be boiled down to a geographically fixed location. Terrorists can, and do, operate across multiple jurisdictional boundaries, by physical movement and by their usage of electronic communication. Moreover, individuals may increasingly become radicalised without needing to leave the comfort of their own homes. The emerging threat of so-called 'lone wolf' and 'self starting' terrorism is now a reality in the United Kingdom, placing intelligence and police agencies with finite resources under greater pressure than ever before.[5]

The Snowden revelations, in particular, identify a key problem with unauthorised disclosures, particularly where they impact beyond the domestic jurisdiction. Whilst acts of spying may be legal and otherwise accepted on justifiable policy grounds by the government and intelligence services in one jurisdiction, such acts may be in breach of another country's laws or accepted standards. As unauthorised disclosures become a globalised issue, a government employee faced with a crisis of conscience must make a judgement as to whether they should leak the information, raise the matter through official channels, or keep quiet. A leak of information may be perceived by the individual to be the best course of action in order to ensure that the concern is addressed. However, in turn, the act can also place the employee at the greatest risk of prosecution. Leaks of information impacting on multiple jurisdictions are particularly difficult to judge. Whilst the alleged activities uncovered by the leaks may be morally justified to some, they can be morally reprehensible to others. An act may be illegal in one jurisdiction and legal in another. Unauthorised disclosures of any kind frequently polarise

---

[4] ECHR, Arts 8 and 10. Note that the Investigatory Powers Tribunal made its first ruling against the intelligence and security services in an action prompted by the Snowden revelations: *Liberty (National Council for Civil Liberties) and others* v. *Secretary of State for Foreign and Commonwealth Affairs and others* [2015] IPT/13/77/H.

[5] A distinction highlighted in a report on the murder of Fusilier Lee Rigby by the Intelligence and Security Committee. The Committee acknowledged a new threat where simpler unsophisticated attacks involving few individuals were difficult to detect. Intelligence and Security Committee, *Report on the Intelligence Relating to the Murder of Lee Rigby*, HC-795 (2014) 237. The threat of lone wolf terrorism has been used to bolster support for increased electronic surveillance powers in the United Kingdom. For general analysis of the topic see Jeffrey D. Simon, *Lone Wolf Terrorism: Understanding the Growing Threat* (Prometheus Books, 2013).

opinion. How can the public interest in the disclosure outweigh the national security justification in keeping the information secret?

Not all work carried out by public servants concerns national security and not all unauthorised disclosures concern national security information. Not all disclosures concern information regarding wrongdoing or malpractice, some concern information regarding a course of action to which the discloser does not agree. Leaks can be released to representatives of an opposing political party to serve as ammunition to gain political advantage at the dispatch box.[6] Leaks can originate from key government sources, some motivated by career ambition with the ultimate aim to usurp authority;[7] others may be officially sanctioned, seen as the best possible way to reveal information to the public without an official announcement. Not all unauthorised disclosures, whether concerning policy matters or national security issues, will be met with the same response. Unauthorised disclosures by members of government and other high level officials are acted upon very differently to unauthorised disclosures by Crown servants.[8] Crown servants face the risk of prosecution under an arguably draconian and increasingly outdated official secrets regime. Even where disclosures are made to a Parliamentary Committee, civil servants may face the risk of investigation using laws designed for countering terrorism and organised crime.[9] The use of

---

[6] Christopher Galley provides one such example. Galley leaked documents to opposition MP Damian Green, both were arrested and the charges were later dropped; Deborah Summers, 'Damian Green leaks civil servant sacked', *Guardian*, 24 April 2009.

[7] In the Westland affair, Leon Brittan instructed an official in his department to leak parts of a letter to undermine fellow Cabinet colleague Michael Heseltine; for discussion see Dawn Oliver and Rodney Austin, 'Political and Constitutional Aspects of the Westland Affair' (1987) 40(1) *Parliamentary Affairs* 20.

[8] For example, disclosures by Claire Short regarding allegations that the United Kingdom spied on then UN Secretary General Kofi Annan did not lead to prosecution; George Wright, Martin Nichols and Matthew Tempest, 'Short Claims UK spied on Annan', *Guardian*, 26 September 2004. Bob Quick, Assistant Commissioner of the Metropolitan Police, allowed himself to be photographed holding a document marked 'SECRET' whilst walking into Downing Street. The contents of the document were visible and prompted the need to bring an anti-terror operation forward. Quick resigned and no further action was taken; Rob Edwards, 'Bob Quick resigns over terror blunder', *Telegraph*, 9 April 2009.

[9] Osita Mba, an employee of Her Majesty's Revenue and Customs (HMRC), made disclosures with regard to the conduct of tax investigations to the National Audit Office and two Parliamentary Committees. Mba was then made

authorised alternatives can provide an answer to this quandary of unauthorised leaking, yet the effectiveness of official mechanisms and the laws designed to protect whistleblowers remain a source of criticism and review.[10]

The purpose of this book is to consider the law of unauthorised disclosure from the United Kingdom perspective. Whilst the text acknowledges that this is a fast moving area, in the United Kingdom very little legislative reform has occurred to the laws which govern the unauthorised disclosure of official documents and there appears to be a lack of momentum for change.[11] This book will therefore provide a thorough assessment of the relevant laws in the light of a new dawn of official leaking. The text will provide an analysis of the law relating to the protection of journalistic sources, with an emphasis on new media outlets; it will consider the impact on secrecy laws, and it will provide case studies of three distinct areas, the UK Civil Service, the Security and Intelligence Services and the UK Armed Forces. These case studies endeavour to provide analysis not only of the unauthorised routes to disclosure but also consideration of authorised whistleblowing mechanisms. The text hopes to take a contemporary approach by considering not only what should happen to an individual as whistleblower but also what should happen to the information. Comparative examples of current laws and practice in a number of legal jurisdictions will be provided throughout the narrative.

This introductory chapter will define terminology before proceeding to consider well established theoretical justifications for public interest expression as well as the justifications for keeping information secret. It will draw upon sources of direct relevance to unauthorised disclosures and whistleblowing in order to provide a framework to test the adequacy of the various laws and procedures in place in the UK jurisdiction.

---

subject to an investigation by HMRC officials using authority obtained under the Regulation of Investigatory Powers Act 2008.

[10]   National Audit Office, *Government Whistleblowing Policies* (2014), available at www.nao.org.uk/report/government-whistleblowing-policies/.

[11]   Where the intent to legislate in this area has been identified it has been left to the common law to rectify anomalies. For example, it was reported by the Intelligence and Security Committee that the government intended to amend the Official Secrets Act 1989 to remove the common law defence of duress of circumstances. The Committee identified in its subsequent report that the judgment in *R* v. *Hasan* [2005] UKHL 22 had removed the need for amendment. See further, Intelligence and Security Committee, *Annual Reports*, Cm 6864 (2005–06) and Cm 7299 (2006–07).

I TERMINOLOGY AND FOCUS

This text will consider the position of public servants who are designated as Crown servants by Official Secrets Act 1989, section 12. The section includes persons employed in the Civil Service, security and intelligence services and Armed Forces. This will be the main focus of the narrative. The book will also discuss Ministers of the Crown, where appropriate, as Ministers are also covered by the definition. For reasons of focus the book will not be discussing the role of police officers or government contractors.[12]

The term 'unauthorised disclosure' is featured in various sections of the Official Secrets Act 1989.[13] In this text the author will use the term beyond the confines of its usage in the Act. The book will be discussing other Official Secrets Acts of relevance and will further be discussing the common law offence of misconduct in public office, as well as the civil tort of breach of confidence. It is therefore appropriate to define the term as simply, 'any disclosure without official authorisation'. At various points in the narrative the terms 'leaking' or 'anonymous disclosures' will be used. This will refer to instances where disclosures have been made to recipients who do not know the identity of the recipient. This should be contrasted with 'confidential disclosures'. Confidential disclosures occur when the identity of the individual is known to a journalist, investigator or conduit and information is then imparted to the general public as the recipient audience without disclosing the identity of the communicator.

The term 'whistleblowing' will be a constant feature throughout the text. The term has undoubtedly received increasing prominence over the last few years. Despite this, there is no 'universally accepted' definition.[14] In academic research, Near and Miceli define whistleblowing as: 'disclosure by organisation members (former or current) of illegal, immoral or illegitimate practices under the control of their employers to persons or organisations who effect action'.[15] The Australian Senate expanded on this to include 'a person or agency capable of investigating the complaint

---

[12] For discussion of whistleblowing and unauthorised disclosure in the police see Ashley Savage, 'Whistleblowing in the Police Service: Developments and Challenges' (2016) 22(1) *European Journal of Current Legal Issues*.

[13] See e.g., Official Secrets Act 1989, ss. 1(4)(b), 2(1)(c), 3(2)(b), 4(2)(b).

[14] David Lewis, 'What is Whistleblowing?' in David Lewis (ed.), *Whistleblowing at Work* (Athlone Press, 2001) 1.

[15] Janet Near and Marcia Miceli, 'Organizational Dissidence: The Case of Whistle-blowing' (1985) 4 *Journal of Business Ethics* 1, 4.

and facilitating the correction of the *wrongdoing*'.[16] Some definitions are particularly restrictive, requiring that disclosures must be made within the public domain.[17]

The types of information which may indicate an act of whistleblowing has taken place and what might constitute the 'public interest' is more difficult to define. In UK legislation, the Public Interest Disclosure Act 1998, which provides employment protection for those who engage in acts of whistleblowing, contains an overarching (but not defined) public interest requirement as well as limiting the types of disclosure to a number of distinct categories which relate to risks to health and safety and the environment, miscarriages of justice, breaches of legal obligations, or a cover-up of any of the matters listed.[18] There is an inherent difficulty in restricting analysis of whistleblowing by Crown servants to the aforementioned categories. This is because disclosures may be made to the public domain which are of a high value to the public interest but do not indicate wrongdoing or malpractice *per se*. Vickers provides a distinction between what she calls 'Watchdog Whistleblowing' and 'Protest Whistleblowing'. 'Watchdog whistleblowing' requires the individual to disclose misconduct or wrongdoing, whereas 'protest whistleblowing' may relate to disclosures of information or policy which, whilst not unlawful, the individual raising the issues has the necessary experience to suggest that the policy complained of is the wrong course of action.[19] It is suggested that situations may arise where it is difficult to ascertain whether or not the action complained of constitutes wrongdoing. It is therefore sensible for the text to encapsulate both the watchdog and protest definitions of whistleblowing whilst highlighting the distinction where appropriate. On occasion, the term 'whistleblower' has been used to describe members of the public, operators of conduit organisations and journalists. For the purpose of this book the author will use the term 'whistleblower' to refer to workers. This chapter will now consider the theoretical arguments relevant to the making of disclosures.

---

[16] Senate Select Committee on Public Interest Whistleblowing, *In the Public Interest* (AGPS, Canberra,1994) [2.2].

[17] Frederick Ellison, *Whistleblowing Research: Methodological and Moral Issues* (Praeger, 1985) cited in Peter B. Jubb, 'Whistleblowing: A Restrictive Definition and Interpretation' (1999) 21 *Journal of Business Ethics* 77, 91.

[18] See Employment Rights Act 1996, Part IVA.

[19] Lucy Vickers, *Freedom of Speech and Employment* (OUP, 2002) 43.

II THEORETICAL JUSTIFICATIONS FOR WHISTLEBLOWING

General Freedom of Expression Theory

Before considering the theoretical arguments for whistleblowing, it is first necessary to acknowledge several justifications which relate to general freedom of expression theory. The first to consider is moral autonomy whereby all individuals must have an unfettered right to free expression. Consequentially, all matters of moral choice must be left to the individual who must decide whether their proposed course of action is right or wrong.[20] The justification is of particular relevance to Crown servants who ultimately choose whether or not to make unauthorised disclosures. However, upon entering employment, Crown servants are conditioned to be aware that certain forms of communication are restricted or considered unacceptable. From a practical standpoint, a new employee upon starting work in any organisation may agree to terms which may restrict his or her right to certain forms of expression to maintain discipline. Crown employees have additional responsibilities. Employees of the UK Civil Service must agree to the Civil Service Code which provides a contractual obligation not to 'disclose official information without authority'; this requirement extends post employment.[21] Employees of the security and intelligence services must sign confidentiality agreements. Service personnel are required to observe regulations relating to forces discipline. All of the above persons may be subject to the Official Secrets Acts.

Moral autonomy, whilst serving as an underpinning justification for unauthorised disclosures, does not account for the possibility of negative impact or harm to others. The argument from self-fulfilment suffers from the same difficulty. Crown servants in the United Kingdom are required to be apolitical; they can and do work for successive governments which are of a different political persuasion to their own.[22] The argument from self-fulfilment advocates that individuals may become active participants in the political process, allowing them to oppose actions which would be

---

[20] Helen Fenwick and Gavin Phillipson, *Media Freedom under the Human Rights Act* (OUP, 2007) 304.

[21] Civil Service Code, available at www.gov.uk/government/publications/civil-service-code/the-civil-service-code.

[22] Evidenced by Civil Service Code, paras. 12–15, which emphasise the importance of impartiality.

detrimental to their own interests.[23] Whilst Crown servants do not face an absolute restriction on being engaged in political activities, the machinery of government would ground to a halt if servants leaked every document with which they did not agree.

Justifications for unauthorised disclosure grow stronger when arguments also take into account the benefit of the communication on the recipient audience. Raz suggests that the benefits to others are the result of the benefit the right brings to the right holder. He identifies the argument that a person's right to freedom of expression is protected not in order to protect him, but in order to protect the public good, a benefit which respect for the right of freedom of expression brings to all those who live in the society.[24] Barendt, in contrast, identifies that a court determining a free speech case would not ignore the speaker's interest in the ability to communicate or share his ideas or information.[25]

The justification that freedom of expression is necessary to enhance the public good provides a strong justification for the communication of 'whistleblowing speech'. Indeed, it may be observed that whistleblowing laws focus upon acts of expression which are for the public good. The UK Public Interest Disclosure Act 1998 covers a number of broad categories whereby the disclosure of information may qualify for protection, including: a breach of health and safety; damage to the environment; a miscarriage of justice; or a breach of a legal obligation. This is further compounded by the addition of an overarching public interest requirement.[26]

In addition to enhancing the public good, expression can enhance democracy. The argument from democracy comprises of two essential ideals. First is the notion that citizens as active participants in the democratic process require information on political issues to engage in open debate and to make informed decisions, thus government should be accountable. Second, in a democracy the government serves at the will of the people. It is therefore vital that citizens have the opportunity to freely

---

[23]   Anthony Mason, 'The Relationship Between Freedom of Expression and Freedom of Information' in Jack Beatson and Yvonne Cripps (eds.), *Freedom of Expression and Freedom of Information, Essays in Honour of Sir David Williams* (OUP, 2000) 237.

[24]   Joseph Raz, 'Free Expression and Personal Communication' (1991) 11 *Oxford Journal of Legal Studies* 303, 305; for an alternative view see Frederick Shauer, *Free Speech: A Philosophical Enquiry* (CUP, 1982) 105.

[25]   Eric Barendt, *Freedom of Speech* (OUP, 2005) 13.

[26]   Inserted into Public Interest Disclosure Act (PIDA) 1998, s. 43B by the Enterprise and Regulatory Reform Act 2013.

communicate their wishes to the government of the day so that its actions accurately reflect the will of the people. The argument places considerable emphasis on equality by suggesting that citizens have an equal right to engage in public debate and exchange information and ideas.[27]

The sovereignty argument is not without its critics. Vickers argues that it does not provide an automatic guarantee to freedom of expression.[28] If this were the case, the electorate could opt for a government which doesn't uphold free speech or one which limits the expression rights of a minority group.[29] Vickers' solution to the sovereignty problem is to allow for wide debate of government actions, effectively enhancing democratic accountability.[30]

The argument from democracy provides a strong justification for whistleblowing disclosures by public servants who can make a valuable contribution to the accountability process. However, if sovereignty is about control, one must consider whether ultimate power resides in the hands of the electorate or in the hands of elected representatives. Fixed Term Parliament Act 2011, section 1(3) dictates that a general election will be held every five years. Public debate may ultimately influence decisions made at the ballot box but it may not, short of a full-scale revolution, prompt immediate institutional change.[31]

As much as the argument from democracy can support public service whistleblowing it also identifies a fundamental problem. Sovereignty is about control: the executive and its departments maintain operational control of official information. Departments dictate the appropriate level of classification and can utilise a number of exemptions in freedom of information legislation to frustrate public access. The executive can control the expression rights of Crown servants. It can dictate what actions should be taken against Crown servants for leaking documents, often resulting in dismissal or prosecution. Conversely, it can decide a course of inaction where leaks originate from within government itself.

---

[27] Barendt, above n. 25, 36.
[28] Vickers, above n. 19, 24.
[29] *Ibid.* 24.
[30] *Ibid.* 25.
[31] By way of illustration, Fixed Term Parliament Act 2011, s. 1(3) dictates that a general election will be held every five years.

Unauthorised Disclosures and Whistleblowing

Bok provides a well-established theory concerning whistleblowing in the context of unauthorised disclosures.[32] She suggests that both unauthorised disclosures and authorised whistleblowing are similar in the sense that both modes can be used to challenge wrongdoing but they can also comprise of false accusations and personal attacks.[33] She recommends that society should draw distinctions between the types of information communicated, questioning its relevance to the public interest.[34] She suggests prospective whistleblowers must first consider whether the public is entitled to know the information in question or whether it comprises of personal information which should remain private; those who raise private matters on the basis that they are a threat to the public may voice their own 'religious or political prejudice'.[35]

Bok favours internal disclosure, at least in the first instance, because it can uphold loyalties owed to both the employer and citizens.[36] Therefore, public disclosures should remain a last resort, where there is insufficient time to go through proper channels or when the organisation is considered so corrupt that the whistleblower will be punished if they attempt to use the regular channels.[37]

Sagar provides a contemporary analysis drawing heavily on recent events concerning Wikileaks and examples from the United States.[38] He poses five conditions which he believes should be met before secrecy laws may be breached. The first is that the disclosure should reveal an abuse of public authority. Sagar recognises that an individual cannot be reliant upon their own interpretation of what wrongdoing means. He suggests that the way to rectify this is to concentrate on when the person exceeded the authority conferred to him.[39] Second, the disclosure must be based on clear and convincing evidence; as an unauthorised disclosure

---

[32] Sisella Bok, *Secrets: On the Ethics of Concealment and Revelation* (Vintage, 1989).

[33] *Ibid.* 219.

[34] *Ibid.* 219.

[35] *Ibid.*

[36] *Ibid.* 221.

[37] *Ibid.* 221.

[38] Raul Sagar, *Secrets and Leaks: The Dilemma of State Secrecy* (Princeton University Press, 2013) 129.

[39] *Ibid.* 129.

may place citizens in harm's way, the act will not be justified without providing convincing evidence.[40]

Third, the disclosure must not pose a disproportionate burden on national security. Sagar suggests that there may be circumstances, such as where the nation is at war or where diplomatic interests outweigh disclosure of an act of wrongdoing. He believes that only 'grave threats' rather than those which are 'vague and remote' can outweigh the disclosure of 'grave wrongdoing'.[41]

Fourth, the disclosure should be 'limited in scope and scale as far as it is possible to do so',[42] a criterion which relates to whom the disclosure is made. Sagar considers disclosures to senior officials and suggests that individuals should determine if it is possible to raise the concern internally and/or with the executive branch. They should consider whether the complaint will likely be heard, the risk of retaliation or that the evidence could be destroyed.[43] If there is a risk, unauthorised disclosures to the public domain may be justified, but he argues that as little of the information should be disclosed as is necessary to convince citizens that wrongdoing has taken place. Fifth, he argues that the individual must be willing to disclose their identity.[44]

Whilst Sagar's criteria are useful, parts of it do not readily cohere to the position of whistleblowers in the United Kingdom. With regard to Sagar's first criterion, the abuse of public authority, the United Kingdom has long encountered difficulty with identifying the limits of executive power. Executive power, unless expressly restrained by statute, is exercised under the royal prerogative. A quirk of the nation's un-codified constitution, it can be both indeterminate and unwieldy. Moreover, from a public law perspective, focussing on whether a member of the Executive has exceeded their authority would be covered by the principle of *ultra vires* in judicial review. This would not, however, account for other grounds of judicial review such as irrationality, disproportionality or a breach of natural justice.[45] In addition, Sagar's criterion are not best suited to disclosures relating to malpractice, i.e. those which concern not wrongful action but wrongful *inaction* or other working practices which, if not stopped, could cause

---

40   *Ibid.* 131.
41   *Ibid.* 131.
42   *Ibid.* 132.
43   *Ibid.* 133.
44   *Ibid.* 135.
45   As discussed in *Council for Civil Service Unions* v. *Minister for the Civil Service* [1983] 6 UKHL 409, per Lord Diplock.

harm. The Public Interest Disclosure Act 1998, therefore extends much wider than wrongdoing *per se*. It includes health and safety and harm to the environment as disclosures qualifying for protection and thus encompasses malpractice as well as wrongdoing.[46]

Sagar's conception of wrongdoing is unlikely to cover instances of 'protest whistleblowing'. Sagar's criterion do not allow for disclosures which are wholly based on the subjective analysis of a prospective whistleblower. Leaks concerning policy initiatives (for example) are commonplace; often these documents do not concern wrongdoing as such, but instead reveal a course of action of which the individual, based on their experience in the workplace, believes the public should be aware. It is here that Sager's concept of whistleblowing and the general justifications from democracy and recipient enhancement diverge. If one applies arguments from recipient enhancement or from democracy, there is a need to at least consider 'protest whistleblowing' as part of a wider theoretical framework relating to public servant whistleblowers.

It is suggested, however, that arguments from recipient enhancement are not without difficulty; for example, one should question whether Bok's recommendation that society should draw distinctions between the types of information communicated may be idealistic. According to Dean, society may not be equipped to make such a distinction. Dean's conception of society involves two types of individuals: those who 'believe through the judgments of others', and the 'few' who 'judge for themselves on the basis of the available information',[47] who may struggle to interpret the messages communicated. The value of the disclosure could be diminished whereby the recipient audience fails to grasp the importance of the information provided to them. Whilst it is not suggested that the recipient audience will lack the intellectual capacity to identify clear information exposing wrongdoing, they may lack the subject expertise to understand and interpret complex documents couched in official language without help.[48]

Conversely, one should question whether a Crown servant will have the capacity to correctly weigh the potential harm of a disclosure against the potential benefit. They could consult with others within the organisation, but may feel inhibited from doing so for fear of later being exposed as

---

[46]   PIDA 1998, s. 43B.

[47]   Jodi Dean, 'Publicity's Secret' (2001) 29(5) *Political Theory* 624.

[48]   For example, the *Guardian*'s coverage of the Manning leaks was accompanied by a glossary of terminology used by the US Armed Forces and expert commentary to assist readers in interpreting the disclosures, see Simon Rogers, 'Afghanistan war logs: the glossary', *Guardian*, 25 July 2010.

the originator behind any subsequent leaks. Official documents may be classified at a certain level and may be accompanied by a special handling instruction to limit access but this does not provide a guaranteed indicator of the risks involved in disclosure. The prospective leaker could believe that the document will not cause harm or that it is a product of over-classification. For security reasons, unbeknown to the individual, the organisation may have only provided one segment of information which if disclosed could allow those with mal-intent to develop a whole picture. Beyond the contents of documents, classification and information garnered from organisational activity, the weighing of harm versus benefit pre-disclosure is highly subjective.

Anonymous Leaking

Faced with leaked information which purportedly originates from a government department, society cannot make an adequate assessment of the value of the speech communicated or the motivation behind the disclosure unless they understand the information communicated to them. Traditionally, the public have been reliant upon traditional media outlets to report on such material. Technological advancements have meant that vast quantities of official documents can be made readily accessible by organisations such as Wikileaks. Despite these developments, traditional media outlets still play a role in presenting and explaining the material to the public, as well as providing their own often-redacted copies of the information.

Difficulties occur when the information is provided to a journalist via a conduit, creating more distance between the source and journalist than ever before. How can journalists be certain that they are not being fed with false information without having access to the source to test the source's motives? Can society assess the value of the information communicated without knowing the identity of the source?

Bok, prefers overt acts of whistleblowing which allow for the information to be checked and the source to be challenged.[49] In weighing the positives and negatives of unauthorised versus overt disclosures, she considers anonymous whistleblowing to be safer as it can be 'kept up indefinitely' whereas the overt whistleblower 'shoots his bolt by going public'.[50] She suggests, however, that the value of the message is diminished when disclosed anonymously because the communicator

---

[49] Bok, above n. 32, 223.
[50] *Ibid.* 223.

cannot explain its importance.[51] Writing in a time well before online disclosure outlets she expressed concern that information can pass through a number of intermediaries before being printed, it can be changed or not printed in its entirety.[52]

Rains and Scott provide a theoretical model of receiver responses to anonymous communication in which they identify that many whistle-blowers elect to remain anonymous to avoid personal or legal retribu-tion.[53] In organisations where mechanisms are provided for anonymous concern reporting, they suggest that such communication has impacted on the credibility of claims and the ability of the accused to respond against them.[54] They suggest that understanding a 'source's qualifica-tions' and 'trustworthiness' are 'central to evaluating his or her mes-sage'.[55] They argue that the identity of the source could be of 'integral importance to assessing the veracity of his or her claims'.[56]

Anonymous whistleblowing highlights the competing interests of the communicator and the recipient audience. Self-identification adds cred-ibility to the information disclosed; identity may help to maximise the value of the message, provided that the person who disclosed it is willing or is indeed able to engage in further dialogue.[57] Further dialogue or explanation may be most needed in instances of 'protest whistleblowing' where the activity complained of is not overtly clear to the recipient audience. Self-identification, therefore, principally serves recipient inter-ests. Questions concerning credibility and value can be answered in other ways. Media commentators can provide views, the authenticity of docu-ments could be checked via outward-facing or back channels, and the audience can make their own assessments. As Bok rightly points out, there is a problem in that the meaning and value of the initial communi-cation can be lost in the way it is presented and reported upon.[58] There is also the problem that the whistleblower rather than the information disclosed can become the story, which may detract from the messages

---

[51]   *Ibid.* 223.

[52]   *Ibid.*

[53]   Stephen A. Rains and Craig A. Scott, 'To Identify or Not to Identify: A Theoretical Model of Receiver Responses to Anonymous Communication' (2007) *Communication Theory* 1, 74.

[54]   *Ibid.* 67.

[55]   *Ibid.* 74.

[56]   *Ibid.* 83.

[57]   If their identity is known it may lead to arrest and the individual may be prohibited from further communication at that stage.

[58]   Bok, above n. 32, 223.

communicated. The publishing of raw and un-redacted documents presents its own risks – it increases the likelihood of harm to individual and or national security and there are also no guarantees that the audience will understand the documents presented to them.

Anonymity principally serves the individual interests of the communicator, there are risks that the communicator will be discovered and will suffer some form of detrimental treatment as a result.[59] Anonymity can, however, serve recipient interests. If the information disclosed is of value, there may be a thirst for further disclosures, which if the communicator is identified and stopped he will be unable to make. To some individuals, anonymity may be seen as the most appropriate and safest option. However, the person may still be uncovered as the originator of the leaks – circumstantial matters, such as the content of the disclosure, can lead to identification.[60] Where documents have only been provided to a small number of individuals, it may be relatively easy for the authorities to track down the originator of the leaks, even where precautions have been taken. Self-identification can allow the whistleblower not only to explain the contents of disclosures but also the motivations behind them. In doing so it allows individuals to engage in political discourse. Political discourse leads to political pressure. Pressure can be exerted by supporters of the leaks in question who can argue that the individual was right to make the disclosures and should not be punished. Pressure can also be felt by the executive and its agencies who may feel it is a more sensible course of action to drop any reprisals against the leaker, first, to safeguard against any further anticipated embarrassment, and, second, to attempt to dim the spotlight of publicity on the leaks if legal action were to be pursued.[61] As the next section will identify, anonymity is most problematical when considering disclosures purportedly motivated by necessity and civil disobedience where self-identification may be considered a prerequisite.

---

[59] Conversely, it would be difficult for a worker to argue that they have suffered detrimental treatment or dismissal for making a disclosure and to receive protection using the PIDA 1998 where contact between the communicator and recipient cannot be proven.

[60] Richard Calland and Guy Dehn, *Whistleblowing Around the World: Law, Culture and Practice* (ODAC, 2004) 8.

[61] For example, prosecutors may decide on advice from the Attorney General that it would be in the public interest not to proceed with a prosecution. This can also be a preventative measure because of fears that court proceedings could reveal further information harmful to national security.

Necessity

Necessity, according to Brudner, most commonly refers to circumstances whereby someone chooses to break the law in order to avoid a greater evil.[62] The evil, it is suggested, must present an immediate threat of harm to the communicator or to others. The appropriate circumstances are the subject of wide academic debate. For Lee, it is not enough that the commission of an offence resulted in 'a lesser evil than the evil avoided through the violation' – it must have been the 'only option the individual had available to address the choice of evils he was facing'.[63] Alternatively, Brudner suggests necessity can be considered as a 'momentary aberration from, rather than an expression of, the accused's moral character' which if accepted should lead to acquittal. Crown servants are placed in a unique position, whereby the disclosure of information may be considered necessary because of a perceived duty of care owed to citizens.[64] Determination of what constitutes the lesser evil, or the most proportionate course of action in the circumstances, requires careful consideration.

Brudner argues that necessity cannot be used as a justification where an individual 'imposes grave risks on the health of persons, regardless of the magnitude of the net saving of lives'.[65] Transposed to the circumstances of unauthorised disclosure of government documents, the release of information identifying that an illegal war is about to take place would be justified, but the whereabouts or identities of the soldiers may not. The Crown servant would be faced with the unenviable task of determining what disclosures of information would be justifiable and to whom.

According to Howard Dennis, the necessity should be restricted to two situations: first, in an emergency situation, and, second, where there is a conflict of duty, giving rise to a 'danger of death or serious injury'.[66] In less serious situations, he believes in regulating the ordering of harms with codified defences. Legislators can delegate the task of ordering harms to the courts. Whilst this is consistent with methods adopted by the

---

[62]   Anthony Brudner, 'A Theory of Necessity' (1987) 7(3) *Oxford Journal of Legal Studies* 340.

[63]   Youngjae Lee, 'The Defence of Necessity and Powers of the Government' (2009) 3 *Criminal Law and Philosophy* 133, 141.

[64]   Brudner, above n 62.

[65]   *Ibid.* 365.

[66]   Ian Howard Dennis, 'On Necessity as a Defence to a Crime, Possibilities, Problems and Limitations of Justification and Excuse' (2009) 3(1) *Criminal Law and Philosophy* 29.

European Court of Human Rights (ECtHR) to weigh competing interests by engaging in detailed proportionality analyses, domestically, the UK courts are constrained in their ability to order harms effectively using the current Official Secrets regime; and where the question of what might constitute necessity has arisen, the executive has later expressed its reluctance to codify the defence.[67] This discussion will now turn to consider civil disobedience.

Civil Disobedience

The Crown servant may feel duty bound to engage in civil disobedience as a means of pursuing a greater good. This in effect becomes an overriding obligation to act.[68] The draconian nature of the Official Secrets Act 1989 and increasing use of the common law offence of Misconduct in Public Office as an alternative to prosecution under the Official Secrets Act means that a Crown servant who decides to disclose official information without authorisation will most likely break the law as a result.

Can a Crown servant make an unauthorised disclosure on the grounds of civil disobedience? In principle, the servant could meet Perry's two objectives. The first is to disobey a law which the individual believes is forbidding them to do what they believe they must. The second is to achieve a good which is greater than the evils entailed by the disobedient act. Perry suggests the aim could be to focus attention on a law or a policy or to protect someone.[69] There is an argument to suggest that civil disobedience should go further than this – that the motivation must be to *change* law or policy, otherwise the good will not be sufficient to outweigh the disobedient act.

Anonymous disclosures are more difficult to justify on civil disobedience grounds. Rawls contends that the act of civil disobedience is both public and political; it is neither covert nor secretive.[70] Therefore, the individual should provide an explanation as to why they chose to break the law and an explanation as to why the action complained of is wrong. Whilst the discloser could provide an anonymous explanation, the

---

[67] This should be considered in the light of the approach taken by legislators in Canada, where Security of Information Act 2001, s. 15, contains a codified defence which takes into account acts of necessity.

[68] Henry David Thoreau, *Walden or Life in the Woods; and on the Duty of Civil Disobedience* (New American Library, 1960) 288.

[69] Michael J. Perry, *Morality Politics and Law* (OUP, 1991) 114.

[70] John Rawls, *A Theory of Justice*, 2nd edn (OUP, 1999) 374.

opportunity for the recipient audience to question the motivation behind the leak or obtain further information is diminished.

Civil disobedience is a form of 'protest speech'. In this context, the explanation as to why the individual broke the law in raising a concern may be considered as significant as the information disclosed. Anonymous disclosures increase the proximity between communicator and recipient, particularly where the disclosures are presented in a raw form without explanation as to their significance. In some circumstances, it may be obvious to the recipient that a document contains information relating to gross wrongdoing. However, in 'protest whistleblowing' cases it may be more difficult to get this message across. The recipient audience may simply fail to understand the significance of the material presented to them.

'Overt' acts of civil disobedience place the communicator at great risk. Once identity is established negative consequences will likely follow. The making of an overt, unauthorised, disclosure can provide the servant with an opportunity to at least get their side of the story across before prosecuting authorities react. Overt acts pit the servant directly against the state and may assist the individual in garnering both political and public support. The strength of this pressure can result in criminal proceedings being dropped, or even a jury acquitting a defendant despite clear directions to the contrary.[71] However, this outcome can never be guaranteed.[72] Even if the servant escapes prosecution, the loss of security clearance and inevitable demotion or dismissal will be difficult to reverse.

Rawls identifies a concept of equal society. Civil disobedience may be regarded as a 'stabilizing device', a 'healthy but illegal method of accountability'.[73] On this basis, disclosures to identify acts of wrongdoing or afford the electorate greater access to official information may be justified. This position is bolstered by justifications from truth or to enhance the public good, justifications which must be counterbalanced with a moral obligation to obey the law, regardless of whether it is

---

[71] For an example of this, see further *R* v. *Ponting* [1985] Crim. LR 318. Discussed further in Chapter 2.

[72] For an example see the conviction of Bradley Manning. Despite receiving support in various countries across the globe, Manning was sentenced to 35 years' imprisonment. For analysis see further Ashley Savage, '35 years for Manning and time for better whistleblowing laws' (21 August 2013), available at https://theconversation.com/35-years-for-manning-and-time-for-better-whistle blowing-laws-17333.

[73] Rawls, above n. 70.

considered to be unjust or bad. This stems from a duty to prevent risk to the legal system and the very principles that govern it.[74] In addition to their duties as a citizen, Crown servants owe enhanced, and at times conflicting, duties to the state as employer, Parliament and the general public. The Rawlsian conception of civil disobedience is problematic as it requires Crown servants to engage in overtly political action where the very nature of their employment ordinarily requires them to be apolitical.

The act of civil disobedience may be acceptable until it reaches the extent that respect for the law of the land and the constitution breaks down. Civil disobedience may appear necessary in rare and individual circumstances, but it can also undermine not only the purpose of the law in question (no matter how invalid it may appear at the time) but the rule of law as a whole. As Thoreau contends, the remedy of civil disobedience may be worse than the evil, an imbalance that should be rectified by the legislature.[75] The question of whether a Crown servant may be justified in disclosing official information without authority should therefore be dependent upon the content of the information itself and the benefits to which such disclosures may confer.

Dworkin identifies three types of civil disobedience. The first is 'integrity based', where a citizen chooses to disobey the law when he feels that the law in question is immoral. The second is 'justice based', where the individual chooses to act in order to assert a right which he feels has been wrongly denied. The third is 'policy based', where the citizen believes that a chosen policy is 'dangerously unwise'.[76] Dworkin opines that this requires the individual to believe that the policy which they oppose is 'bad for everyone, not just for some minority'.[77] Dworkin makes a distinction between persuasive and non-persuasive strategies. Persuasive strategies require the individual to attempt to convince the majority that the policy in question is wrong in order for it to 'disfavour the program it formerly favoured'.[78] In contrast, non-persuasive strategies require the individual to 'make the majority pay so heavily for its actions without having been convinced' by the need for change.[79] Non-persuasive

---

[74] John Finnis, *Natural Law and Natural Rights* (Clarendon, 2011) 383.
[75] Thoreau, above n. 68, 289.
[76] Ronald Dworkin, *A Matter of Principle* (Harvard University Press, 1985) 107.
[77] *Ibid.* 110.
[78] Dworkin, above n. 76.
[79] *Ibid.* 111.

strategies attack the 'roots and foundations' of the principle of majority rule, because to be successful, the act requires 'minority coercion' of the majority.[80]

Dworkin makes a significant distinction between different forms of policy protest, contrasting the civil rights movement in the United States with the trespass of Greenham Common in order to protest the deployment of nuclear missiles in Europe, which is a more difficult act to justify because the arguments for nuclear deployment are complex. Parallels may be drawn here to the unauthorised disclosures made by civil servant Sarah Tisdall, who disclosed information regarding the arrangements for the missiles at the base.[81] Dworkin argues that such acts are going to make the general public 'pay less attention' to 'complex issues' because it will be motivated to follow the policy its leaders have adopted because any change to that policy would result in 'giving way to civil blackmail'.[82] He identifies that there is a contrast between the types of policy and the justification for civil disobedience in which he believes that non-persuasive action taken to highlight bad economic policy may not be justified.[83]

Unauthorised disclosures by Crown servants may result in the disclosure of information regarding what the servant considers to be a dangerous policy decision. It may be argued, based on Dworkin's hypothesis, that these disclosures should be considered as non-persuasive. However, there is a counter-argument to suggest that circumstances may arise where the information communicated is complex in nature yet the substance of the documents may be highly persuasive. Understanding of the messages can be improved with explanation by the communicator, by journalists or supporters.

Anonymous disclosures may provide the general public with information regarding bad policy decisions or even illegality but they can also be more difficult to justify on civil disobedience grounds where the communicator does not explain to the recipient audience why they oppose a particular policy. The mass disclosure of numerous documents which detail different policies is, by its nature, a non-persuasive act designed to prompt those in power to pursue a different course. The content of the information communicated and the method by which the communication takes place will therefore be highly relevant to this consideration.

---

[80] *Ibid.* 111.
[81] *R* v. *Tisdall* (Unreported, 23 March 1984).
[82] Dworkin, above n. 76.
[83] *Ibid.*

III JUSTIFICATIONS FOR LIMITING EXPRESSION RIGHTS

Restricting Expression which Causes Harm

It is often the case that following an act of unauthorised disclosure or public whistleblowing by an official, the immediate response by the employer and the government of the day is to identify that the act was irresponsible and has harmed national security. In considering restrictions of speech, J.S. Mill argued that the only legitimate justification for the limitation of an individual's free speech rights is the prevention of harm to others.[84] Barendt states that a free speech principle may not confer absolute protection but the principle does mean that governments must show strong grounds for interference.[85] Dworkin suggests that limitation to the right to freedom of expression may be justified if the state demonstrates 'a clear and substantial risk' that the exercise of the right will do great damage to the person or property of others.[86] The practical difficulty with disclosures pertaining to national security is that traditionally, at least from the perspective of courts in the United Kingdom, what constitutes national security is a matter for the agencies in question and the government of the day. It is difficult for the non-expert public to evaluate these claims. There has been a general reluctance by both the courts and indeed oversight bodies to question claims that an act of unauthorised disclosure has harmed or could cause subsequent harm to national security. Courts decline to forensically question the claims, in part due to fears that to do so may cause further harm to national security and because to do so may require judges to take an unwelcome step into the domain of an elected representative.

Shauer identifies that speech can and frequently does cause harm; thus, an individual saying something to a group of people may cause them to be harmful to society by disobeying the law.[87] Such reasoning can be transposed to the unauthorised disclosure of information harmful to national security. A leak of information may be useful to the 'enemy', it may also provide encouragement to colleagues working in the same field also to leak information. It may be argued therefore that the existence of

---

[84] John Stuart Mill, *On Liberty* (Cosimo, 2001, first published 1889) ch. 2.
[85] Barendt, above n. 25, 7.
[86] Ronald Dworkin, *Taking Rights Seriously* (Harvard University Press, 1978).
[87] Shauer, above n. 24, 10.

an Official Secrets Act which limits the freedom of expression of the Crown employee is necessary to protect the information concerned and to act as a deterrent effect.

The United States Supreme Court in *Schenke v United States* developed a 'clear and present danger' test whereby speech may be restricted when 'used in such circumstances as to create a clear and present danger that they will bring about the substantive evils which Congress has a right to prevent'.[88] The subsequent decision in *Abrams v United States*[89] adopted a 'bad tendency' principle, which enabled the restriction of speech by government if it believed that it had the sole tendency to incite or cause illegal activity. Oliver Wendel Homes, dissenting, opined that regardless of whether the speech in question had been communicated in a time of war or any other time the principle would 'always be the same'.[90] Thus, he suggested that Congress could 'only limit the expression of opinion' where the 'present danger of immediate evil or intent to bring it about warranted the intervention'.[91]

The decision in *Abrams* was overturned following *Brandenburg v Ohio*. The court adopted a new standard of review which authorises the restriction of speech where the circumstances give rise to 'imminent lawless action'. Mr Justice Douglas, concurring, was critical of the 'clear and present danger' test, suggesting that application of the principle could result in decisions where 'the threats were often loud but always puny' and 'made serious only by judges so wedded to the status quo that critical analysis made them nervous'.[92]

According to the aforementioned decisions and theoretical reasoning, in order for the state to restrict the expression of a citizen it must first establish an overriding justification, such as the prevention of harm or the security of the state. A court must have the opportunity to test this justification based upon a pre-determined analytical framework. Article 10 of the European Convention on Human Rights (ECHR) provides for such a framework. Article 10(2) provides a number of potential restrictions on the right to freedom of expression provided that they are 'prescribed by law' and 'necessary in a democratic society'. Barendt argues that 'necessary in a democratic society' can only be determined in the light of all the circumstances. The process, therefore, does not only require judges to determine the importance of the relevant state interest

---

[88]   249 US 49, 51 (1919).
[89]   250 US 616 (1919).
[90]   *Ibid.* 628.
[91]   *Abrams*, above n. 89, 628.
[92]   395 US 444 (1969).

and the degree of danger threatened by the expression but further enables them to examine the 'precise character of the speech'.[93] Based upon this reasoning, it is suggested that it is insufficient for the government of the day or an executive department to argue that speech ought to be restricted because it relates to national security, or is necessary to prevent crime. It must provide a justification as to why, in the particular circumstances complained of, the speech would cause harm. A court must subsequently be provided with the ability to rigorously test this justification.

Unfortunately, the doctrinal reasoning does not align itself with the current reality in the United Kingdom. In the judicial sense, whilst it is recognised that courts are required to rigorously balance competing interests and thus challenge why speech should be restricted, the Official Secrets Act 1989 and the harm tests associated with it do not allow for thorough analysis to take place; where certain sections of the Act provide harm tests, these may be easily satisfied without allowing for the determination of the benefit of any disclosure. The next section will consider the theoretical justifications for secrecy.

Concepts of Secrecy and Security

It may be suggested that the maintenance of secrecy is appropriate and necessary. Neocleous, for one, argues that the tendency towards secrecy is endemic to all states.[94] Thus, if a situation arises whereby the ideal course of action is to preserve the state it is the statesman's task to discern this course and as a consequence determine which information should be suppressed in the public interest.[95] Lustgarten and Leigh draw a clear distinction between the concepts of national security and secrecy, whereby they argue that in a democracy national security matters should be 'at the forefront of public discussion'.[96] Whether something should be secret, they suggest, should be based on a determination of the content of information rather than the position of officials.[97] On this basis, information which concerns the identity of individual agents or sources at risk of harm should be kept secret, whereas information regarding policy should not necessarily be kept secret unless these policies depend on secrecy for their success.[98] Colaresi does not distinguish between

---

[93]   Barendt, above n. 25, 20.
[94]   Mark Neocleous, 'Privacy, Secrecy, Idiocy' (2002) *Social Research* 69.
[95]   *Ibid.* 97.
[96]   Laurence Lustgarten and Ian Leigh, *In from the Cold* (OUP 1994) 30.
[97]   *Ibid.*
[98]   *Ibid.*

'national security' and 'secrecy' but acknowledges that secrecy can be used as a category to classify both security and non-security related content.[99]

In the United Kingdom it is evident that the distinction between the two concepts can be blurred. In 2008, Christopher Galley, a young civil servant working in the Home Office, was arrested for leaking documents to then opposition MP Damian Green, who was also arrested as recipient. Highly controversial searches of Green's home, constituency and parliamentary offices ensued and the episode was justified on 'national security' grounds. Despite a police investigation which reportedly cost £5 million, proceedings were dropped on the basis that the leaks did not comprise of national security information and that the information concerned was neither secret nor harmful.[100]

Bok suggests that the conflicts over secrecy between state and citizen are conflicts of power. It may be argued that the citizen's acceptance of state secrecy, and as a consequence state power, is a natural extension of Hobbes' concept of the social contract: the surrender of natural rights to accept the jurisdiction of the sovereign.[101] Part of a citizen's acceptance of secrecy – or the government's justification for it – may lie in the inability of the public to adequately assess and understand information. Bok suggests we are limited by our 'capacity to perceive and remember' and that if provided with information our capacity to make judgement is 'severely limited' and is 'subject to bias from all directions'.[102]

In discussing justifications for secrecy in contrast to arguments for publicity, Dean identifies Bentham's proposition that some individuals may 'defend government secrecy' on the basis that the public 'lacks of capacity for judgment'.[103] Dean further develops Bentham's reasoning, suggesting that the public is split into three classes. The first, those 'who do not have time for public affairs'; the second, those who 'believe through the judgements of others'; and the third 'few' who 'judge for themselves on the basis of the available information'.[104] Dean suggests

---

[99] Michael P. Colaresi, *Democracy Declassified: The Secrecy Dilemma in National Security* (OUP, 2014) 46.

[100] Crown Prosecution Service, 'Decision on Prosecution: Mr Christopher Galley and Mr Damian Green MP', Press Release, 16 April 2009.

[101] Thomas Hobbes, *Leviathan* (OUP, 2008, first published 1651) ch. 14; and Ian Mcleod, *Legal Theory*, 5th edn (Palgrave, 2010) 53.

[102] Bok, above n. 32, 104.

[103] Dean, above n. 47, 649.

[104] *Ibid.* 649.

that it is the second class, those who believe in the judgement of others, who most require publicity to ensure that they are not misled.

Part of the difficulty is the requirement to keep a check on government control of secret information.[105] Neocleaous identifies that civil society lacks a 'sense of equality' or 'reciprocity' with the state as it has 'no spying machine'. The best it can hope for is some kind of 'left opposition' to keep tabs on it but it will always be at a 'serious technical and organisational disadvantage'.[106] However, whilst he suggests that the way to combat secrecy is to combat the state collectively, Szikinger is highly critical of this assertion, identifying that it would most likely result in the collapse of the state itself.[107] If such action were to succeed, he suggests, greater openness based on 'collective knowledge' and 'collective efforts' would not result in 'challenging' the 'oppressive tendencies of the state'.[108] Fenster considers the notion of transparency by providing a modern interpretation of Bentham's Panopticon, a means of allowing the public to view the actions of their political rulers.[109] In doing so he identifies that the motivation for such a design is to create a structure whereby the subject is unable to recognise when he is being watched. This creates a feeling of 'permanent surveillance' leading the subject to regulate 'discipline and organise behaviour and thought'.[110] Fenster argues that a truly 'panopticised state' would be difficult to achieve but serves as a metaphor for transparency and open government.[111]

The author suggests that the benefits associated with a 'panopticised state', namely, that executive malpractice is less likely to occur for fear of the wrongdoer being found out, should be contrasted with the potential damaging consequences of transparency controlling behaviour. The principles of collective Cabinet responsibility and candour have been developed to ensure that members of the Cabinet may speak freely without fear that their words may result in future criticism, and so that civil servants can provide full and frank advice. The 'panopticised' ideal, if

---

[105] As exemplified by the court's handling of secret material. See further Lord Hope, dissenting: 'secret justice at this level is really no justice at all'. *Bank Mellat* v. *HM Treasury (No. 1)* [2013] UKSC 38, [68].

[106] Neocleous, above n. 94, 86.

[107] Istvan Szikinger, 'Privacy, Secrecy, Idiocy: A Response to Mark Neocleous' (2002) 69 *Social Research* 1.

[108] *Ibid.*

[109] Mark Fenster, 'Seeing the State: Transparency as Metaphor' (2010) 62 *Admin. L Rev.* 669.

[110] *Ibid.*

[111] *Ibid.*

implemented, could have a detrimental impact on the machinery of the state, resulting in delayed or hesitant decision-making or decisions made which do not best serve the public interest. In the national security sphere, it has been suggested that the benefits of transparency may be diminished where agencies are effectively forced into the spotlight and thus construct policies to garner political support.[112] At the other end of the spectrum, Bok identifies that the notion of 'collective secrecy' can diminish the sense of 'personal responsibility for joint decisions' resulting in 'skewed' or 'careless judgement' and the taking of 'needless risks'.[113]

The aforementioned doctrinal analysis identifies that a delicate balance must be achieved between the need to communicate official information to the public and the need to keep certain information secret. Whilst similarities may be drawn between justifications for and against publicity and justifications to promote and restrict expression, there are differences. Publicity primarily and predominantly serves community interests, whereas expression, and in particular the justifications for autonomy and individual enhancement, can serve the interests of the communicator alone. The concepts of publicity, national security and secrecy are primarily matters for the government of the day and its organisations. However, these responsibilities, if not properly discharged, can lead to over-classification, misuse of secrecy or mislabelling of national security matters. As Lustgarten and Leigh have established, the Hobbesian concept of security would support an authoritarian regime.[114] If Hobbes' sovereignty argument is to have any place in modern democratic society, citizens must be provided with sufficient information to appreciate how the executive and its agencies are working in practice. Instances of wrongdoing or malpractice are unlikely to be uncovered unless the executive and its agencies acknowledge and publicise their mistakes or they are uncovered by official (via parliamentary, regulatory or enforcement) or unofficial (media and investigative journalist) scrutiny channels. Whistleblowers can provide assistance to these channels; however, in

---

[112] See generally Anthony Glees and Philip H.J. Davies, *Spinning the Spies: Intelligence, Open Government and the Hutton Inquiry* (Social Affairs Unit, 2004). Conversely, the Intelligence and Security Committee's efforts to televise evidence sessions attended by the directors of the intelligence agencies can arguably be seen as an advancement in openness, see session of 7 October 2013. A transcript of the evidence is available at the ISC's website, http://isc.independent.gov.uk/public-evidence?offset=10.

[113] Bok, above n. 32, 109.

[114] Lustgarten and Leigh, above n. 96, 9.

doing so they place themselves at risk of reprisal or criminal sanction. It is suggested that in determining the expression rights of whistleblowers, care must be taken to identify potential harms caused by a disclosure because this can serve as an initial indicator as to the harm which the whistleblower may incur as a result.[115]

Whilst Mill's justification to restrict expression which causes harm provides a useful starting point, it should be acknowledged that if we are to equate harms caused by the expression to potential harm caused to the whistleblower, a more detailed appreciation of what information may cause harm, which recognises the breadth of work undertaken in the different spheres of Crown service and the rights and responsibilities attributed to those spheres, must be provided. The author will now propose a communitarian approach to reconcile these considerations.

A Communitarian Approach to Unauthorised Disclosures

It is necessary to align the various competing theoretical positions to the practical realities of working life. Unauthorised disclosures may be justified on the grounds of autonomy in its purist form, however, without consideration of the impact of the disclosure by an employee creating both personal and organisational risks. Communitarianism grounds the rights of individuals in the context of the community to which they belong.

Etzioni provides a liberal communitarian perspective when considering leaks to the press.[116] In doing so, he identifies that a balance should be struck between individual rights and social responsibilities; he suggests that neither concept can trump the other and thus eschews the advocacy argument which would allow the strongest competing claim to succeed over the weakest.[117] Etzioni's liberal communitarian stance instead requires a balance between the public's 'right to know' and national security.

The liberal communitarian perspective is preferable to general expression theory in the sense that it provides consideration of an individual's responsibility to the community. It is therefore suggested that this provides scope for a more detailed determination of competing interests

---

[115] It is acknowledged that the justification for any subsequent proceedings against a whistleblower may not reflect the reality and that responses may be excessive in contrast to the content of information disclosed.

[116] Amaiti Etzioni, *The New Normal: Finding a Balance Between Individual Rights and the Common Good* (Transaction, 2015) ch. 1.

[117] *Ibid.*

beyond the Millian speech versus harm principle. Etzioni's concept, however, concerns a balance between the public's right to know and national security, thus conflating the arguments from publicity, secrecy and expression. Whilst there are similarities between the concepts of publicity and expression they are two different, albeit complementary, ideals. If we are to conflate the principles, discussion of the general expression theory earlier in this chapter identified arguments for recipient enhancement, truth and democracy. The situation is therefore arguably more complex than a choice between raising a concern or not because of a responsibility to the community.

It is suggested that a Crown servant will need to effectively consider two communities. They have both an obligation to their *intramural community*, by virtue of their employment position, and a pre-existing obligation to the *extramural community*, by virtue of their status as citizens in democratic society.

Case for Intramural Communities

Citizens do not leave the extramural community as a result of gaining employment in public service. However, several indicators suggest that they join intramural or sub-communities which result in the modification of rights and responsibilities. First, all Crown servants, regardless of organisation, sign the Official Secrets Act 1989; many if not all will sign express confidentiality agreements and will be subject to implied duties of confidence; all Crown servants undergo some form of vetting, from the lowest level 'baseline personnel security standard' to the highest 'developed vetting' clearance needed to work in positions involving intelligence and national security matters. The very nature of the work Crown servants undertake and the information they are party to places them in a different position to that of an ordinary citizen. Crown employees develop a unique insight into public life and a skill-set which would not otherwise be available to the ordinary citizen. The special status of public servants has been identified by the European Court of Human Rights in a body of case law which suggests that upon entering employment, public servants agree to a voluntary restriction of their ECHR, Article 10 rights in respect of their work.[118]

---

[118] *Vereniging Rechtswinkels Utrecht* v. *Netherlands*, Application No. 11308/84, ECtHR, 13 March 1986; *Glasenapp* v. *Germany*, Application No. 9228/80, ECtHR, 26 August 1986; *Rommelfanger* v. *Germany*, Application No. 12242/86, ECtHR, 6 September 1989.

Unauthorised disclosures of information can present both risks and rewards to both the servant's intramural community and the extramural community. They can challenge wrongdoing and lead to greater openness and accountability and they can cause reputational damage to the organisation and cause potential harm to individuals. Whilst the afore-mentioned paragraph highlights similarities across the spectrum of Crown employment, differences in the nature of employment in the Civil Service, the security and intelligence services and Armed Forces suggest the need to identify 'community specific' challenges relevant to these groupings. As Crawford suggests, the scope of freedom of expression ought to vary between communities on the basis that moral standards are at their most meaningful when 'rooted in community traditions and notions of the common good'.[119] Individuals working in the three groupings have different responsibilities due to the nature of the work that they undertake; moreover, they are required to conform to different rules concerning workplace discipline. Unauthorised disclosures from those particular organisations are likely to engage different benefit/harm analyses. Whilst it is acknowledged that the nature of public employment will result in some cross-sector harms overlapping, it is necessary to identify three distinct intramural communities. These intramural com-munities will be the subject of three case studies later in the text.

Civil Service

The first community concerns the Civil Service. Civil servants are obliged to observe the Civil Service Code, the Official Secrets Acts and common law restrictions on speech. Civil servants in particular positions of influence may be required to observe further, more rigorous, standards of political impartiality.[120]

The government, and in particular, government Ministers, need to maintain trust in the Civil Service to deliver their objectives. If civil servants leak information there is a danger that this trust will be eroded. At the highest level, the government operate a policy of candour in Cabinet meetings. Candour is seen as essential. If Ministers fear their words will be leaked they will be inhibited from making important decisions.

Leaks concerning national security may place individuals or the public as a whole at risk. Leaks about politically sensitive negotiations with

---

[119] Mark Crawford, 'Regimes of Tolerance: A Communitarian Approach to Freedom of Expression and its Limits' (1998) 48 *University of Toronto Faculty of Law Review* 4.

[120] For further discussion see Chapter 5.

other states are likely to result in lost confidence and reputational harm. Leaks of commercially sensitive information may harm state interests and impede the ability of the United Kingdom to compete on a world stage.

Security and intelligence services

The second intramural community concerns the security and intelligence services. Employees of the security and intelligence services face the most stringent vetting procedures of all Crown servants, known as 'developed vetting'. The restriction on expression increases as does the risk of prosecution for the making of an unauthorised disclosure. Employees in this community are subject to a lifelong ban on speaking about their work unless they are able to obtain prior authorisation. Employees are also subject to confidentiality agreements enforceable before the civil courts.[121]

An unauthorised disclosure may lead to a loss of confidence in the agency and subsequent reluctance of intelligence partners and agencies based in other jurisdictions to share information. By convention, agencies do not openly discuss the recruitment of informants on the basis that to do so would discourage future recruitment. Disclosures regarding the identities or information obtained by informants would likely discourage others from coming forward in the future. By convention, agencies neither confirm nor deny information relating to their activities and where leaks do occur, the security and intelligence services are left in the difficult position of attempting to deal with the fall out whilst maintaining this.[122]

Armed Forces

The third intramural community concerns the armed forces. In the UK Armed Forces, the restriction on expression is at the highest level to maintain discipline. Expression is restricted both inside and outside of the organisation, with strict rules on engagement with the media and use of social networking. Service personnel are subject to a rigid command structure where individuals higher up the chain of command have more opportunity to engage in overt public expression than the lower ranks.

---

[121]   See generally *Attorney General* v. *Blake* [2000] UKHL 45.

[122]   For example, see the stance taken by the government and security and intelligence services in *Liberty and others* v. *GCHQ and others* [2014] UKIP-Trib. 13_77-H. As a comparator see Department of Defense (US), 'Information Security Program', DoD Directive 5200.1, 10-101 (C) which instructs staff to neither confirm nor deny leaks to the media.

The risk of prosecution for unauthorised disclosure is slightly lower that the security and intelligence services because service personnel are generally not subject to Official Secrets Act 1989, section 1,[123] and leaks are likely to be covered by sections relating to damaging disclosure tests, however the risk is still high. Unauthorised disclosures may be harmful to the community if they identify operational matters (such as troop movements) or information concerning the capability of forces which is not known to opposing forces. Unauthorised disclosures are likely to undermine discipline which is seen as a fundamental requirement in armed service, particularly in times of conflict. Paradoxically, service personnel risk disciplinary sanctions and potential breaches of military law if they communicate concerns internally.

IV WHEN CAN UNAUTHORISED DISCLOSURES BE JUSTIFIED?

Crown servants face a myriad of competing community interests. Whilst it is clear that they observe community-specific values upon entering their respective intramural community, it is suggested that the basic values obtained as a result of being a citizen in democratic society may come into conflict with activities conducted within the intramural community. An unauthorised disclosure can be defended when the interests of society so clearly outweigh the need to keep the information secret that there is no option but to disclose. Because all Crown servants face strong obligations of loyalty to their respective intramural communities, it is suggested that the information in question must identify matters which fundamentally conflict with societal values, where the problem has been raised internally but has not been rectified or because the culture of the organisation is so rotten that the very fabric of the intramural community will break if something isn't done. Society should seek to support these disclosures. Public and political support can provide a degree of protection to the communicator. However, the fact remains that unauthorised disclosures require a subjective assessment by the communicator who must be prepared to face an inevitable subjective assessment by the recipient audience. Justification for protection and assessment as to the value of the information will always be a consideration *post facto*, meaning that the position of the whistleblower will always be uncertain.

---

[123] Unless notified by a Secretary of State.

Where possible it is suggested that individuals should therefore consider unauthorised disclosures as an avenue of 'last resort'.

V CONCLUSION

The argument from moral autonomy provides a strong justification for the right of individuals to raise concerns, in particular the right to make unauthorised disclosures of official information. In exercising the right to moral autonomy, the individual would not feel inhibited by social norms, legal restrictions or contractual obligations. The difficulty with the argument is that by bypassing the restrictions placed upon the individual as an employee or a citizen in democratic society, the argument fails to consider the practical realities of modern life. Upon entering employment, Crown servants agree to abide by rules of conduct in relation to political activities, legal obligations in relation to the law of confidence and the Official Secrets Acts, and the implied contractual term existing in all contracts of employment that the employer and employee will maintain trust and confidence. Failure to abide by the aforementioned restrictions is likely to result in the civil servant losing his or her employment, or being prosecuted under the Official Secrets Acts.

The argument that whistleblowing communication enhances the individual may be more easily justified. The communication of a political policy which is legal and which does not identify wrongdoing may still be justified to allow the individual to become a participant in political debate. The arguments from moral autonomy and to enhance the individual share close similarities in that both may provide strong justifications to allow 'protest whistleblowing'. As neither argument requires a benefit conferred upon the recipients of the information, it is submitted that anonymous whistleblowing would be justified.

Neither argument, however, allows for consideration as to the value of the communication to the recipient audience or to wider public debate. Such communication may be harmful to colleagues or to democratic society as a whole. The argument that freedom of expression is justified to enhance the public good provides a stronger justification for whistleblowing speech, because it concentrates on the contribution the communication makes to society as a whole. The discovery of truth will provide an important justification for whistleblowing, particularly where members of the public have been misled. Where there has been a cover up of information or if false information has provided, the Crown servant may be best placed to provide such information.

The argument from participation in a democracy supports the argument from truth. In a democratic society it is vital that citizens are provided with sufficient information to engage in and enhance political debate, to decide who to elect based upon clear and informed decision-making, and ultimately so that they can be aware on what actions are taken in their name. The arguments from truth and from democracy identify benefits to both the communicator of the information and the recipient audience. The argument that citizens should have a right of access to information is closely linked to the justifications from truth and democracy. Ultimately, where information has been suppressed from the public and such information could lead to truth or a better more informed electorate, a Crown servant may be justified in releasing such information. In these cases the interests of the extramural community will prevail.[124] Conversely, information which discloses the private lives of individuals may not provide a contribution to the public debate and the disclosure of such material should be questioned.[125]

In a theoretical justification for whistleblowing, the public interest in the speech communicated is as important as the act of whistleblowing itself. Thus, as Bok identifies, society must test the information to determine whether it is in the public interest. Determination of the value of the information is central to considering whether the suppression of whistleblowing speech may be justified. Both Barendt and Dworkin identify that governments must show strong grounds for interference, a clear and substantial risk that the speech will harm people or property. The unauthorised disclosure of national security information may cause grave harm to individuals and may provide a justifiable restriction on speech but must be tested and weighed against the benefit of the disclosure. The disclosure of secrets which are not harmful to national security may still be harmful to the public interest if routine disclosure leads to a 'panopticised' regime whereby public officials feel unable to make decisions in the national interest for fear of recrimination, undermining the purpose of government in democratic society. Conversely, the disclosure of national security information as an act of necessity must be counterbalanced against the disclosure of bureaucratic secrecy. Where necessity is used as a justification, the act should not create more harm to individuals than the threat the whistleblower is trying to prevent.

---

[124] It can also be argued that the intramural community may also benefit by strengthening the long-term integrity of the organisation.
[125] According to Bok, above n. 32, 219.

The difficulty with information perceived to be confidential or pertaining to national security is that the act of interpreting the speech and balancing the public interest in the information often takes place *post facto*. It is therefore submitted that before deciding to make an unauthorised disclosure, a Crown servant should consider what official channels are available. Thus, external, unauthorised disclosure should be considered as a last resort, where the official mechanisms available cannot deal with the concern, are not viable or may lead to suppression of the speech, or where the matter is urgent and there is not time to use those official channels.

Where unauthorised disclosures are made to the public, the individual should identify himself to the audience and should be available to explain the contents of the information and his motivations for the disclosure. This should be preferred as an alternative (where possible) to anonymous leaking. Anonymous leaking may prevent the recipient audience from making an assessment as to the value of the information communicated. It may therefore be detrimental to the aims identified in the justifications from truth and from participation in a democracy. Anonymous leaking should be reserved to 'last resort' situations where the individual feels that she or he will suffer grave reprisals for raising the concerns if identified.

2. The consequences of making an unauthorised disclosure

Secrecy can be used to safeguard national security but it can also be used as a tool to hide deception.[1] Secrecy comes at a price. There is an inevitable imbalance between the executive, who are considered to be best placed to determine risks to national security,[2] and the state who need a degree of access to official information to be informed, active participants in a democratic society.[3] The Freedom of Information Act 2000 was intended to redress the balance. However, the resulting Act is subject to a number of exemptions.[4] Government departments can

---

[1] Michael P. Colaresi, *Democracy Declassified: The Secrecy Dilemma in National Security* (OUP, 2014) 75.

[2] See generally: 'Those who are responsible for the national security must be the sole judges of what the national security requires': *The Zamora* [1916] 2 AC 77, [107], per Lord Parker. See also *Council for Civil Service Unions* v. *Minister for the Civil Service* [1984] 3 All ER 935, [28], per Lord Roskill, where he identified that it was for the government of the day and not the courts to determine whether national security should prevail over fairness in particular cases.

[3] Birkinshaw discusses general right to freedom of information, Patrick Birkinshaw, *Freedom of Information: The Law, the Practice, the Ideal* (Butterworths, 2001) 16. Parallels can also be drawn to John Stuart Mill's concepts of truth and audience enhancement. John Stuart Mill, *On Liberty* (Longman, 1889) ch. 1. For further discussion, see Chapter 1.

[4] Freedom of Information Act (FOIA) 2000, Part II, contains 24 exemptions; information may also be exempted if to collate the information would cost more than £600 for government departments (FOIA 2000, s.12). For an overview of the various exemptions see Patrick Birkinshaw, *Freedom of Information: The Law, the Practice and the Ideal* (4th edn, CUP, 2010). Ministers also have the power to override decisions of the Information Commissioner and the Information Tribunal by using FOIA 2000, s.53. For analysis of the impact on accountability see further Ashley Savage, *Publication of the Black Spider Memos: A Hollow Victory?* (Halsbury's Law Exchange, 13 June 2015), available at www.halsburyslawexchange.co.uk/publication-of-the-black-spider-memos-a-hollow-victory/; and Ashley Savage, *Untangling the Spider's Web: Evans at the Supreme Court* (Halsbury's Law Exchange, 11 March 2015), available at

frustrate the process further by choosing to delay responses.[5] As citizens suffer from the effects of imbalance in the extramural community, Crown servants likewise encounter imbalances in their respective intramural communities. Crown servants in the Civil Service, Armed Forces, police and security and intelligence agencies are subject to Official Secrets Act 1989, section 12.

Whilst other Crown servants must seek authorisation to disclose official information, Ministers are self-authorising.[6] All Crown servants undergo some form of security vetting before they can begin employment and access official documents, Ministers are not vetted.[7] The maintenance of secrecy at ministerial level is therefore reliant upon a degree of trust, self-responsibility, and for those with a seat in Cabinet, membership of the Privy Council.[8] This archaic remnant of the United Kingdom's monarchical system requires an oath of allegiance to the Queen – those in breach of the oath could until 1999 be tried for treason.[9] In reality, the

---

www.halsburyslawexchange.co.uk/untangling-the-spiders-web-evans-at-the-supreme-court/.

[5] Department for Education, Department for Work and Pensions, Cabinet Office, Home Office, Crown Prosecution Service, Highways Agency, Ministry of Justice, Government Equalities Office and Rural Payments Agency have all been subject to monitoring by the Information Commissioner due to delays at some point during the period 2010–15.

[6] Official Secrets Act 1989, s.7, concerns authorisation for disclosure.

[7] All Crown servants with access to government assets (applicants for the Civil Service and Armed Forces) are subject to the Baseline Personnel Security Standard; those with long-term access to 'SECRET' information and occasional access to 'TOP SECRET' information are required to undergo a more extensive 'Security Check'. Developed vetting is required where individuals are in posts which require frequent and uncontrolled access to 'TOP SECRET' information. See further Ministry of Defence Guidance (2014), available at www.gov.uk/guidance/security-vetting-and-clearance. The Prime Minister may still, of course, receive briefings from the security service regarding potential ministerial appointments. For example, see further point of order raised by Dale Norman Campbell-Savours MP regarding the suitability of six Conservative MPs to hold office, Hansard, HC Deb., vol. 145, col. 1041, 25 January 1989.

[8] See further David Rodgers, *By Royal Appointment: Tales from the Privy Council, the Unknown Arm of Government* (Biteback, 2015). Note also that the Leader of the Opposition must be made a member of the Privy Council to be provided with intelligence briefings from Whitehall. Labour leader Jeremy Corbyn was initially resistant to pledge an oath to the Queen. See further Matt Dathan, 'Jeremy Corbyn will have to kneel before the Queen and kiss her hand – despite wanting to abolish the monarchy', *Independent*, 15 September 2015.

[9] *Ibid.*

consequences for Ministers who leak information are likely to be very different to those in Crown service. Ministers can be pressured to resign their post but will remain a salaried Member of Parliament.[10] Crown servants can be subject to disciplinary action, dismissal and possible civil or criminal action.[11]

Prosecutions for unauthorised disclosures are relatively few.[12] When they do occur, the cases are considerably high profile in nature and place the spotlight back on the disclosed information, something which the official secrets regime seeks to avoid. There is an incentive, to pursue the investigation and punishment of some leakers whilst refraining from action against others. Some leaks can be self-serving[13] whereas others can be officially sanctioned by government or officials to highlight policy issues without an official announcement.[14]

In 2014, the government introduced a new security classification scheme. The number of classifications were reduced from six ('UNCLASSIFIED', 'PROTECT', 'RESTRICTED', 'CONFIDENTIAL', 'SECRET' and 'TOP SECRET') to three: 'OFFICIAL', 'SECRET' and 'TOP SECRET'.[15] A key motivation behind the reform was to bring a system originally engineered to govern the handling of paper-based materials in line with the realities of twenty-first century working

---

[10]   This is consistent with the doctrine of Ministerial Responsibility and the Ministerial Code. Note that even if the MP 'loses the party whip' and ceases to be under the control of the parliamentary party, they will still remain an MP until the electorate chooses to remove them or they choose to resign.

[11]   See further below.

[12]   For data, see further below.

[13]   Leon Britain ordered a civil servant to leak a memo during the Westland Affair to discredit Michael Heseltine. See Colin Pilkington, *The Civil Service Today* (Manchester University Press, 1999) 57.

[14]   Pozen calls this act 'pleaking', see further David E. Pozen, 'The Leaky Leviathan: Why the Government Condemns and Condones Unlawful Disclosures of Information' (2013) 127 *Harvard Law Review* 512, 565. For a UK perspective see also the comments by Dianne Abbot and others regarding use of the 'Chapman Pincher route', Hansard, HC Deb., vol. 145, col. 1078, 25 January 1989. For further analysis of the debates regarding the Official Secrets Bill, see generally John Griffith, 'The Official Secrets Act 1989' (1989) 16(2) *Journal of Law and Society* 280.

[15]   See further Cabinet Office, *Government Security Classifications*, version 1.0 (2013), available at www.gov.uk/government/uploads/system/uploads/attachment_data/file/251480/Government-Security-Classifications-April-2014.pdf.

practices.[16] Despite the reforms, the laws which underpin the scheme have remained unchanged.[17] Unauthorised disclosures are criminalised primarily by the Official Secrets Act 1989 drafted in an age of paper-based leaks. The government may also seek to bring a civil claim for breach of confidence to restrain publication and recover any profits made from the disclosures. In the Internet age, both methods suffer from the same difficulty: extraterritorial application and enforcement.

The aim of this chapter is to focus upon the consequences of unauthorised disclosures for Crown servants. The first section will provide in-depth analysis of unauthorised disclosures in government departments and agencies by drawing upon extensive information obtained using freedom of information requests. The second section will provide an assessment of the laws used to prosecute individuals for making an unauthorised disclosure in the light of the *Guja* v. *Moldova* and *Bucur* v. *Romania* decisions.[18] The third and final part of the chapter will consider the common law remedy of breach of confidence, Convention compliance and whether the remedy is still useful in the age post the Manning and Snowden disclosures.

I STATE OF UNAUTHORISED DISCLOSURES

The purpose of this section is to provide an insight into the frequency of leaking and leak inquiries in government departments and agencies. The author sent freedom of information requests to 91 government departments and agencies who employ civil servants.[19] The author developed a standardised request asking organisations employing civil servants for information. Out of the responses received, 48 responses provided useable data and information.[20] The Scottish Government provided an

---

[16] Cabinet Office, *Government Security Classifications: Supplier Briefing* (2013), available at www.gov.uk/government/uploads/system/uploads/attachment_data/file/251481/Government-Security-Classifications-Supplier-Briefing-Oct-2013.pdf.

[17] See above n. 15, 4.

[18] Official Secrets Act 1911, s.1, as well as the offence of misconduct in public office.

[19] Based on the organisations who took part in the 2013 Civil Service People Survey, available at www.civilservice.gov.uk/about/improving/employee-engagement-in-the-civil-service/people-survey-2013.

[20] The National Crime Agency identified that it was exempt from the Freedom of Information Act 2000. Organisations are also able to apply exemptions where the information requested would not be possible to retrieve within

aggregated response which included data from its own department as well as six executive agencies under its control.[21]

Signing the Official Secrets Act

Departments and agencies were asked whether civil servants working for their organisation were required to sign the Official Secrets Act and, if so, to provide a blank copy of the agreement. When Crown servants sign the Official Secrets Act they surrender their expression rights in respect of information protected by the Act. In reality, signing of the Act represents little more than an acknowledgement of the various obligations.[22] All Crown servants are subject to the Official Secrets Act 1989; all individuals within the jurisdiction of the UK courts are subject to Official Secrets Act 1989, section 5 and the Official Secrets Act 1911.[23]

Twenty four of the 48 responses identified that the Official Secrets Act declaration is included as part of the civil servant's contract of employment. There was a variation in the wording used in the contracts. For example, the United Kingdom Debt Management Office provides a clause in the contract of employment which states 'as a Civil Servant you owe duties of confidentiality and loyal service to the Crown and are subject to the Official Secrets Act 1989 (and any subsequent enactment)'.[24] In contrast, the Charity Commission provides a bullet-point list of Acts of Parliament to which the civil servant is to be subject as well as identifying that a fact sheet on the Official Secrets Act will be provided.[25] It was not clear from all of the responses provided as to whether an explanatory fact sheet on the Official Secrets Act 1989 was provided to civil servants prior to signing the contract of employment.

---

the £600 cost limit. Exemptions also can be applied on grounds of national security and confidentiality.

[21]   The executive agencies included were Disclosure Scotland, Education Scotland, Student Awards Agency for Scotland, Transport Scotland, Accountant in Bankruptcy, Scottish Housing Regulator.

[22]   Although it could be used to bolster the argument that a contractual duty of confidence existed between the Crown servant and the organisation, see further e.g. *Attorney General* v. *Blake* [2000] UKHL 45, discussed below.

[23]   Note that individuals do not need to sign the Act to commit an offence under Official Secrets Act 1989, s.5, this further compounds the point that 'signing' the Act is a symbolic gesture rather than a legal necessity.

[24]   UK Debt Management Office, FOI response, received 6 May 2015.

[25]   Charity Commission, FOI response, received 12 May 2015.

Three of the 48 responses identified that civil servants sign the Act. In these cases a standardised fact sheet is provided explaining the Official Secrets Act 1989 which the civil servants must sign to acknowledge that they have read it. It was not clear from the responses whether those organisations make reference to the Official Secrets Acts in the contract of employment.

Seven of the 48 responses identified that civil servants in their respective organisations do not sign the Official Secrets Act. The response from the Scottish Government, comprising of information from the organisation and its six executive agencies (Disclosure Scotland, Education Scotland, Student Awards Agency for Scotland, Transport Scotland, Accountant in Bankruptcy, Scottish Housing Regulator) identified that civil servants did not sign the Act. At first sight there would appear to be no logical explanation for why civil servants in the aforementioned organisations do not sign the Act. However, the Welsh Government in its response identified that:

> information we have access to that is covered by the Officials Secrets Act comes from other government departments and relates to non-devolved matters. Any information would only be released by the government department concerned e.g. MOD, Home Office or Cabinet Office.[26]

Defence and national security issues are not currently devolved to the Scottish and Welsh administrations. It may therefore be sensible that civil servants working for those administrations do not need to sign the Act. The Office for the Scottish Charity Regulator, Scottish Prison Service, the Office for National Statistics, the Medicines Health Regulation Agency, the Land Registry, Food Standards Agency, Food and Environment Research Agency, also all identified that civil servants are not required to sign the Official Secrets Act. This therefore raises the question as to why other organisations require civil servants to sign the Act despite the work of the organisations in question appearing to have little to do with work covered by the Official Secrets Act 1989. For example, it is difficult to see how civil servants working for the Animal Plant Health Agency or the Rural Payments Agency may be party to information which could fall within the provisions of the Official Secrets Act 1989.[27]

---

[26] Welsh Government, FOI response, received 15 May 2015.
[27] For full explanation of the sections see further below.

There is an argument for a consistent approach across the Civil Service. Where all civil servants are subject to the Official Secrets Act 1989, it is not clear why some organisations require signing of the Act when some do not. The Official Secrets Act can serve as a deterrent to the making of unauthorised disclosures even where such disclosures would not concern information under the Act. Unauthorised disclosures which do not breach the criminal law may be protected by the Public Interest Disclosure Act 1998. Requiring civil servants to sign the Official Secrets Act, particularly where they are not working on defence and national security matters, is an unnecessary and disproportionate restriction on expression.

In addition to the above, none of the responses received made reference to the common law offence of misconduct in public office, despite the offence being used in attempted prosecutions of civil servants, either as an alternative to the Official Secrets Acts where the information disclosed was determined not to be covered by the Official Secrets Act 1989,[28] or as an additional charge. No reference is made to the misconduct in public office offence in law. Moreover, the explanatory fact sheets which provide information on the Official Secrets Act 1989 do not identify that individuals who make unauthorised disclosures may also be subject to the alternative offence.

Signing Confidentiality Agreements

The signing of an express confidentiality agreement is, again, an act of symbolism. There is already an implied duty of confidence. Moreover, the Civil Service Code makes it clear that civil servants owe a duty of confidence and that this is a contractual duty.[29] As with the signing of the Official Secrets Acts, responses to the request identify that there is a variation of approaches taken by departments and agencies. Twenty-two

---

[28] As was the case in the arrest of Christopher Galley. Information disclosed to the author by the Crown Prosecution Service indicates that the offence is used as an additional count where charges have been brought for unauthorised disclosure under the Official Secrets Act 1989. Also, note that following allegations regarding payments of public officials for information supplied to journalists, several officials were charged with misconduct in public office offences.

[29] Civil Service Code (March 2015), available at www.gov.uk/government/publications/civil-service-code/the-civil-service-code.

of the 48 responses identify that a confidentiality agreement is included in the contract of employment. Three organisations answered that they require civil servants to sign confidentiality agreements. Two of those respondents identified that this was linked to the Official Secrets Act agreement.[30] Seventeen responses identified that civil servants were not required to sign a confidentiality agreement at all. One must therefore question why additional confidentiality agreements are needed when the Civil Service Code is in place. Well established common law principles identify that unauthorised disclosures may be made in the public interest, particularly where the information concerned involved evidence of iniquity.[31] This is supported by Public Interest Disclosure Act 1998, section 43J. Requiring civil servants to sign confidentiality agreements when they are already subject to the Civil Service Code is unnecessary and may act to dissuade civil servants from bringing important concerns to the attention of regulators or the general public.

Reported Leaks and Subsequent Investigations

The Crown Prosecution Service, Department for Communities and Local Government and HM Treasury refused to provide an exact figure but indicated that there had been less than five unauthorised disclosures during the period. The Department for Work and Pensions only held information for the year 2014 but identified that there had been 15 unauthorised disclosures in that year. HMRC reported 130 unauthorised disclosures had occurred over the four-year period and were able to provide a detailed breakdown of the number of incidents per year.

Generally, where leaks had been reported the same number of recorded leaks had been investigated. This would indicate that departments and agencies are investigating reported leaks. For example, the Department for Environment, Food and Rural Affairs identified that there had been 12 reported leaks and 12 leak investigations during the period. However, there were two notable discrepancies in the responses provided. Not all of the responses identified that the number of reported leaks matched the number of reported leak investigations. The Department for Education

---

[30] Royal Parks, FOI response, received 9 April 2015; and Office for National Statistics, FOI response, available at www.ons.gov.uk/ons/about-ons/business-transparency/freedom-of-information/what-can-i-request/previous-foi-requests/government/unauthorised-disclosures-of-official-information/index.html.
[31] *Gartside* v. *Outram* (1857) 26 LJ Ch. 113; *Initial Services Ltd.* v. *Putterill* [1968] 1 QB 396; *Lion Laboratories* v. *Evans* [1984] QB 526.

stated that it did not hold information on the number of reported leaks, however the Department disclosed that there had been 23 leak investigations during the period. Similarly, the Crown Office and Procurator Fiscal disclosed that there had been one recorded incident of unauthorised disclosure but identified that eight leak investigations had taken place. There is a need for consistent recording of unauthorised disclosures to journalists and to the wider public.[32] Information on leaking can provide an indication that the official reporting mechanisms for concerns are not effective in dissuading individuals from, or providing an alternative to, unauthorised leaking.[33]

Disciplinary and Dismissal

Whilst this chapter is primarily concerned with the legal consequences of unauthorised disclosures, at the lowest level civil servants may be subject to disciplinary action or dismissal as a result of making unauthorised disclosures. The number of disciplinary or dismissal actions across the departments and agencies who provided information was generally low. The Department for Education reported that ten people had been disciplined. The Department for Work and Pensions were able to provide a detailed breakdown of the number of civil servants disciplined for unauthorised disclosures, identifying that 2,237 individuals had been disciplined between 2010 and 2014.[34]

Scope for Reform

Overall, the wide variation in approaches used across the departments and agencies that provided information suggests that there is a need for greater consistency. Of principal concern is the signing of the Official Secrets Act. Signing of the Act pre-dates the Official Secrets Act 1989

---

[32] Where the disclosures do not contain personal data, they fall outside of the remit of the Data Protection Act 1998. Breaches of the Data Protection Act 1998 must be reported to the Information Commissioner.

[33] In Chapter 5, the author reports on whistleblowing disclosures across government departments and agencies; because of the way in which the information on whistleblowing and unauthorised disclosures have been reported it is not possible to accurately draw direct comparisons from analysis of this data.

[34] Department for Work and Pensions, FOI response, received 30 April 15. The number of unauthorised disclosures appears high in relation to other government departments and agencies who provided information and must therefore be viewed with a degree of caution.

and is indicative of a time when all disclosures of official information, regardless of whether they concerned national security matters or not, could be subject to criminal action under the old Official Secrets Act 1911, section 2. Signing of the Act by all civil servants should no longer have been considered necessary when the categories of protected information were narrowed in the 1989 Act. Regardless of this, even pre the 1989 Act, signing of the Official Secrets Act was never necessary because all Crown servants could be prosecuted for offences regardless of whether they had signed the Act or not. All Crown servants remain subject to the Official Secrets Act 1989 regardless of whether they 'sign the Act' or not. It is submitted that the process of signing the Act should be reviewed to determine whether or not it is still necessary, and whether it is creating an unnecessary barrier to the expression of public interest concerns.

If signing the Act is to remain common practice it is suggested that a review is needed to identify whether it is necessary to require individuals not in security sensitive posts to sign the Act. Any contract and guidance should also make reference to, and provide explanation of, the offence of misconduct in public office if it is to continue to be used to prosecute civil servants for unauthorised disclosures. Another option would be to reduce the number of individuals signing the Act only to those involved in national security matters. The difficulty with this option as it currently stands is that the Official Secrets Act 1989 still has the potential to cover information classified at the lowest level 'OFFICIAL' because (as identified above), the classification of documents is not linked to the protected categories of information. The following section will now proceed to discuss criminal disclosures.

II CRIMINAL DISCLOSURES

Unauthorised disclosures are criminalised primarily by the Official Secrets Act 1989 which replaced Official Secrets Act 1911, section 2.[35] The old section 2 offence was hastily drafted in an afternoon in response to concerns that enemy spies were operating in Dover Harbour prior to

---

[35] Note that for reasons of focus and due to space limitations, this analysis will not consider the very large number of other statutory provisions which may apply to Crown servants working in particular areas.

the outbreak of the First World War.[36] The offence was so broadly drafted that it effectively criminalised all official information. An attempted prosecution of the then journalist Jonathan Aitken prompted the government to commission a review of the legislation.[37] The Franks Committee (chaired by Lord Franks) recommended extensive reforms to the 1911 Act on the classification and handling of documents.[38] The report received a lukewarm response from Edward Heath's Conservative Government. Home Secretary, Robert Carr, accepted the recommendations of the report but stated that the government needed further time to consider them.[39] The Conservative Government was defeated at the 1974 general election before any reforms could be implemented.[40] The Labour Party manifesto had detailed plans to abolish section 2 and replace it with a new 'Official Information Act' which would be based upon the recommendations of the Franks Committee Report; however, once in power, the Labour Government failed to go further than giving backing to a Private Member's Bill introduced by Liberal MP Clement Freud.[41]

A series of controversial and high profile cases followed. In 1983, Sarah Tisdall was the first person to be sent to prison for unauthorised disclosure under section 2 since 1970.[42] Then in 1984, the Crown failed to successfully prosecute Clive Ponting for leaking documents to opposition MP Tam Dalyell identifying that the government had misled Parliament over the circumstances surrounding the sinking of the *General*

---

[36] For the history of the 1911 Act, see generally David Hooper, *Official Secrets: The Use and Abuse of the Act* (Secker & Warburg, 1987).

[37] *R* v. *Aitken* (1971, unreported), see further Jonathan Aitken, *Officially Secret* (Weidenfield and Nicolson, 1971).

[38] *Report of the Departmental Committee on Section 2 of the Official Secrets Act 1911*, Cmnd 5104 (1972).

[39] For discussion of this see Hooper, above n 36, 293. For the House of Commons debate on the Franks Committee Report see Hansard, HC Deb., vol. 858, col. 1885, 29 June 1973.

[40] Most interestingly, Andrew states that as Prime Minister, Edward Heath was 'even more secretive about intelligence matters than the Secret Service itself' and when intelligence chiefs requested that their successes were publicised he would refuse, see further Christopher Andrew, *Secret Service* (Hienmann, 1985) 696. This may suggest that if Heath's government had remained in power the reforms may not have been forthcoming.

[41] Official Information Bill, 1978–79, Bill 96.

[42] Tisdall leaked documents concerning arrangements regarding nuclear missiles at Greenham Common; she later pleaded guilty to the offence and was sentenced to six months' imprisonment. *R* v. *Tisdall* (1984, unreported).

Belgrano during the Falklands conflict. Ponting's defence was that it was in the 'interests of the state' for Parliament to be informed that it was being misled by Ministers. Despite being directed to convict Ponting, the jury acquitted him. Following the case, the Crown was understandably reluctant to risk another prosecution using section 2, and in 1985 it decided not to prosecute Cathy Massiter, a former intelligence officer in the security service, who made claims in a television documentary that MI5 had bugged the telephones of trade union members. There were two further unsuccessful attempts to introduce new legislation by Richard Shepherd MP and Lord Bethell in 1988.[43] When Peter Wright's book *Spycatcher* was published, the government chose to take action in the civil courts by bringing multiple breach of confidence actions, which were costly and ultimately unsuccessful.[44] The following section will consider the Act which replaced section 2 of the 1911 Act, the Official Secrets Act 1989.

Official Secrets Act 1989

The Official Secrets Act 1989 replaced the complete ban on the unauthorised disclosure of all official information by servants of Her Majesty by limiting the information to six categories. Section 1 concerns security and intelligence information; section 2 concerns information regarding defence; section 3 concerns international relations; section 4 concerns crime and special investigations (which includes information regarding interception of communications); section 5 concerns information resulting from unauthorised disclosures or entrusted in confidence; and section 6 concerns information entrusted in confidence to other states or international organisations. During the course of the following analysis, the author will provide data identifying the number of defendants proceeded against under each section of the Official Secrets Act 1989 between the

---

[43] Richard Shepherd's proposed Official Information Bill would have included a public interest test and the use of ministerial certificates to certify the severity of any unauthorised disclosure. See further, Hansard, HC Deb., vol. 125, col. 564, 15 January 1988, and HL Deb., vol. 495, col. 1566, 20 April 1988. For further discussion see Lucinda Maer and Oonagh Gay, *Official Secrecy*, SN/PC/02023 (Parliament and Constitution Centre, 30 December 2008).

[44] *Attorney General v. Guardian Newspapers Ltd (No. 2)* [1988] UKHL 6. For discussion see further Fiona Patfield, '*Spycatcher* Worldwide: An Overview' (1989) 11(6) *European Intellectual Property Review* 201.

years 1999 and 2013.[45] The information provided is based upon analysis of data obtained through freedom of information requests made by the author.[46]

Unauthorised Disclosures of Security and Intelligence Information

Official Secrets Act 1989, section 1(1)(a), provides that a current or former member of the security and intelligence services or notified person will be guilty of an offence if they disclose any information which is or has been in their possession in the course of their work.[47] Any unauthorised disclosures made by employees of the security and intelligence services and notified persons will constitute an offence, regardless of the classification of document, the harm caused by the disclosure or any public benefit. Employees of the security and intelligence services are also exempt from the Public Interest Disclosure Act.[48]

During debate on the Official Secrets Bill at Committee stage, section 1(1) received considerable criticism. It was suggested that the life-long duty of non-disclosure was imposed as a reactionary measure after the government's failure to suppress the Peter Wright book, *Spycatcher*.[49] The resulting Act would have the potential to make a member or former member of the intelligence services criminally liable for writing a book about their experiences without authorisation.[50] Of principal relevance to

---

[45] Prior to this date the exact section was not recorded, in 1991 one individual was found guilty for an offence under the Act. In 1993 two individuals were proceeded against, Ministry of Justice, FOI Response, received 18 May 2011.

[46] Note that the data provided may also include defendants who were from the police or government contractors and fall outside of the scope of this study.

[47] Official Secrets Act 1989, s.1(1)(b) includes 'persons notified' of the provisions contained in s.1. Persons who are most likely affected by such a notification are members of the Joint Intelligence Committee and the Intelligence and Security Committee, whose work brings both committees into contact with information regarding national security and intelligence matters.

[48] Persons notified would need to be exempted from the provisions by the issue of a ministerial certificate.

[49] See comments by Roy Hattersley MP, Hansard, HC Deb., vol. 145, col. 1049, 25 January 1989.

[50] The Official Secrets Act 1989 did not prevent the former Director General of MI5, Dame Stella Rimington, from publishing her memoirs. Despite controversy caused by the publication, the Home Office did not go further than voicing 'regret and discontent' for her decision to publish; see further Serverin Carrell, 'Rimington calls for independent vetting of spy memoirs', *Independent*, 9 September 2001. The publication of official memoirs is considered below.

this analysis, Members of Parliament also expressed reservations that the section would prevent individuals from raising concerns regarding wrongdoing or malpractice and would ultimately be unable to raise concerns to Parliament. The government refused to include a public interest defence on the basis that it would give *carte blanche* to individuals to make unauthorised disclosures. As an alternative, the government presented staff with an authorised alternative, the Independent Staff Counsellor, a role which at that time was very much in its infancy.

Employees of the security and intelligence services still lack access to Parliament. Despite the establishment of the Intelligence and Security Committee (ISC) in 1994,[51] the successor to the Security Commission,[52] and enhanced statutory oversight powers following the Justice and Security Act 2013, there is no known official channel for individuals in the security and intelligence services to raise concerns with the Committee.[53] At the time of writing, the ISC is yet to provide any form of publically accessible assessment as to how the Counsellor role is working in practice.[54] Perhaps the most notable prosecution under Official Secrets Act 1989, section 1 so far has been that of David Shayler.[55] Shayler made unauthorised disclosures to the *Mail on Sunday* alleging that the Secret Intelligence Service (MI6) had plotted to assassinate Colonel Gaddafi; that MI5 had conducted surveillance on a number of key figures in the Labour Party who, at the time of the disclosures, had become key ministerial figures; and that MI5 had failed to pass on intelligence which could have prevented terrorist bombings in London. Shayler was found guilty and sentenced to six months' imprisonment.[56] Between the years

---

[51] Established by Intelligence Services Act 1994, s.10.

[52] For consideration of the work of the Security Commission see further Laurence Lustgarten and Ian Leigh, *In From the Cold: National Security and Parliamentary Democracy* (OUP, 1994).

[53] For the author's evidence to the Committee on this point see Ashley Savage, Submission to the Intelligence and Security Committee: Privacy and Security Inquiry, 12 March 2015, available at http://isc.independent.gov.uk/public-evidence.

[54] A conclusion based upon the author's analysis of the Committee's annual reports and special reports. Note that reports are often partly redacted.

[55] *R* v. *Shayler* [2002] UKHL 11, discussed further below and in Chapter 6.

[56] *Ibid.*

1999 and 2013, a total of only two (out of three) defendants have been found guilty of Official Secrets Act 1989, section 1(a) and (b) offences.[57]

Damaging Disclosures of National Security and Intelligence Information

Official Secrets Act 1989, section 1(3) concerns Crown servants who are not otherwise employees of the security and intelligence services but whose work involves security and intelligence information. Fenwick and Phillipson highlight the difference in treatment between employees of the security and intelligence services who are subject to the all-encompassing provision in section 1(1) (a) and (b), and, ordinary Crown servants subject to the damaging disclosure test in section 1(3), suggesting that the section is aimed at 'underpinning the culture of secrecy in the security services rather than ensuring that no damaging disclosure is likely to be made'.[58] Regardless of motivation, there is an alternative explanation for why employees in intelligence and security should be subject to an absolute prohibition on disclosure.[59] Arguably, any disclosure of information emanating from the security and intelligence services may be harmful, regardless of its content. Innocuous information which on its own does not appear to cause a risk to national security may contribute to other pieces of intelligence, leading to the formation of a much more detailed and potentially harmful picture.[60]

A disclosure of such information is held to be damaging if it causes damage to the work of any part of the services or would be likely to

---

[57] 1997: one individual found guilty; 2000: one individual proceeded against; 2002: one individual found guilty: Ministry of Justice, FOI response, received 18 May 2011, and Ministry of Justice, FOI response, received 7 January 2015.

[58] Helen Fenwick and Gavin Phillipson, *Media Freedom under the Human Rights Act* (OUP, 2007) 932. There is also another key distinction: unless the 'ordinary' Crown servant has been expressly exempted by a ministerial certificate, they will be able to obtain employment protection using the Public Interest Disclosure Act 1998 unless they are convicted of a criminal offence in making the disclosure.

[59] Save for the opportunity to seek authorisation to disclose information as per Official Secrets Act 1989, s.7 and to challenge any refusal to disclose before the Investigatory Powers Tribunal, following *A* v. *B* [2009] UKSC 12.

[60] Known as 'mosaic theory', discussed further in David E. Pozen, 'The Mosaic Theory, National Security and the Freedom of Information Act' (2005) 115 *Yale Law Journal* 628. It could also provide metadata that can be used by others to identify operatives.

cause such damage or 'falls within a class or description' likely to have such an effect.[61] The test is both widely defined and easily satisfied. The White Paper (*Reform of Section 2 of the Official Secrets Act 1911*, Cm 408 (1988)) indicated that the public interest is relevant as to whether a disclosure is damaging. In considering the evidential burden on the prosecution to prove the necessary harm to satisfy the test, the government stated that 'evidence may need to be adduced' which involves 'a disclosure which is as harmful as or more harmful than the disclosure which is the subject of the prosecution'. The argument provided a justification for not adducing such evidence in court. Instead it was held to be sufficient to state that the document or information concerned was of a 'certain class or description'. The question of what constitutes a damaging disclosure of a certain class or description, or indeed of who decides which documents belong to which class, remain unclear.

The majority of the sections in the 1989 Act contain 'damaging disclosure' tests. Rather than affording the court the opportunity to assess the damage caused by any disclosure, the information concerned need only relate to the categories of information so prescribed in the respective category. Beyond this, the 'potential to cause damage to the work of or any part of the security and intelligence services' is also a test easily satisfied. For example, arguably any unauthorised disclosure of material protected under the Official Secrets Act 1989 can be said to cause damage to the services. The drafting of the Act identifies a paradoxical situation faced by the legislators, governments and intelligence services, who do not wish for information to be disclosed in court as to do so may reveal sensitive material; likewise, judges are traditionally reluctant to make assessments as to what constitutes a risk to 'national security' as this is seen as a matter for the government of the day.[62]

The classification of documents is an established and integral feature of the control of official information but they cannot be used in evidence to provide evidence of the damage caused by the disclosure. The White Paper expressly stated that the classification of the document will not be of 'evidential relevance' to the jury or of the degree of harm caused by the leaks. The classification therefore only provides evidence of the person's opinion of the importance of the document at the time of classification. The White Paper also stated that the classification of the

---

[61]   Official Secrets Act 1989, s.1(4).

[62]   For an example, see the discussion in *Council of Civil Service Unions* v. *Minister for the Civil Service* [1985] AC 374, [393] per Lord Fraser. This is further demonstrated in cases concerning Public Interest Immunity certificates. See e.g. *Burmah Oil Co. Ltd* v. *Bank of England* [1980] AC 1090.

document may provide evidence to suggest that the defendant knew that his unauthorised disclosure was likely to cause harm but the prosecution would be required to adduce further evidence to prove that the disclosure was likely to be harmful. This approach is significantly different to that proposed by the Franks Committee which recommended, first, that the classification of documents should be enshrined in statute. Second, prior to any prosecution taking place, the Minister responsible for the document(s) in question would have to determine whether the information had been classified at the right level and that its disclosure would cause 'serious injury to the interests of the nation'.[63] The Minister would have been required to issue a certificate to the court and would be responsible before Parliament if the document was over-classified.[64] A similar proposal was made by Richard Shepherd MP in the unsuccessful Official Information Bill.[65] Two defendants were proceeded against for offences under Official Secrets Act 1989, section 1(3) between 1999 and 2013, with one individual being found guilty of the offence.[66]

Unauthorised Disclosure of Defence Information

Official Secrets Act 1989, section 2, concerns the damaging disclosure of defence information. The section provides that a disclosure will be damaging if it damages the capability of the armed forces to carry out their tasks or leads to loss of life, injury or serious damage to equipment or installations, endangers the interests of the United Kingdom abroad or endangers the safety of British citizens. The test for damage in section 2 is far more specific than the test relating to the damaging disclosure of security and intelligence information.[67] The section clearly defines the potential of harm to members of the Armed Forces and their equipment. However, endangering the 'interests of the United Kingdom abroad' remains undefined. Bailin argues that the phase is 'troublingly wide' and questions whether it could be used to cover up the disclosure of information concerning the treatment of prisoners by British soldiers.[68] During debates on the Bill, it was suggested that the wording of the

---

[63]   See above n. 38. For further discussion see Chapter 8.
[64]   *Ibid.* The workability of such a model is considered further below.
[65]   See above n. 41.
[66]   Both cases were in 1998: Ministry of Justice, FOI response, received 18 May 2011, and Ministry of Justice, FOI response, received 7 January 2015.
[67]   Official Secrets Act 1989, s.1(3).
[68]   Alex Bailin, 'The Last Cold War Statute' (2008) 8 *Criminal Law Review* 625–6.

section set the bar deliberately low on the basis that the 'Government distrusted the jury system'.[69] Arguably, it may be suggested that Clive Ponting would have been caught by the section, suggesting that section 2 does not learn the lessons from the jury nullification in that case. Three defendants were proceeded against between 1999 and 2013 for offences under section 2(1), with two of the individuals being found guilty.[70]

Disclosure of Information Relating to International Relations

Official Secrets Act 1989, section 3, concerns the damaging disclosure of international relations information or 'any confidential information, document or other article which was obtained from a State other than the United Kingdom or an international organisation'. Section 3(6) gives a definition of 'confidentiality':

> For the purposes of this section any information, document or article obtained from a state or organisation is confidential at any time while the terms on which it was obtained require it to be held in confidence or while the circumstances in which it was obtained make it reasonable for the state or organisation to expect that it would be so held.

The wording of the section provides for an easily satisfied harm test. Section 3(6) is particularly restrictive in scope. First, the section gives no indication as to the circumstances in which documents should be held in confidence and in the absence of express instruction from another state on how the information is to be handled, the section infers that any disclosure of information obtained from other states is damaging. Second, the lack of a clear definition in the wording of section 3(6) is a cause for confusion. This chapter has already indicated that there is a classification system for official documents, in which the classification 'CONFIDENTIAL' is no longer used. However, under the definition of section 3(6) information harmful to international relations is to be regarded as confidential. This gives no recognition to the classification system already in place, nor does it fully recognise the substance of the information concerned. Moreover, it does not recognise the differing foreign classification systems.[71] The information may be of particularly

---

[69]   For discussion see Griffith, above n. 14, 283.

[70]   1999: one person found guilty; 2000: one person proceeded against; 2011: one person found guilty. Ministry of Justice, FOI response, received 18 May 2011, and Ministry of Justice, FOI response, received 7 January 2015.

[71]   See e.g., United States, Executive Order 13526 on classifying information, 29 December 2009.

low level importance, yet this is not taken into account by the section. Furthermore, information which is protected by the Official Secrets Act 1989 may not be protected in the same way by the other states' domestic legislation. Indeed, the other state may not have an equivalent to the UK Official Secrets Act, it may not protect information concerning international relations and any such legislation may have a public interest defence.

The controversial trial of Derek Pasquill brought the use of section 3 into question. Pasquill was a civil servant in the Foreign and Commonwealth Office (FCO). He was charged with six breaches of Official Secrets Act 1989, section 3, after leaking several documents to Martin Bright, a journalist who used the information to write several articles in the *Observer* and *New Statesman*.[72] He leaked information regarding top secret extraordinary rendition flights of terrorist suspects by the US Central Intelligence Agency, which also identified that the flights had landed on UK soil to refuel. The case was dropped at trial after it was admitted by counsel for the government that there was 'no realistic prospect of conviction'. This followed disclosure of a series of internal written papers within the FCO which indicated that the leaks had not been damaging and had instead promoted positive debate. The documents were not disclosed to the defence until the day before the case was dropped, 20 months after the police investigation had started.[73]

Disclosure of Information Relevant to Criminal Proceedings

Official Secrets Act 1989, section 4 makes it an offence for a person who is or has been a Crown servant or government contractor to disclose any information relevant to criminal proceedings to which section 4(2) applies. In order to understand the interrelationship between the sections it is necessary to quote the provisions in their entirety. Section 4(2) states that:

---

[72]   *R* v. *Pasquill* (2008, unreported). See Richard Norton Taylor, 'Civil servant who leaked rendition secrets goes free', *Guardian*, 10 January 2008.
[73]   It should be noted from the data provided from the Ministry of Justice that it would appear that this is the only case to have been proceeded against under this section between 1999 and 2013: Ministry of Justice, FOI response, received 18 May 2011, and Ministry of Justice, FOI response, received 7 January 2015.

This section applies to any information, document or other article;

(a) the disclosure of which—
    (i)   results in the commission of an offence; or
    (ii) facilitates an escape from legal custody or the doing of any other act prejudicial to the safekeeping of persons in legal custody; or
    (iii) impedes the prevention or detection of offences or the apprehension or prosecution of suspected offenders; or
(b) which is such that its unauthorised disclosure would be likely to have any of those effects.

It can be observed that the above provisions contained in section 4 do not provide a test for harm. Instead, for an offence to be committed under section 4 it is required that the disclosure results in the commission of an offence, escape from custody, etc. under section 4(2)(i) to (iii). This has the effect of creating an implied harm test, yet this too can be easily satisfied. An unauthorised disclosure of information which is leaked to a journalist or a publisher would mean that the person in receipt of the information would commit an offence under Official Secrets Act 1989, section 5 (see below).[74] Information relating to electronic surveillance activities which is disclosed by Crown servants or government contractors, such as the type of information disclosed by Edward Snowden, would be covered by section 4(3)(a) of the Act.[75] As well as being charged with an offence under Official Secrets Act 1989, section 1, David Shayler's actions also fell under section 4(3) because one of his disclosures concerned information obtained from a wiretap.[76]

Information Resulting in Unauthorised Disclosures or Entrusted in Confidence

Official Secrets Act 1989, section 5 applies to persons who have received information entrusted in confidence by a Crown servant or government contractor and have then disclosed the information. An offence is committed when a person makes an unauthorised disclosure of the information which is damaging and which he knows or has reasonable cause to believe would be damaging under sections 1 to 3, provided that the disclosure is an offence under those sections. Section 5 carries a

---

[74] Or possibly be liable for aiding and abetting misconduct in public office, see further below.
[75] See also Regulation of Investigatory Powers Act 2000, s.54, which makes it an offence to 'tip off' individuals who are subject to a surveillance warrant; this extends to 'every other person who is aware of it or its contents'.
[76] See further, *R* v. *Shayler*, above n. 55.

further means of protection whereby persons in receipt of information as a result of a breach of Official Secrets Act 1911, section 1 will be subject to the provision. It is important to note that section 5 does not criminalise those who are in receipt of information unless they choose to make a further disclosure of information.[77] This should be considered in contrast with the old Official Secrets Act 1911, section 2, which criminalised the recipients of information.

The section could technically be used to prosecute individuals for conducting acts of spying by passing on documents to 'the enemy'. However, Official Secrets Act 1911, section 1, is more likely to be used for that purpose. The targets of section 5 are journalists and others who receive unauthorised disclosures from Crown servants and publish the information in the public domain. Despite this, there are no special procedures contained within the provisions for dealing with cases involving journalists.[78] In practice, section 5 is used more for the threat of prosecution in order to attempt to restrict the publication of leaked documents or to determine the source of the leak.[79] Disclosures by Members of Parliament, or even a defendant's legal counsel, if the information were to be repeated outside of conference, could potentially be captured by the section.[80] At the time of writing there has only been one conviction for a section 5 offence: Lee O'Connor, a researcher working for a Member of Parliament, was sentenced to three months' imprisonment for passing documents on to the MP that he had received from a civil servant.[81]

---

[77] In contrast, the US Espionage Act 1917 can be used to prosecute both the discloser and recipient of information.

[78] Whilst it is acknowledged that Official Secrets Act 1989, s.11(3), imports special procedures for obtaining search warrants when the suspected person is a journalist, the procedures do not extend to s.5.

[79] For example, a search warrant could be obtained for suspected offences under Official Secrets Act 1989, s.5. Note that any search warrant concerning the media will be subject to the special provisions contained in Official Secrets Act 1989, s.11(3).

[80] However, note that MPs enjoy the protection of parliamentary privilege for words said in Parliament. Whilst it was expressed by Lord Hope (in discussing Official Secrets Act 1989, s.1) in the *Shayler* judgment that there is an implied right to seek legal counsel, this right is unlikely to extend to subsequent disclosures made by an individual's legal counsel.

[81] Considered further below. Analysis of prosecutions also based on data obtained from FOI requests: Ministry of Justice, FOI response, received 18 May 2011, and Ministry of Justice, FOI response, received 7 January 2015.

Whilst it is a defence for an individual to show that they believed that the information in question was not damaging, the damage tests are taken from the foregoing provisions of sections 1(3), 2(1) and 3(1) which are applied to Crown servants and government contractors. One must consider whether this is a realistic expectation on the recipients of information. Crown servants and government contractors are arguably more likely to be able to determine whether the information concerned is likely to be damaging to national security because of their experience in working with the information concerned than a journalist.[82] As Fenwick and Phillipson correctly identify, the court will need to give substantial consideration to free speech rights of the press by utilising Human Rights Act 1998, section 3 to 'read down' provisions to bring Official Secrets Act 1989, section 5 into line with Article 10 of the European Convention on Human Rights (ECHR). A proportionality test will therefore be engaged under which the public interest in disclosure will be weighed against the public interest in non-disclosure. It is submitted that journalists are likely to be placed in a stronger position than ordinary citizens because of the considerable weight that the European Court of Human Rights (ECtHR) places on the right of journalists to undertake their 'vital role as watchdog'.[83] Journalists could take information concerning wrongdoing to the police (for example), however this is likely to have a significant impact on their journalistic source.[84]

There is a key distinction between section 5 which impacts on recipients of the information who chose to make a disclosure and Crown servants who are subject to other sections contained in the Act. In *Shayler*, the court was satisfied that the Official Secrets Act 1989 was compliant with Article 10 ECHR on the basis that civil servants had the opportunity to seek authorisation to disclose the information or to report information to the authorities.[85] Recipients who are not Crown servants are therefore placed at a strategic disadvantage. Section 7, which concerns authorisation, is limited only to Crown servants, government

---

[82] Conversely, there is a policy argument to suggest that journalists who publish information without determining whether disclosure will be harmful to national security should be punished. This argument is further explored in Chapter 2.

[83] See generally, *Observer and Guardian* v. *United Kingdom*, Application No. 13585/88 (ECtHR, 29 November 1991).

[84] Moreover, regardless of the s.5 offence, journalists could still be subject to the offence of aiding and abetting misconduct in public office.

[85] *R* v. *Shayler*, above n. 55, [30].

contractors and persons notified; recipients of information (such as journalists) cannot seek official authorisation for disclosure.[86]

The question remains open as to whether citizen journalists would be able to convince the court that they too should deserve the enhanced protection. Section 5 could also be used against individuals who are part of online disclosure outlets such as Wikileaks. Journalists who are part of an established media organisation and those who have a good media presence or the means to generate considerable media coverage are likely to be in a stronger position. The Attorney General must determine whether or not is in the public interest for a case to be prosecuted. Any prosecution, particularly where the disclosed information is considered to be of public interest value, is likely to result in public and political pressure. Additionally, if a case were to proceed to trial and the court was not prepared to utilise HRA 1998, section 3, to make Official Secrets Act 1989, section 5 ECHR compatible (or it was not convinced there was sufficient need to) a jury could, of course, decide to acquit the defendant even if they were directed otherwise.

Ultimately, whilst the police and the Crown Prosecution Service are subject to Human Rights Act 1989, section 6, they are not expressly required to follow Strasbourg jurisprudence or to conduct lengthy proportionality analyses. Public authorities will not be in breach of section 6 where the primary legislation does not afford the opportunity to act differently or where the primary legislation cannot be read or given effect to in a way which is compatible with the Convention.[87] Regardless of the outcome of any prosecutorial decision or trial, journalists may still be arrested. The threat of arrest may therefore be said to create a chilling effect on journalists and journalistic sources.

Safeguarding Information

Official Secrets Act 1989, section 8, is a summary offence with a maximum penalty of imprisonment for a term not exceeding three months or a fine not exceeding level 5 on the standard scale or both. The offence is committed where a Crown servant or government contractor has a document or other article which would be an offence to disclose under any of the 'foregoing provisions' of the Act and they either retain

---

[86] Official Secrets Act 1989, s.1(a) and (b). Journalists could still seek advice on disclosure by contacting the Defence and Security Media Advisory Notice Committee, although this will not protect them from liability. See further DSMA website, www.dsma.uk.

[87] Applying Official Secrets Act 1989, s.6(2)(a), (b).

the document, fail to comply with a direction to dispose of or return it, or fail 'to take such care to prevent the unauthorised disclosure of the document or article as a person in his position may reasonably be expected to take'.[88]

The case of *R* v. *Jackson* would appear to be the first time that a person in England and Wales has been brought before the courts and found guilty for an offence under Official Secrets Act 1989, section 8.[89] Jackson, a senior civil servant on secondment from the Ministry of Defence, mistakenly took two reports, one marked 'top secret', the other classified at a lower level, from his office but then also left the documents on the train. The documents were discovered by a concerned member of the public who passed the folder on to the BBC's security correspondent. Jackson pleaded guilty to the offence and received a fine of £2,500; he was reportedly able to carry on working in the organisation but in a lower position without a security clearance.[90] The year 2008 saw an unprecedented level of official information being lost. Several instances could potentially have been covered by the 'foregoing provisions' detailed in the Official Secrets Act 1989 and would therefore constitute an offence under section 8.[91] In January 2008, the loss of data regarding 600,000 persons interested in joining the UK Armed Forces by the Ministry of Defence may have constituted a damaging disclosure of defence information contrary to section 2.[92] In June 2008, the theft of a laptop owned by then Cabinet Minister Hazel Blears which contained details relating to religious extremism, resulted in calls from the Conservative opposition for a police investigation under section 8 on the basis that Ms Blears should not have held the information on the laptop in the first instance.[93] Furthermore there have been several reported instances of laptops owned by members of the security services being lost or stolen, and in September 2008 a mobile telephone sold on the Internet auction website eBay was found by the new owner to have

---

[88]   *Ibid.* s.8(1)(b).

[89]   *R* v. *Jackson* (unreported, 2008); see Mark Tran, 'Civil servant fined for leaving documents on train', *Guardian*, 28 October 2008.

[90]   Jackson was allowed to retain a position at the Ministry of Defence, albeit at a much lower level, and lost his security clearance.

[91]   'MOD admits loss of secret files', BBC News, 18 July 2008, available at http://news.bbc.co.uk/1/hi/uk/7514281.stm.

[92]   'MOD computer hard drive missing', BBC News, 10 October 2008, available at http://news.bbc.co.uk/1/hi/uk/7662604.stm.

[93]   'Blears PC loss', BBC News, 17 June 2009, available at http://news.bbc.co.uk/1/hi/uk_politics/7459579.stm.

photographs and information relating to terrorism investigations which had not been deleted by the previous owner, an operative in MI6.[94] Such instances would be covered under section 1, the disclosure of security and intelligence information. Despite clear breaches of Official Secrets Act 1989, section 8, the individuals were not prosecuted. The case highlights the need for consistency in the way in which unauthorised disclosures of information covered by the Official Secrets Act 1989 are handled.[95]

Authorisation to Disclose

The circumstances whereby a Crown servant is deemed to have made a disclosure with lawful authority are detailed in Official Secrets Act 1989, section 7. With regard to Crown servants, section 7(3) states that a disclosure is deemed lawful 'if and only if' it is made:

(a) to a Crown servant for the purposes of his functions as such; or
(b) in accordance with an official authorisation.

In the *Shayler* judgment, Lord Bingham considering the making of disclosures in the public interest and suggested that if a Crown servant had information relating to malpractice or abuse he could seek authorisation to disclose the information. This was particularly important in cases whereby the information would reveal matters 'scandalous or embarrassing' but would not damage any national security or intelligence interest. It was suggested that in considering a request for authorisation officials should make a decision:

> bearing in mind the importance attached to the right of free expression and the need for any restriction to be necessary, responsive to a pressing social need and proportionate.[96]

The aforementioned suggestion provides a solution to the difficulties posed by disclosures in the public interest by utilising the existing statutory framework. However, the solution is reliant upon an official making an objective judgement. The authorisation decision is likely to involve a senior civil servant and the relevant Minister of the department

---

[94] 'MI6 photos sold on auction site', BBC News, 20 September 2008. available at http://news.bbc.co.uk/1/hi/uk/7643374.stm.

[95] Individuals or the organisation may also be liable for offences under the Data Protection Act 1998.

[96] *R* v. *Shayler*, above n. 55, [29].

in question, or in the case of the security and intelligence services, a senior member of those services. In the *Shayler* judgment, Lord Bingham arguably placed undue reliance upon the effectiveness of authorisation to disclose as a method for getting concerns addressed. He stated:

> One would hope that, if disclosure were made to one or other of the persons listed above, effective action would be taken to ensure that abuses were remedied and offenders punished. But the possibility must exist that such action would not be taken when it should be taken or that, despite the taking of effective action to remedy past abuses and punish past delinquencies, there would remain facts which should in the public interest be revealed to a wider audience. This is where, under the OSA 1989 the second condition comes into play: the former member may seek official authorisation to make disclosure to a wider audience.[97]

The authorisation process does not, at present, appear to be sufficient to merit the restriction of an individual's Article 10 rights. The process does not appear in accordance with the law as there is no criteria by which an authorisation application can be judged. Lord Bingham's 'second condition' would effectively place the decision to authorise disclosure back into the hands of the head of an organisation, who will be either a government Minister or a senior official. The decision-maker could be complicit in the wrongdoing, but either way the person will have a vested interest in safeguarding the organisation against reputational damage. Moreover, in order to be compliant with Article 10, the decision to disclose information is far too complex to be taken by one official and requires careful consideration of the legal principles.

This potential problem extends much wider than consideration of the security and intelligence services. Research conducted by the author indicates that all government departments and agencies who responded to a request for information (a total of 48 responses) identified that the decision to authorise disclosure would be taken by either the Minister in charge of the department or an agency Chief Executive.[98] It should also be noted that if an individual did not commit an offence under the Official Secrets Act 1989 he or she may be able to obtain protection under the Public Interest Disclosure Act 1998 which allows for disclosures outside of the organisation without prior authorisation.[99]

---

[97]   *Ibid.*
[98]   For further information on methodology see further above.
[99]   Note that Public Interest Disclosure Act 1998 exempts members of the Armed Forces and the security and intelligence services: see further Public

One way of alleviating the potential for a conflict of interest would be to introduce a 'Publications Review Board', as in an unsuccessful amendment to the Official Secrets Bill which would have formed an independent body to view requests to publish memoirs of former members of the security and intelligence services.[100] Lord Bingham indicated that if a request is denied under the current framework, the Crown servant would be entitled to seek judicial review, a course which the Official Secrets Act 1989 does not 'seek to inhibit'.[101] Following the *A* v. *B* decision, employees of the security and intelligence services must now challenge refusals to authorise disclosure before the Investigatory Powers Tribunal.[102] This discussion will now proceed to consider defences for unauthorised disclosures.

Defences

Expressly defined in statute

A common feature throughout the sections of the Official Secrets Act 1989 is the defence available, namely, that it is a defence for a person charged with the offence to prove that he 'did not know and had no reasonable cause to believe that the information, document, or article in question related to (the relevant provision)'.[103] *R* v. *Keogh* provides the most up-to-date judgment on defences contained in the Official Secrets Act 1989.[104] It involved the leaking of a memo detailing communications between President George W. Bush and the former Premier Tony Blair and was alleged to contain discussions of the situation regarding the war in Iraq. Keogh passed the memo to O'Connor, a researcher working for the Labour MP Tony Clarke who had voted against the war in Iraq. O'Connor gave the memo to Clarke who immediately contacted the

---

Interest Disclosure Act 1998, s.11 and Employment Rights Act 1996, s.193 (as amended by Employment Relations Act 1999).

[100] A Publications Review Board exists in the United States to authorise the disclosure of CIA memoirs, for example. For discussion see further John Hollister Headley, *Secrets, Free Speech and Fig Leaves* (Centre for the Study of Intelligence, 2007), available at www.cia.gov/library/center-for-the-study-of-intelligence/kent-csi/docs/v41i3a01p.htm.

[101] See above n. 55, [31].

[102] [2009] UKSC 12. For discussion see further below, and see also Ashley Savage, and Paul David Mora, 'Security Service Memoirs and the Jurisdiction of the Investigatory Powers Tribunal: The Supreme Court's Decision in A v B' (2010) 21(5) *Entertainment Law Review* 196.

[103] See further Official Secrets Act 1989, ss.1(5), 2(3), 3(4), 4(4), and 8(2).

[104] [2007] EWCA Crim 528.

police. David Keogh was convicted and sentenced to six months' imprisonment for offences under Official Secrets Act 1989, sections 2 and 3.[105] The defence had appealed the decision of the preparatory hearing on the basis that the defences contained in section 2(3) and (4) were incompatible with the presumption of innocence guaranteed by Article 6 ECHR. Lord Phillips held that the sections should therefore be 'read down' so as to be compatible with the Convention right as per Human Rights Act 1998, section 3; this has the effect that the accused has only an evidential burden rather than a legal burden.[106] Because the wording of the defence is a common feature of all provisions of the Official Secrets Act 1989 which require damaging disclosures, the judgment should therefore be seen as applicable to all defences under each section. Despite the defendant only being required to carry the evidential burden, the aforementioned damaging disclosure tests are still easily satisfied. It would be particularly difficult for a Crown servant to assert that he did not know that his disclosure would be damaging. It is suggested that the drafting of the sections would make it particularly difficult to read these down to ensure compliance with Article 10 ECHR. This chapter will now focus on the common law defence of necessity to consider whether such a defence is available under the Official Secrets Act 1989.

Implied necessity defence
In *R* v. *Shayler*, the Court of Appeal sought to determine whether an implied defence of necessity could apply to the Official Secrets Act 1989.[107] The court considered the issue at length. Lord Woolf, identifying the principle established in *R* v. *Wright*, held that the defence may be applied to threats concerning an individual's immediate family or 'to some other person, for whose safety the defendant would reasonably regard herself as responsible'.[108] This determination is consistent with the author's determination in Chapter 1 that individuals may feel that they have obligations to the wider extramural community. However, Lord Woolf was unconvinced with Shayler's necessity argument for two key reasons. First, whilst Lord Woolf determined that the defendant did not need to name specific individuals to whom he had a responsibility, he did at least need to 'describe the individuals by reference to the action which

---

[105]   O'Conner was convicted and sentenced to three months' imprisonment for committing an offence under s.5 of the 1989 Act.
[106]   See above n. 104, [33].
[107]   [2001] EWCA Crim 1977.
[108]   *Wright* [2000] Crim LR 510, [22], per Kennedy LJ, and *ibid.* [61].

is threatened would be taken which would make them victims absent avoiding action being taken by the defendant'.[109] Second, Shayler's claims regarding the security service were *post facto,* he was not raising concerns regarding an act which he was trying to prevent but was instead drawing attention to the past conduct of members of MI5.[110]

Shayler appealed to the House of Lords.[111] Lord Bingham was unconvinced by the circumstances surrounding Shayler's disclosures holding that they were 'not within measurable distance of affording him a defence of necessity or duress of circumstances'.[112] Following the decision it was announced that the government would seek to reform the Act to remove the possibility of an implied defence being used.[113] The government decided to abandon the reform following *R* v. *Hasan.*[114] Post *Shayler,* the defence of necessity for alleged offences under the Official Secrets Act 1989 is yet to be tested. In *Hasan,* Lord Bingham used the opportunity to effectively clarify and narrow the duress of circumstances defence. Lord Bingham identified that the defence would only apply where there is a threat of death or serious injury directed at the defendant, the defendant's family or persons close to him.[115] Lord Bingham did, however, make reference to a 2003 specimen direction by the Judicial Studies Board which effectively widened the scope of the defence to include 'person for whose safety the defendant would reasonably regard himself as responsible'.[116] He went on to say:

> The correctness of such a direction was not, and on the facts could not be, in issue on this appeal, but it appears to me, if strictly applied, to be consistent with the rationale of the duress exception.[117]

The above statement is significant because it identifies that Lord Bingham would have been prepared to consider the Practice Direction but that the facts of the instant case did not merit him doing so. There are material differences between the *Hasan* and *Shayler* judgments. In *Hasan,* the defendant claimed that he had been pressured into committing

---

[109]   See above n. 107, [63].
[110]   *Ibid.* [65].
[111]   *R* v. *Shayler,* above n. 55.
[112]   *Ibid.* [17].
[113]   Intelligence and Security Committee, *Annual Report,* Cm 68–64 (2005–06).
[114]   [2005] UKHL 22.
[115]   *Ibid.* [21].
[116]   *Ibid.* [21].
[117]   *Ibid.* [21].

two burglaries because his family had been threatened with violence if he refused. This distinction may identify scope for future legal challenges regarding the Official Secrets Act 1989. Part of the difficulty is because the English and Welsh courts have expressed a willingness to conflate the defences of duress and necessity.[118] Lord Woolf in *Shayler* made reference to *Archbold* (*Criminal Pleading, Evidence and Practice*) which identified that duress of circumstances meant 'a crime of force by circumstances' rather than by 'physical coercion'.[119] The court in the *Hasan* case did not refer to the Court of Appeal decision in *Shayler*. Furthermore, whilst Lord Bingham identified that the defence could not be used in murder or treason cases, the court did not make reference to the Official Secrets Acts.[120]

Prior to the *Hasan* judgment, the government dropped a case against Katherine Gun which would have likely provided an opportunity to test the defence in a case concerning the Official Secrets Act 1989.[121] Gun was a GCHQ translator who disclosed a request by the US National Security Agency to intercept the communications of countries voting on whether to take action against Iraq at the United Nations. She was charged with offences under Official Secrets Act 1989, section 1. When the case advanced to trial the prosecution declined to offer evidence. It emerged that the day before the trial, the defence had asked the government for disclosure of any documentation relating to the advice it had received as to the legality of the war in Iraq. This would have enabled the defence to argue necessity, in that the reason for the disclosure was to stop an illegal war and thus prevent loss of life. Gun's defence would not have been without difficulty; it may be argued that Gun failed to show sufficient proximity of the persons in 'imminent peril' and the persons who would prevent the war. Gun's argument may be considered to comprise of three stages: first, the disclosure will be published; secondly, the publication will lead to overwhelming public pressure; and thirdly, the public pressure will prevent war. Media speculation at the time suggested that the prosecution had been dropped because of fears that evidence surrounding the legality of the war in Iraq

---

[118]   As evidenced in *R* v. *Pommell* [2005] Cr. App. R 607.
[119]   See above n. 107, [56].
[120]   See above n. 114, [21].
[121]   *R* v. *Gun* (2004, unreported); see also 'GCHQ translator cleared over leak', BBC News, 26 February 2004, available at http://news.bbc.co.uk/1/hi/uk/3485072.stm.

would be made public.[122] This discussion will now turn to consider prosecutorial decisions and the role of the Attorney General.

Prosecutorial Decisions

In the United Kingdom, the Crown Prosecution Service (CPS) has the responsibility for determining whether a defendant should be prosecuted. Official Secrets Act 1989, section 9, requires the Attorney General to consent to any prosecution before it may proceed; in cases concerning Official Secrets Act 1989, section 4(2), consent must be provided by the Director of Public Prosecutions. Information provided to the author, obtained by a freedom of information request to the CPS, identifies that 24 cases were considered between late 2006 and mid-2014.[123] Out of the 24 cases, two individuals pleaded guilty. One individual received a caution for the offence.[124] The data appears to suggest that in the timeframe provided the CPS has chosen not to proceed to trial. This information is significant as, read in conjunction with the data obtained from the Ministry of Justice on the number of cases proceeded against before magistrates' courts and found guilty in all courts, it highlights the small number of prosecutions. It also highlights that the majority of individuals in the dataset were arrested but were not proceeded against further. An arrest will undoubtedly impact on an individual's career. This was most notably identified in *Stankovic* v. *Chief Constable of Ministry of Defence Police*.[125] Stankovic, a major in the British Army, was arrested

---

[122]   See generally, Mark Oliver, 'GCHQ whistleblower cleared', *Guardian*, 25 February 2004, available at www.theguardian.com/uk/2004/feb/25/iraq.press andpublishing.

[123]   Crown Prosecution Service, FOI response, received 6 February 15. The CPS were unable to provide data for cases before late 2006 due to the way in which the information had been recorded. Note that this data may include government contractors as well as persons notified. The CPS were unable to provide details as to the exact sections of the Act which were at issue in each individual case.

[124]   Twelve of the cases were not proceeded against because the 'essential legal element was missing'. Two cases were not proceeded against because of 'exhibit or other evidence not available'. Two cases were not proceeded against because there was a 'conflict of evidence'. Three cases were not proceeded against and were listed as 'Pre-chg Investigation (Police) conclusion without charge'. One case was not proceeded against because it was determined not to be in the public interest on the basis that there was a 'very small or nominal penalty'. Ibid.

[125]   [2007] EWHC 2608 QB.

for offences under the Official Secrets Act 1989; searches were conducted and he lost his security clearance. After two and a half years the
matter concluded when no charges were brought against him. Stankovic
resigned his post and successfully brought proceedings against MOD
police.[126] The number of individuals arrested for offences under the
Official Secrets Act 1989 across the United Kingdom remains unknown.

The Crown Prosecution Service provides guidance to prosecutors on
handling cases where unauthorised disclosures have been made to
journalists. The guidance states:

> It is important that a breach of confidence that might best be considered as a
> disciplinary matter should not be elevated to a criminal offence simply by
> virtue of the fact that the person leaking the information is a public servant.

Whilst this guidance is welcome it should be reiterated that the Official
Secrets Act 1989 does not take into account the classification of official
documents. Because, as the aforementioned analysis in this chapter has
identified, it is relatively easy to meet the damaging disclosure tests or
the catch all provisions in Official Secrets Act 1989, sections 1 and 4; it
is suggested that it will be difficult to determine whether the matter
should or rather should not constitute a criminal offence. Moreover, there
are difficulties in equating a breach of confidence to the Official Secrets
Act 1989. Technically all unauthorised disclosures could constitute a
breach of confidence. The key difference is that breach of confidence
actions can be subject to a public interest defence whereas there is no
public interest defence to breaches of the Official Secrets Act 1989. It
would be more appropriate therefore to identify unauthorised disclosures
considered as a breach of professional codes or an employment contract
rather than a breach of confidence. It is argued that the guidance, written
in 2014, is out of date. It fails to acknowledge the key ECtHR decisions
of *Guja* v. *Moldova*,[127] *Heinisch* v. *Germany*[128] and *Bucur and Toma* v.
Romania.[129] In order for the CPS to be compliant with their obligations
under Human Rights Act 1998, section 6, it is arguably important that
these decisions are taken into consideration in any prosecutorial decision.

In addition to the considerations raised by the Crown Prosecution
Service, the Attorney General must make the ultimate decision whether

---

[126]   For further discussion on this case see Chapter 7.
[127]   *Guja* v. *Moldova*, Application No. 14277/04 (ECtHR, 12 February 2008).
[128]   *Heinisch* v. *Germany*, Application No. 28274/08 (ECtHR, 12 July 2011).
[129]   *Bucur and Toma* v. *Romania*, Application No. 40238/02 (ECtHR, 8
January 2013).

to prosecute an individual for offences under the Act. In the United Kingdom, the Attorney General is a government Minister; in effect the role requires a politician to make decisions on an apolitical basis. In making their determination the Attorney General may consult Cabinet colleagues in what is known as a 'Shawcross Exercise' whereby it is acceptable to obtain the opinions of others as long as they do not tell the Attorney General what decision to make.[130] It is difficult to see how the Attorney General cannot be motivated by political factors. The controversial positioning of the role has led to criticism over a number of years.[131] The Attorney General has in the past made decisions which would appear to be based on government policy or national security objectives, for example, when the Director of the Serious Fraud Office discontinued an investigation into the alleged bribery of Saudi officials by BAe Systems after representations from the Attorney General.[132] The Attorney General released a statement the same day which argued that there was a strong public interest in upholding and enforcing the criminal law but that there was a distinction between this public interest and considerations of national security and 'our highest priority foreign policy objectives in the Middle East'.[133] The decision to halt the prosecution of Katherine Gun despite clear evidence of a breach of the Official Secrets Act was arguably politicised due to the fact that it would have led to the disclosure of documents pertaining to the legal advice provided prior to the invasion of Iraq.[134]

The Attorney General's consent requirement is arguably advantageous to those at risk of prosecution particularly where the accused person can obtain strong political and public support. The more politically controversial the subject matter of disclosure is, the higher the likelihood that the government will be resistant to taking matters further. Not only would this create a risk of reputational damage but it may also lead to the jury returning with a not guilty verdict as they did in the *Ponting* case. In

---

[130]   Hansard, HC Deb., vol. 483, cols 683–4, 29 January 1951.

[131]   See e.g. Constitutional Affairs Committee, *Constitutional Role of the Attorney General*, HC-306 (2006–07); see also John Llewelyn Jones Edwards, *The Law Officers of the Crown* (Sweet & Maxwell, 1964) 224.

[132]   See further Zeray Yihdego and Ashley Savage, 'The UK Arms Export Regime: Progress and Challenges' [2008] *Public Law* 546, 558 and Transparency International (UK) Briefing Note, *British Aerospace Systems, Al Yamamah and the UK Serious Fraud Office* by (15 January 2006).

[133]   Clare Dyer, 'Clash of interests highlighted by decision to halt investigation', *Guardian*, 15 December 2006.

[134]   See further: 'GCHQ translator cleared over leak at GCHQ', 26 February 2004, available at http://news.bbc.co.uk/1/hi/uk/3485072.stm.

addition, if the content of the leaked information requiring disclosure to the defence team would be more harmful than the leak itself, there is a greater potential likelihood that the information may not be disclosed.[135] As Andrews suggests, where matters of state interest are at risk the only way of achieving fairness for the defendant without giving the defence access to the information is to drop the case, and the extent to which criminal investigations and subsequent proceedings are aborted because of national or political pressure is unknown.[136] However, whilst this may be a safeguard against an unfair trial, as has been indicated elsewhere in this chapter, those arrested for offences under the Official Secrets Act 1989 have still waited a considerable amount of time for the charges against them to be dropped and they may still lose their security clearance and/or job as a result of the action.[137]

Compliance with Article 10 ECHR Values

In *Shayler*, when Lord Bingham considered the appropriate ECtHR jurisprudence, he identified the Court's reasoning that the 'special nature of their work' imposes duties on employees of the security and intelligence services within the meaning of Article 10(2) ECHR. Lord Bingham then suggested that a 'blanket ban' which 'permitted no exceptions' to the rule of non-disclosure would be inconsistent with Article 10(1). It would not, he opined, survive the 'rigorous scrutiny' required to give effect to Article 10(2). Lord Bingham held that the fact that unlawfulness and irregularity could be reported to a number of authorities prescribed by the Act, if properly applied, was sufficient to be Convention compliant. For this reason, Lord Bingham held that the Official Secrets Act 1989 did not provide a blanket ban against disclosure because the employee, or former employee, could seek official authorisation from his superiors to disclose the information and if it were to be refused he could challenge the decision by way of judicial review.

Lord Bingham held that if the wording of the Official Secrets Act 1989 were incompatible with Shayler's Convention rights, the incompatibility

---

[135] This is a risky strategy and should not be considered as a viable alternative to reform of the legislation. Conversely, this may increase the motivation to punish an individual for making the disclosure.

[136] John Andrews, 'Public Interest and Criminal Proceedings' (1988) 104 *Law Quarterly Review* 413.

[137] For example, Major Stankovic waited two and a half years for the matter to conclude. Derek Pasquill waited 20 months from the police investigation until the prosecution offered no evidence at trial.

must be left to Parliament to resolve. He did not believe that the legislation could not be interpreted compatibly with Human Rights Act 1998, section 3.[138] Whilst Lord Bingham identified that there may be some doubt as to whether a whistleblower could persuade the authorities to take allegations seriously, he suggested that the effectiveness of the system had not been tested as Shayler had chosen not to use the mechanisms available. Furthermore, he noted that the Act was defective in that it did not identify the criteria that officials should follow when deciding whether information should be authorised, but was still satisfied that the Act was Convention compliant. Lord Bingham did not seek to identify whether the official mechanisms were effective.

It is submitted that because Lord Bingham placed such a strong emphasis on the availability of the authorised mechanisms, he neglected to consider whether the Official Secrets Act 1989 could be compliant with the Convention even though the various sections contain little, if any, scope for analysis of the public interest value of the speech. Neither Official Secrets Act 1989, section 1 nor section 4 provide the opportunity to test the value of the information; this is inconsistent with Article 10 values which aim to protect information of a high value to the public interest. Proportionality balancing thus requires a court to thoroughly assess the public interest in the disclosure against the public interest in non-disclosure. If it is impossible for the legislation to provide such scope for analysis by reading down the sections to align them with Article 10 ECHR values, the court should then make a declaration of incompatibility, as per Human Rights Act 1998, section 4.

Post *Guja* v. *Moldova*[139] and *Bucur and Toma* v. *Romania*,[140] it is submitted that a domestic court will need to place emphasis upon the effectiveness of the mechanisms available. In *Shayler*, both Lord Bingham and Lord Hope placed great emphasis on the fact that Shayler had not attempted to use those mechanisms but did not fully question why this was the case. Applying the proportionality framework used in the *Guja* decision and later applied in *Bucur*, a public servant may bypass the official mechanisms if he believes that he will suffer mistreatment as a result of raising the concern. Public disclosure would also be acceptable 'as a last resort'. The *Guja* framework does not fully account for disclosures concerning national security information, however the ECtHR was required to make a full determination on the unauthorised disclosure

---

[138] See above n. 53, 55.
[139] *Guja* v. *Moldova*, above n. 127.
[140] *Bucur and Toma* v. *Romania*, above n. 129.

of information in the *Bucur* case. In *Bucur*, the applicant had chosen not to raise his concern to a parliamentary oversight body for the Romanian Intelligence Service on the basis that it was considered to be ineffective. Bucur's disclosures regarding illegal surveillance were held to be within the protection of Article 10 ECHR despite Bucur's failure to use the official routes available to raise his concerns.[141]

It is submitted that in the proportionality analysis the special nature of employment in the security and intelligence services will shift the balance strongly in favour of the requirements identified in Article 10(2). However, where the information concerned is disclosed as a 'last resort' it may be sufficiently high to outweigh the special duty of confidence owed by the servant. Lord Bingham drew reference to the fact that the Official Secrets Act did not prevent *Shayler* from mounting a duress of circumstances defence, whereby the disclosure would be necessary to prevent the immediate risk of harm. Yet by placing emphasis on the requirement in the Act that prior authorisation is needed for disclosure, both Lord Bingham and Lord Hope failed to adequately consider whether the lack of a codified public interest defence rendered the Official Secrets Act incompatible. Following the *Guja* and *Bucur* decisions it is increasingly likely that the lack of a codified public interest defence will make the Official Secrets Act 1989 incompatible with the Convention.

A domestic court may seek to disregard the reasoning in *Guja* and *Bucur* on the basis that national security information falls within the 'special circumstances' principle established in *Ullah* v. *Special Adjudicator*.[142] It should also be noted that in *Shayler* Lord Hope had identified that a regime which favours official authorisation subject to judicial review is 'within the margin of discretion which ought to be accorded to the legislature'.[143] In *Financial Times* v. *United Kingdom*, the Grand Chamber of the European Court of Human Rights reiterated that margin of appreciation will be circumscribed by the interest of a democratic society in a free press and that such an interest would weigh heavily in the proportionality analysis.[144] This reasoning if transposed to cases involving public servant whistleblowers suggests that the interest of a democratic society in whistleblowers who disclose information of a high value to the public interest would outweigh the margin of appreciation owed to the domestic authority. This is because in *Financial Times* v. *United Kingdom* and *Guja* v. *Moldova*, the effects of

---

141   *Ibid.*; for further discussion see Chapter 4.
142   [2004] UKHL 26.
143   *R v Shayler*, above n. 55, [83].
144   Application No. 821/03 (ECtHR, 15 December 2009).

restraining such expression were markedly similar; thus in the context of journalistic sources, the 'chilling effect' caused by the grant of an order for source disclosure may dissuade individuals from providing the press with public information. In the context of the employee as a whistle-blower, the dismissal of an employee for raising concerns may cause a 'chilling effect' dissuading other potential whistleblowers from raising concerns.[145]

Application Outside of the Jurisdiction

Official Secrets Act 1989, section 11 identifies that legal proceedings may be taken in any place in the United Kingdom. Official Secrets Act 1989, section 15 extends the extraterritorial reach of the Act to include 'acts done abroad'. In order to be captured by this section the unauthor-ised disclosure must have been made by a British citizen or Crown servant or any colony. The Act further extends to Northern Ireland, the Channel Islands, the Isle of Man or any colony. Section 15 is clearly aimed at Crown servants and government contractors working abroad, for example in embassies. Effectively, it will not matter in which jurisdiction the disclosure is made provided that the person who made the disclosure is a Crown servant or a British citizen. Therefore, if a British intelligence official left the United Kingdom in order to make unauthorised dis-closures from the safety of a foreign jurisdiction (in a similar way to Edward Snowden) they would still be guilty of an offence under the Official Secrets Act 1989.

In the post Wikileaks and Snowden age, Official Secrets Act 1989, section 5(4) may identify a lacuna where the information is shared beyond one individual. Section 5 requires a Crown servant or government contractor (person 'A') to make a disclosure to person 'B' or 'another'.[146] Person B must then make a disclosure to be captured by the section 5 offence. However, section 5(4) requires the original disclosure by person A to have been made by a British citizen or for the disclosure to take place in the United Kingdom, the Channel Islands or a colony. If person A makes a disclosure to person B and they make a disclosure to person C, then both person A and person B will be liable. However, if the disclosure is made outside of the jurisdictions listed in section 5(4) and person B is not a British citizen, then person C will not be liable for an

---

[145]   *Ibid.* [70].
[146]   Official Secrets Act 1989, s.5(1).

offence. This identifies a significant potential weakness in the extra-territorial application of the law. Person B could be acting as a conduit whilst person C could either release documents to the entire world by an online platform such as Wikileaks, whilst it may be argued that the most harm will be caused by the original leaker, who puts the information into the position where it can be used; arguably, person C could cause considerable harm by publishing and widely disseminating it and yet would not be guilty of an offence.[147]

Where prosecution under the Official Secrets Act 1989 is possible (whether it be prosecution of a Crown servant, government contractor or a person covered by section 5) the difficulty will be for the domestic prosecuting authority to prosecute an individual based outside the juris-diction. Domestic courts have an obligation to ensure that a defendant has a fair hearing; the natural law principle of *audi alteram partem* has been an established part of the United Kingdom's legal system for many years prior to the incorporation of Article 6 ECHR. It is unlikely that a trial will therefore take place with the defendant *in absentia*.[148]

A European Arrest Warrant (EAW) may be issued by an EU Member State to request another state to arrest and deport an individual for the purposes of conducting a criminal prosecution.[149] For an EAW to be issued, the alleged crime with which the warrant is concerned must carry a custodial sentence of 12 months.[150] Both the country who issues the EAW and the country receiving the EAW must be compliant with the Charter of Fundamental Rights of the European Union. The Member State therefore has an obligation to have regard to Article 10 ECHR.[151] Based upon the aforementioned Strasbourg jurisprudence in *Guja* and *Bucur and Toma*, it is submitted that another jurisdiction may resist execution of an EAW on the basis that to do so will place the jurisdiction in breach of Articles 10 and 5 (on the basis that any detention will be

---

[147]   Crimes Act 1961 (New Zealand), s.78, applies to everyone whether 'inside or outside' of New Zealand, however the section is restricted to those who owe 'allegiance to the Sovereign' of New Zealand. In contrast, the US Espionage Act 1917 is not limited by territorial reach.

[148]   See *R* v. *Jones* [2003] 1 AC 1.

[149]   EU Council Framework Decision on the European Arrest Warrant and the surrender procedures between Member States, 2002/584/JHA (EAW Framework Decision'). For discussion of the information exchange process in cross-border proceedings, see generally Ángeles Gutiérrez Zarza, *Exchange of Information and Data Protection in Cross-border Criminal Proceedings in Europe* (Springer, 2015).

[150]   EAW Framework Decision, art. 2(1).

[151]   *Ibid.* art. 1(3).

unlawful).[152] Moreover, a country may resist execution of the warrant where it can be determined on an objective basis that the purpose of the warrant is to punish an individual for their political opinions.[153] The French courts refused to accede to the extradition of David Shayler on the basis that the prosecution against him was politically motivated.[154] Shayler was detained in a French prison for four months before being set free.[155] He did not face trial until he voluntarily re-entered the United Kingdom.

Outside of the European Union, extradition will be dependent upon whether the country has signed a treaty agreement with the United Kingdom.[156] The extradition request will be likely to be blocked if the country in question does not have an applicable official secrecy law. This is identified as the principle of 'dual criminality'.[157] Again, a further bar to extradition may exist if the extradition is considered to be politically motivated. The circumstances surrounding Edward Snowden suggest that even where extradition and requests for assistance are issued this will not guarantee a successful outcome for the jurisdiction issuing the request. Disclosures made to a Norwegian newspaper indicate that the United States had made extradition requests to countries in Europe to seek Snowden's extradition.[158] The High Court in Ireland refused the extradition request on the basis that the court was unable to determine whether

---

[152] It would also engage Art. 11 of the EU Charter of Fundamental Rights 2000.

[153] See further, EAW Framework Decision, Introduction, [12].

[154] The French courts based their reasoning on European Convention on Extradition 1957, Art. 3, and domestic law. Note that the Convention pre-dates the Council Framework Decision. See further 'UK officials study *Shayler* ruling', BBC News, 19 November 1998, available at http://news.bbc.co.uk/1/hi/uk/216795.stm.

[155] For discussion see Jane Dickson, 'Point of no return: David Shayler', *Independent*, 22 October 2011.

[156] The United Kingdom has signed over 100 treaties with jurisdictions around the world. For a list of the treaties and for further information, see www.gov.uk/guidance/extradition-processes-and-review.

[157] See generally, Stephen David Brown, *Combating International Crime: The Longer Arm of the Law* (Routledge Cavendish, 2008).

[158] 'USA asked Norway to extradite Edward Snowden', NRK News, 27 August 2015, available at www.nrk.no/fordypning/usa-asked-norway-to-arrest-edward-snowden-1.12521802. The *Guardian* provided an interactive guide at the time to identify which countries Snowden could effectively enter which did not have a bilateral treaty with the United States: 'A Guardian guide to extradition', *Guardian*, 2 July 2015, available at www.theguardian.com/world/interactive/2013/jul/02/guardian-guide-extradition-interactive.

the alleged offences had been committed within the United States' jurisdiction; if not the Court would have had to be satisfied that the US offences had extraterritorial effect and that there was an equivalent law which also had extraterritorial effect.[159]

Attempts to prevent Snowden from leaving Hong Kong to travel to Russia failed. At the time of writing Snowden is currently based in Russia where he has successfully sought asylum. It would appear that awareness of Snowden's whereabouts and his identity as the leaker of the documents emerged because he gave a self-identified interview to the media. It may be argued that an individual wishing to make unauthorised disclosures could circumvent any attempts to prosecute under the Official Secrets Act 1989 by travelling to a jurisdiction either without an extradition treaty and or one which will offer asylum and may evade detection further by not providing their identity. This could also be achieved by visiting an embassy on UK soil, as occurred with Julian Assange.[160] The British authorities would have very little opportunity to prevent the disclosures from taking place or to successfully prosecute the person who made them.

Official Secrets Act 1911

It is important to note that individuals who make unauthorised disclosures of information may still be liable for an offence under Official Secrets Act 1911, section 1. Those who 'sign' the Official Secrets Act 1989 also 'sign' the 1911 Act. Section 1(c) is of particular relevance. It concerns any person who:

> obtains (collects, records, or publishes) or communicates to any other person any sketch, plan model, article, or note, or other document information which is calculated to be or might be or is intended to be directly or indirectly useful to an enemy.

Whilst prosecutions for unauthorised disclosures are more likely to be dealt with using the 1989 Act, there may be advantages to using Official Secrets Act 1911, section 1, which extends to 'any person' not just Crown servants. It also extends to persons who 'obtain' information. Therefore the section could be use to punish the recipients of information without the need for further disclosure. The extraterritorial reach of the

---

[159]   *Attorney General* v. *Snowden* [2013] IEHC 308.
[160]   Andrew Hough, 'Julian Assange: WikiLeaks founder seeks political asylum from Ecuador', *Telegraph*, 19 June 2012.

1911 Act also appears to extend further than the 1989 Act. Whilst section 10(1) of the 1911 Act applies to 'acts committed by officers or British subjects in His Majesty's dominions or elsewhere', section 10(2) extends the reach of the Act to circumstances where an offence under the Act if 'committed elsewhere' may be determined by 'any competent British court ... in England'. Prosecuting authorities may seek to argue that disclosures or the publication of unauthorised disclosures are useful to the enemy. Whilst this may seem an unrealistic proposition it should be noted that in the *Miranda* case the authorities were able to convince the court that the Snowden disclosures could assist terrorism and could merit use of the Terrorism Act to detain David Miranda.[161] Arguably, any disclosure of official documents could be 'directly or indirectly useful to an enemy' where they are made accessible to all. The wording of the section is particularly broad: it need only be shown that the disclosures 'might be' useful to the enemy. Whilst the Official Secrets Act 1911 is also subject to the same protections under Article 10 ECHR as the 1989 Act, the 1911 Act at the very least provides the scope to arrest suspects and to seek extradition of persons based outside of the jurisdiction. Moreover, the 1911 Act provides scope for a much harsher penalty: the maximum penalty for an offence under the 1989 Act is two and a half years' imprisonment whereas the maximum penalty for offences under the 1911 Act is 14 years' imprisonment.

Misconduct in Public Office

The difficulty with the common law offence of misconduct in public office is that, unlike the Official Secrets Act 1989, there is no prescribed class of information.[162] This means that, in theory, any person who as a public officer makes an unauthorised disclosure of official information may be liable to prosecution, regardless of the content of the information concerned.[163] In *Attorney General's Reference No. 3 of 2003*, Lord Justice Pill summarised the requirements of the offence:

---

[161] *Miranda* v. *Secretary of State for the Home Department* [2014] 1 WLR 3140.
[162] For information on the offence and its uses, see generally Lucinda Maer, House of Commons Research Note, *Misconduct in Public Office*, SN/PC/04909 (2008).
[163] Parallels may be drawn with Official Secrets Act 1963 (Eire), s.4, which effectively makes any unauthorised disclosure of information an offence, regardless of content.

(a) A public officer acting as such, (b) [w]illfully neglects to perform his duty and/or willfully misconducts himself, (c) [t]o such a degree as to amount to an abuse of the public's trust in the office holder, (d) without reasonable excuse or justification.[164]

The *Attorney General's Reference* sets the bar very high, identifying that there must be a 'serious departure from proper standards' and that this must be 'not merely negligent but amounting to an affront to the standing of the public office held'.[165] The offence has increasingly been used as a means to arrest and/or prosecute public officers for leaking information.[166] In 2007, Thomas Lund-Lack, a civilian worker at Scotland Yard, was convicted and sentenced to eight months' imprisonment for leaking information about a planned al-Qaeda attack on the West to a journalist at the *Sunday Times*.[167] Lund-Lack pleaded guilty to an offence of misconduct in public office and not guilty to an offence under the Official Secrets Act 1989. The fact that both offences were run side by side is a worrying development.

In *R v Kearney*,[168] a former Thames Valley Police detective, Mark Kearney, was charged with misconduct in public office for disclosing information to Sally Murrer, a journalist for the *Milton Keynes Citizen*. Murrer was charged with aiding and abetting misconduct in public life, alongside another journalist Derek Webb and Mr Kearney's son Harry. The information had concerned the bugging of conversations between Sadiq Khan MP and a terrorist suspect at Woodhill Prison in Milton Keynes. The trial collapsed because the judge held that the prosecution had breached the right to freedom of expression under Article 10 ECHR. The case is worrying because it illustrates that the offence is capable not only of extending criminal liability to the person who leaks the information but also to the person who receives it.

The Damian Green/Christopher Galley incident has resulted in confusion between the safeguarding of national security information, and use

---

[164]　[2004] EWCA Crim 868, [61].

[165]　*Ibid.* [56].

[166]　The offence may also be used to prosecute the recipients of disclosures for 'aiding and abetting a misconduct in public office'. Note that unlike Official Secrets Act 1989, s.5, no further disclosure would be necessary.

[167]　'Police worker admits secrets leak', BBC News, 18 July 2009, available at http://news.bbc.co.uk/1/hi/uk/6763377.stm.

[168]　*R* v. *Kearney* (unreported, 2008); see 'Detective Sergeant Mark Kearney: "Refusing to bug inmates made me a thorn in their side"', available at www.timesonline.co.uk/tol/news/uk/crime/article5254216.ece.

of the Official Secrets Act 1989 and misconduct in public office.[169] It was stated that the justification for the arrests was that national security had been put at risk as a result of the leaks. However, David Davis told the BBC that if the leaks were a risk to national security then charges should have been brought under the Official Secrets Act 1989.[170] The *New Statesman* suggested that there were yet to be any charges brought under the Official Secrets Act 1989 and this suggested that 'the leaks were not especially serious'.[171] Such confusion highlights a difficult contradiction between the two offences.

The Public Administration Select Committee Report, *Leaks and Whistleblowing and Whitehall*, stated that the use of the misconduct in public office offence to prosecute Crown servants who leak information meant that the 'boundaries established by the 1989 Act may be becoming blurred' and that it was important that the offence is not used to 'subvert the clearly expressed will of Parliament' in 'limiting the scope of offences under the Official Secrets Act'.[172] Since the report, there have been a number of investigations against public officials as part of Operation Elvedon where members of the press have been alleged to have made payments to public officials in exchange for information.[173] At the time of writing, approximately 28 public officials have been convicted of misconduct in public office offences for these acts. There is a danger that individuals who make whistleblowing disclosures will be prosecuted for misconduct in public office offences. It may be argued that the act of payment to officials for information may be distinguished

---

[169] For discussion see Anthony Bradley, 'The Damian Green Affair: All's Well That Ends Well?' [2012] *Public Law* 396, 407.

[170] Jon Swain, 'Tories colluded over leaks, Mandleson claims', *Telegraph*, 3 December 2008. This assertion would accord with the decision of the House of Lords in *R* v. *Rimmington* [2006] 1 AC 459, [30]: 'Where Parliament has defined the ingredients of an offence, perhaps stipulating what shall and shall not be a defence, and has prescribed a mode of trial and a maximum penalty, it must ordinarily be proper that conduct falling within that definition should be prosecuted for the statutory offence and not for a common law offence which may or may not provide the same defences and for which the potential penalty is unlimited', per Lord Bingham.

[171] 'Government needs secrecy but the public needs whistleblowers', *New Statesman*, 4 December 2008, available at www.newstatesman.com/politics/2008/12/green-british-information.

[172] Public Administration Select Committee, *Leaks and Whistleblowing in Whitehall*, HC 83 (2009) [46].

[173] For discussion, see Lord Justice Leveson, *An Inquiry into the Culture, Ethics and Practices of the Press*, HC 780-1 (2012) vol. 1, 423.

from the unauthorised disclosure of documents to raise concerns about wrongdoing or malpractice.[174] Where it is clear that payments have not been made to officials, it is arguable that use of the misconduct in public office offence is inappropriate. The Court of Appeal in *R* v. *Chapman* and others[175] has improved matters by introducing a requirement for the jury to consider whether a defendant's conduct had the effect of harming the public interest.[176] However, the offence still remains overly broad and carries the potential to criminalise disclosures, regardless of content and regardless of the individual's motivation for making it. The following section will proceed to consider suggestions for reform of the regime pertaining to official secrets.

Suggestions for Reform

In discussing the Official Secrets Bill, then Home Secretary, Douglas Hurd MP, stated that 'there could not conceivably be a prosecution under the Bill on the ground of embarrassment to a British minister'.[177] Available data on the number of individuals prosecuted identifies that the Act is rarely used. However, questions still remain as to the number of individuals being arrested for offences under the 1989 Act. Whilst the severity of the sanction is arguably less where individuals are not proceeded against to trial, it is submitted that an arrest can still have a detrimental impact on the careers of individuals who are likely to lose their security clearance as a result of any leak allegations. Beyond this, the impact of the Official Secrets Act 1989 appears to be largely symbolic. The low number of prosecutions could indicate, for example, that Crown servants are being deterred from leaking information for fear of prosecution. Part I of this analysis identified that there is a lack of consistency in the number of organisations who require Crown servants to sign the Official Secrets Acts. One must consider how many of those individuals are coming into contact with information which would be covered by the Official Secrets Act 1989. Moreover, despite narrowing the scope of the information to distinct categories there is no direct link to the classification of documents; this can only add to the uncertainty of

---

[174] Applying *Guja* v. *Moldova*, the motivation of the individual who made the disclosure will be taken into account when considering good faith; focus will particularly be made on whether or not the individual made the disclosure for personal gain. *Guja* v. *Moldova*, above n. 127), [95].

[175] EWCA Crim 539.

[176] *Ibid.* [39].

[177] Hansard, HC Deb., vol. 147, col. 428, 15 February 1989.

risk of a potential prosecution. Is not clear how far this symbolism is acting to deter individuals from raising concerns regarding wrongdoing or malpractice in the workplace. Post the *Guja* and *Bucur and Toma* decisions, there is a strong likelihood that any attempt to prosecute individuals under the Official Secrets Act 1989 will fail. It is suggested that new legislation is needed to ensure Convention compliance as well as to accurately reflect current information handling practices.[178]

Harm tests

This chapter has identified that the courts are reluctant to make determinations on whether information is harmful to national security; however, in considering cases concerning Article 10 ECHR, the ECtHR is required to conduct a proportionality test which weighs the harm against the public interest benefit of any disclosure. The *Bucur and Toma* case in particular identifies that where national security is an issue, the Court will still conduct rigorous balancing of these competing interests. It is therefore suggested that the damaging disclosure tests in the Official Secrets Act 1989 should be replaced with harm tests. Parliament should consider whether it would be appropriate to base these harm tests on the descriptions attached to the current classification of official documents. As discussed above, there is currently no direct link between the provisions of the Official Secrets Act 1989 and the classification of documents. This creates the uncertainty that potentially the unauthorised disclosure of any government document, provided it fits within the class or description of the sections, could result in an offence. The Franks Committee Report on the reform of Official Secrets Act 1911, section 2, recommended that the classification of documents should be enshrined in a new Official Information Act.[179] A government Minister responsible for the document would need to issue a certificate to the court that the document was correctly classified before any prosecution could be brought (in addition to the Attorney General's consent to prosecute).

---

[178] In addition to the recommendations in this section, it is submitted that various improvements are possible to the official whistleblowing mechanisms and other authorised routes. Full consideration of the mechanisms available to civil servants will be provided in Chapter 5, to employees of the security and intelligence services in Chapter 6, and to the Armed Forces in Chapter 7.

[179] *Report of the Departmental Committee on Section 2 of the Official Secrets Act 1911*, above n. 38, vol. I, [59].

Whilst it is acknowledged that there is a risk of individuals over-classifying documents, the ministerial certificate considered in conjunction with new harm tests and the other recommendations in this section would help to mitigate against this.

Authorisation to disclose

As identified above, the *Shayler* judgment placed particular emphasis on the ability of individuals to be able to seek authorisation for disclosures, particularly where other avenues to raise concerns have failed. Currently, authorisation depends on the head of the organisation agreeing to the disclosure. If disclosure is refused they challenge the decision by judicial review. As Fenwick and Phillipson argue, this would place a fetter on the expression rights of individuals. It is suggested that it would be appropriate to consider the introduction of an 'Authorisations Review Board' or similar.[180] The board could comprise of senior officials but with the requirement of membership of a lay member or a retired judge.[181] Appeals from the Board could be made to the Information Tribunal or to the Investigatory Powers Tribunal for cases concerning the authorisation of information from the security and intelligence services.[182]

Public interest defence

This chapter has identified that the Official Secrets Act 1989 places undue reliance upon officially available mechanisms. As identified in the *Bucur and Toma* and *Guja* decisions, the existence of effective mechanisms will not be sufficient to mitigate against a disproportionate restriction of Article 10 rights. Parliament should therefore consider the need for a public interest defence. As discussed above, attempts to introduce such a defence have failed largely on the basis of fears that the disclosures will result in allowing individuals to make unauthorised

---

[180] The remit of the Board could also be widened to include applications from journalists.

[181] It is suggested that the individuals could be made 'persons notified' under Official Secrets Act 1989, s.1, if required. Composition of the Board would be critical. The CIA Review Board has come under fire for decisions regarding redactions of publications. See further Gregg Miller and Julie Tate, 'CIA probes publications review board over allegations of selective censorship', *Washington Post*, 31 May 2012, available at www.washingtonpost.com/world/national-security/cia-probes-publication-review-board-over-allegations-of-selective-censor ship/2012/05/31/gJQAhfPT5U_story.html.

[182] Employees of the security and intelligence services are required to bring claims before the Investigatory Powers Tribunal following *A* v. *B* [2009] UKSC 12.

disclosures *carte blanche*. A defence which is narrow in scope and potential application is more likely to achieve state buy-in. Security of Information Act 2001 (Canada), section 15, provides protection where an individual discloses information where they reasonably believe an offence 'has been, is being or will be committed' by an official in the performance of their duties and that 'the public interest in the disclosure outweighs the public interest in non-disclosure'.[183] In a similar way to the proportionality framework used in *Guja* and subsequent whistle-blowing cases before the ECtHR, the court will be required to assess the public interest in the disclosure and the harm caused by it; whether the individual raised their concern prior to making the disclosure; and the extent of the exigent circumstances in making it.[184] Whilst the section requires prior disclosure to the Deputy Attorney General of Canada, a person may raise their concern with the Security and Intelligence Review Committee or the Communications Security Establishment Commissioner if they have not received reasonable time. Ultimately, no prior disclosure is needed if the communication was 'necessary to avoid grievous bodily harm or death'.[185] In effect this would provide a codified necessity defence.

Need for new policy
The aforementioned analysis has identified a need for new policies and procedures. At the organisational level, it is suggested that the number of individuals being required to sign the Act should be limited to those engaged in matters involving national security; it should also be considered whether the signing of the Act is necessary at all. At the enforcement level, it is suggested that guidance is needed to determine where it is appropriate to arrest individuals for Official Secrets Act offences because of the potential consequences on an individual's right to freedom of expression and the potential loss of their security clearance. The appropriateness of using the misconduct in public office offence where there is no suspicion of payment for the unauthorised disclosure should be reviewed. At the prosecutorial level, the CPS guidance should be urgently updated to reflect the Strasbourg decisions in *Bucur and Toma* and *Guja*. Moreover, the current guidance refers to unauthorised disclosures of information to journalists. It is suggested that the guidance should be updated or additional guidance produced to include online

---

[183] Security of Information Act 2001, s.15(a) and (b).
[184] *Ibid.* s.15(4).
[185] *Ibid.* s.15(6).

disclosure outlets, to reflect the changing nature of unauthorised disclosures post Wikileaks. Where the disclosures do not pertain to information which is harmful to national security, at all levels the suggested guidance should make clear that disciplinary action or civil action for breach of confidence is a more appropriate response than criminal prosecution. The next part of this analysis will consider civil actions.

III CIVIL CONSEQUENCES

Breach of Confidence

The purpose of this final section is to consider breach of confidence. Whereas the Official Secrets Act 1989 is used as a means to prosecute after an unauthorised disclosure has been made, the civil remedy of breach of confidence allows for the possibility of obtaining an injunction both at the interim stage, and later, once a full trial has been decided, to prevent further disclosures from taking place. In this sense, breach of confidence may be considered as an alternative protection of official information to the Official Secrets Act 1989. Advancements in technology mean that it is now very easy for an employee to make an unauthorised disclosure to an online outlet such as Wikileaks, leading to the swift dissemination of material across the globe. As a consequence, this analysis will consider whether the traditional remedy is now obsolete.

Inevitable parallels may be drawn with the Official Secrets Act 1989. The requirement to sign the Official Secrets Act was used in *Attorney General* v. *Blake* by Lord Nicholls to illustrate that Blake had a contractual duty of confidence.[186] Beyond the sanctions available, there are two key differences between the Official Secrets Act 1989 and breach of confidence. First, there is a very well established common law defence against breach of confidence actions.[187] Second, an individual can still be prosecuted under the Official Secrets Act 1989 even if the information is already in the public domain, whereas in breach of confidence actions prior disclosure will provide an argument that the information disclosed

---

[186]   The government sought an injunction to restrain publication of Blake's memoirs. Blake, a former officer in MI5, was exposed as a member of the infamous Cambridge Spy Ring, [2001] 1 AC 268, [14].

[187]   *Gartside* v. *Outram* (1857) 26 LJ Ch. 113; see also *Initial Services Ltd* v. *Putterill* [1968] 1 QB 396 and *Lion Laboratories* v. *Evans* [1984] 3 WLR 539.

does not have the necessary quality of confidence to justify the grant of an injunction.

Prior to the Human Rights Act 1998, during the 1980s, the government made several attempts to prevent the publication of the *Spycatcher* a book written by former MI5 officer Peter Wright. The book contained a number of allegations of wrongdoing, including that the head of the Security Service was a KGB mole.[188] The Attorney General sought to restrain publication by obtaining injunctions in the United Kingdom and Australia. During the case Lord Griffiths identified that:

> if a member of the service discovered that some iniquitous course of action was being pursued that was clearly detrimental to our national interest, and he was unable to persuade any senior members of his service or any members of the establishment, or the police, to do anything about it, then he should be relieved of his duty of confidence so that he could alert his fellow citizens to the impending danger. However, no such considerations arise in the case of *Spycatcher*.[189]

Lord Griffith's comments provide a consideration for the actions of the whistleblower intending to expose iniquity. However, even if an employee of the security and intelligence services were to be protected under the law of breach of confidence they would not have access to a public interest defence against prosecution under the Official Secrets Act 1989.

Following unsuccessful attempts to have the injunctions lifted despite widespread publication of the book outside of the jurisdiction, the *Observer* and *Guardian Newspapers* applied to the ECtHR.[190] The Court held that the injunctions which were in force before the publication of the book in the United States were proportionate in order to prevent the publication of material which may have caused harm to the security service. The material in question contained allegations which related to events that had occurred several years ago and could therefore not be regarded as 'urgent'.[191] The injunctions granted after the publication of the book in the United States were regarded as disproportionate, as the

---

[188] There were two House of Lords decisions; the first, *Attorney General* v. *Guardian Newspapers Ltd* [1987] 3 All ER 316, dealt with interlocutory injunctions; the second, *Attorney General* v. *Guardian Newspapers (No. 2)* [1990] 1 AC 109 dealt with permanent injunctions.

[189] *Attorney General* v. *Guardian Newspapers (No. 2)* [1990] 1 AC 109, [795]. Further consideration of the *Spycatcher* litigation is provided below.

[190] *Observer and Guardian* v. *United Kingdom*, Application No. 13585/88 (ECtHR, 26 November 1991).

[191] *Ibid* [64].

Attorney General's aim became more of an exercise in the preservation of the secret service's reputation and to deter other officers or former officers from making such disclosures.[192] The information had become readily available in the public domain.

Post Human Rights Act 1998, the case of *Attorney General* v. *Times Newspapers*[193] concerned a former Secret Intelligence Service (SIS) officer, Richard Tomlinson. After leaving the SIS, Tomlinson served six months' imprisonment for breaching Official Secrets Act 1989, section 1, by sending a synopsis to a publisher. After he was released he published the book, which was made available in Russian on a relatively small scale. The Attorney General then applied for an injunction to prevent further publication. *The Times* had intended to publish information contained in the book. The Court of Appeal applied a more liberal approach than seen in the *Spycatcher* litigation, holding that whilst it was preferable for a newspaper to consult with the SIS prior to publication, a requirement to do so would place a disproportionate fetter on freedom of expression. It was therefore a matter for the editor to decide. Based on the aforementioned reasoning, even where publication has been made on a small scale, it will be difficult for the government to obtain an injunction. However, a distinction must be made between the expression rights of a journalist and the expression rights of an employee of the security and intelligence services. Arguably, the failure of an employee to obtain authorisation prior to disclosure will be a factor in the proportionality analysis. As identified in *Guja* v. *Moldova*, courts should consider the duty of loyalty owed by public servants to their employer.[194] The next section will now consider the protection afforded by Human Rights Act 1998, section 12, with particular reference to interim applications.

Injunctions

Had the *Spycatcher* litigation happened today, the UK government may have faced significant difficulty in obtaining an injunction against publication. Books can very often be purchased in an electronic format from anywhere in the world. Documents can be made accessible for download by individuals located all over the world with relative ease. Unless prior notification of the disclosure is made, so that a government may seek an injunction prior to publication, there will be little point in granting an

---

192   *Ibid.* [69].
193   [2001] EWCA Civ 97.
194   *Guja* v. *Moldova*, above n. 127, [71].

injunction at the interim stage. This makes the obtaining of a permanent injunction once the full trial has been conducted a highly unlikely outcome.

Human Rights Act 1998, section 12, applies in any proceedings where a court granting relief could impact on the right to freedom of expression. This section will primarily focus upon injunctive relief, however it should be noted that the provision of damages awarded against an individual or a newspaper would also be covered by section 12.[195] Section 12(2) provides a safeguard whereby relief will not be granted unless the court is satisfied that the applicant has taken 'all practical steps to notify the respondent' or that 'there are compelling reasons why the respondent should not be notified'. The purpose of this section is to provide a safeguard whereby an interim injunction is sought on an *ex parte* basis. If interim relief is granted without the knowledge of the respondent, the individual will be prevented from further communicating on the subject and will not have been provided with the opportunity to make his representations known as to why the information should not be subject to an injunction.

Ex parte hearings require the most careful scrutiny by the courts, as the courts will need to have regard to the high standard of protection the ECtHR affords to Article 10 and will need to determine the public interest value of the communication without giving the respondent an opportunity to make representations as to why the particular information is of value. Section 12(4) bolsters the protection afforded by section 12(2) by requiring that the court must have particular regard to the importance of the Convention right to freedom of expression and, where the proceedings relate to material which the respondent claims 'or which appears to the court to be':

> journalistic, literary or artistic material (or to conduct connected with such material), to:
>
> (a) the extent to which—
>   (i)   the material has, or is about to, become available to the public; or
>   (ii) it is, or would be, in the public interest for the material to be published;
> (b) any relevant privacy code.

It is submitted that courts should consider section 12(4) when making determinations concerning information obtained as a result of an unauthorised disclosure by a Crown servant where publication of the

---

[195] Supported by application of the reasoning in *Tolstoy and Miloslavsky* v. *United Kingdom*, Application No. 18139/91 (ECtHR, 13 June 1995).

information is intended. With regard to information disclosed to a traditional media outlet based in the domestic jurisdiction, the court must apply section 12(4) as the information concerned could be argued to be journalistic material. There is considerable scope to argue that online disclosure outlets (such as Wikileaks) should still be protected under section 12(4). If a respondent is provided with an opportunity to make their case as to why an injunction should not be granted and is encountering difficulty in convincing the judge that the information was for a journalistic purpose, section 12(4) also covers 'conduct connected with such material', thus providing disclosure outlets with the opportunity to argue that their conduct is in support of journalistic activities and as a result they should not be subject to an injunction. This conduct could be argued to include Wikileaks or a similar organisation acting as a conduit to provide information to a traditional media outlet as a partner. If an online disclosure outlet has already published unauthorised material and the information has been downloaded and disseminated across the globe by the time that the interim hearing has been reached, it is unlikely that an injunction will be granted, as section 12(a)(i) requires the court to have regard to the extent to which the information has been, or is about to be, made available to the public.

Extraterritorial Application

When granting an injunction against an online disclosure outlet based outside the jurisdiction the question of whether such an injunction can be effectively enforced will undoubtedly arise. If an application for injunctive relief is made prior to the disclosure of the information it is likely that the court will be faced, first, with questions relating to service of the court order and, secondly, with whether the injunction will be recognised by the jurisdiction in question. Civil Procedure Rules, Part 40.4 identifies that once a judgment or order has been made by the court it must be served on the respondent. Despite the fact that the respondent may reside outside of the jurisdiction, UK courts have been particularly flexible in allowing service to be conducted by electronic means. Civil Procedure Rules, Part 6.2(e) allow for service by fax or 'other electronic communication'. Therefore service could be conducted by communication over the Internet.[196]

Service of a court order may not prove difficult but the enforcement of such an order is likely to be problematic. Brussels Regulation I, article 2,

---

[196] However, applications for service of an order outside of a jurisdiction may encounter difficulty because of the applicable laws of the state in question.

allows a judgment made in one EU Member State to be enforced in another. Yet article 34 identifies that a judgment may not be enforced where recognition of it is 'manifestly contrary to public policy in the Member State in which recognition is sought'. The problem with extraterritorial enforcement is that it will of course take time for the respective procedures to take place and for proceedings to begin. With regard to online outlets, the enforcement of an order becomes very much a moot point if an organisation chooses to disregard an order and goes ahead and publishes the material anyway. The nature of the Internet means that the information can be swiftly published and disseminated. The question of service and enforcement becomes even more difficult when the first publication has been made online and an injunction has been sought to prevent further publication. The court will be faced with attempting to serve orders against potentially unknown actors in multiple jurisdictions, creating many difficulties for subsequent enforcement.

Section 12(3) specifically concerns the grant of interim relief and states that no such relief is to be granted to restrain publication before trial unless the court is satisfied that the applicant is 'likely to establish that publication should not be allowed'. Interpretation of this section was considered at length in *Cream Holdings* v. *Banerjee*.[197] Lord Nicholls identified that there may be circumstances where a lesser degree of likelihood will suffice, such as where the adverse consequences of disclosure would be 'extremely serious such as a grave risk of personal injury to a particular person'. Lord Nicholls gave an example of an individual who had given evidence against a defendant in a criminal trial and had received threats. In such circumstances, according to Lord Nicholls, the consequences of the disclosure may be serious whereas the applicant's claim to confidentiality may be weak. Lord Nicholls' assessment of the test in section 12(3) is problematic and will require close scrutiny by courts if the correct balance between competing interests is to be achieved. Applying the reasoning to applications for injunctions to prevent the publication on a website such as Wikileaks identifies that if the information in question could cause harm, an injunction could still be granted at the interim stage. The Wikileaks disclosures resulted in the publication of personal details relating to the names and addresses of individuals who had assisted the US government by acting as informants. The publication of the diplomatic cables contained information regarding the private lives of public officials. Such information, if it were in reach

---

[197] *Cream Holdings Ltd v. Banerjee & Others* [2004] UKHL 44. The case concerned a former employee who passed documents allegedly showing wrong-doing to a local newspaper.

of the jurisdiction of the ECtHR and a UK domestic court, would likely engage Article 8 ECHR. Here the court should apply the 'new methodology' test developed in *Re S*.[198] In cases where Article 8 is determined to outweigh Article 10, it is likely that an interim injunction will be granted.

It is clear that breach of confidence, a body of common law principles developed at a time of paper-based publication, is not sufficient to prevent disclosures utilising social media or online outlets such as Wikileaks. The general futility of attempting to restrain the publication of information in the Internet age must also be considered. For example, a so-called 'super-injunction' aimed at restricting the identity of footballer Ryan Giggs from being revealed as an individual engaged in an extra-marital affair did not prevent the information from being widely circulated on the social networking site Twitter.[199]

As a consequence, 'traditional' breach of confidence actions are likely to be concerned first and foremost with the obtaining of damages, rather than the obtaining of an injunction. In legal proceedings whereby a government department seeks to obtain damages against a civil servant for breach of confidence, the motivation for doing so could be to deter other employees from making unauthorised disclosures.[200] Breach of confidence actions may provide a viable alternative to prosecutions for misconduct in public office where the disclosure has been made for the purposes of monetary gain.

IV CONCLUSION

All of the legal measures discussed in this chapter are intended to restrict freedom of expression. With regard to the Official Secrets Acts, as J.S. Mill suggested, the restrictions imposed on Crown servants not to reveal such information may be justifiable to prevent harm to others. As Dworkin identifies, however, the state must be able to demonstrate 'a clear and substantial risk' of great harm to people or property. The difficulty with the Official Secrets Acts is that, even though the 1989 Act limited harmful information to certain specified categories, the Act does not provide sufficient scope for a court to test whether a certain

---

[198]   [2004] UKHL 47.

[199]   *CTB* v. *News Group Newspapers and Imogen Thomas* [2011] EWHC 3099.

[200]   See the approach of the House of Lords in *Attorney-General* v. *Blake* [2001] 1 AC 268 and the US Supreme Court in *Snepp* v. *United States* 444 US 507 (1980).

document perceived to fall within the specified document is in fact harmful. In contrast, the civil law remedy of breach of confidence does allow for such analysis to take place.[201] The most draconian legal protection is provided by the common law offence of misconduct in public office. The offence does not allow for any determination as to whether the information is harmful but instead focuses on the act of disclosure by an individual, who because of their position in public employment should not have communicated the information.

In order to be Convention compliant it is suggested that courts must consider the proportionality framework used in *Guja* v. *Moldova* and *Bucur and Toma* v. *Romania* where an unauthorised disclosure has been made by a Crown servant. In doing so the court will consider the severity of the sanction. Criminal prosecution for disclosure is the heaviest sanction available. It is suggested that actions taken against an individual to obtain damages for breach of confidence are arguably less severe, thus requiring the information disclosed to be of a sufficiently high value to the public interest to outweigh the sanction imposed. However, in providing reference to *Vogt* the court in *Guja* suggested that dismissal was also a 'very harsh measure'.[202] The framework also considers the detriment to the organisation. Crown servants who have been dismissed, prosecuted or made subject to a breach of confidence action, after raising concerns where there has been little damage to the organisation, will most likely attract the protection of Article 10.[203] The reasoning in *Observer and Guardian* v. *United Kingdom* suggests that where a public organisation is principally motivated to protect its reputation it is unlikely to succeed.[204]

Considerable reform is needed to ensure that the laws which are used to safeguard official information are complaint with the ECHR. Reform is also required to the way in which government departments and agencies restrict the expression rights of public employees. As this chapter has identified, the extraterritorial enforcement of the criminal law

---

[201] As Feldman identifies, a court will be required to determine the public interest in the information, where they would not be able to do so in a criminal case involving the Official Secrets Act 1989; David Feldman, *Civil Liberties and Human Rights in England and Wales* (2nd edn, OUP, 2002) 669.

[202] *Vogt* v. *Germany*, Application No. 17851/91 (ECtHR, 26 September 1995); *Guja* v. *Moldova*, above n. 127, [95].

[203] *Ibid.* [90].

[204] *Observer and Guardian* v. *United Kingdom*, above n. 190.

and court orders obtained for breach of confidence are unlikely to prevent the unauthorised disclosure of documents outside of the legal jurisdiction. It is therefore vital that public organisations provide their employees with viable authorised alternatives.

3.   Protection as a journalistic source

The making of unauthorised disclosures to journalists provides an alternative to making whistleblowing disclosures using official channels. Provided that the individual can remain anonymous from their organisation, they can continue to leak information and potentially avoid any workplace reprisals.[1] The press perform a vital function in democratic society and can provide whistleblowers with a voice which may have gone unheard if they had chosen to use an official route. Journalists need sources and those sources need protection.[2] Where journalists are compelled to reveal a source, their role as watchdog is undermined.[3] Individuals are deterred from coming forward, resulting in a lasting 'chilling effect'.[4] The threat of prosecution to both journalists and their sources is a problem shared across the globe.[5]

---

[1]   Sisella Bok, *Secrets: On the Ethics of Concealment and Revelation* (Vintage, 1989) ch. 14. Brian Martin, 'Strategy for Public Interest Leaking' in Greg Martin, Rebecca Scott Bray and Miiko Kumar (eds), *Secrecy, Law and Society* (Routledge, 2015) 219. However, note that if an individual is anonymous it will be more difficult for them to obtain protection using the Public Interest Disclosure Act 1998, see further Ashley Savage and Richard Hyde, 'The Response to Whistleblowing by Regulators: A Practical Perspective' (2015) 35(3) *Legal Studies* 408. By making unauthorised disclosures the individual will also risk prosecution or dismissal if found out. For further consideration see Chapter 2.

[2]   For theoretical consideration of the journalist and source relationship, see further Damian Carney, 'The Theoretical Underpinnings of the Protection of Journalists' Confidential Sources' (2009) 1 *Journal of Media Law* 97.

[3]   *Goodwin* v. *United Kingdom*, Application No. 17488/90 (ECtHR, 1996).

[4]   *Ibid.*

[5]   For example, in the United States, the Department of Justice seized telephone records of Associated Press in order to determine the source of leaked classified information concerning a CIA operation: Charlie Savage and Scott Shane, 'Justice Dept. defends seizure of phone records', *New York Times*, 14 May 2013. In Japan, the Special Intelligence Protection Act 2013 was passed with the aim of combatting leaks. Public servants can be sentenced to ten years' imprisonment whilst journalists can be subject to five years' imprisonment for encouraging the leaks.

Conversely, whilst anonymity can offer protection to the source, it presents potential challenges for the recipient audience. The information concerned may consist of 'a mixture of substance and disinformation'.[6] The recipient audience of have little way of checking the accuracy of the information, placing significant importance on the role of journalists to check information before publication and to provide explanations as to the importance of the disclosures in question.[7] Furthermore, it has also been suggested that members of the public will 'confuse self-protective instincts with cowardice and deceitfulness'.[8] The traditional relationship between journalist and source is changing. Wikileaks and other online disclosure platforms now act as a conduit, working in collaboration with several media outlets across the globe.[9] Disclosures may be made to newspapers based outside of an individual's home jurisdiction.[10] Unauthorised disclosures are as likely to end up on a blog, disclosure website or circulated via Twitter and other social media as they are to be published by the traditional print media.[11] The legal protections protecting journalistic sources were drafted several years prior to this transformation, with traditional print media in mind. Conduit disclosures can

---

[6]   Helen Fenwick and Gavin Phillipson, *Media Freedom under the Human Rights Act* (OUP, 2006) 311.

[7]   National Union of Journalists, *Code of Conduct* (2013), available at file:///C:/Users/Home1/Downloads/nuj-code-of-conduct%20(1).pdf emphasises the importance of accurate reporting. Bok argues that where anonymous whistleblowing occurs, journalists and intermediaries will be faced with the task of determining whether the information received from a source should be published in its entirety, and whether it should be used at all if the accuracy of the information is in doubt. Bok, above n. 1, 223.

[8]   Yvonne Cripps, *The Legal Implications of Disclosure in the Public Interest* (Sweet & Maxwell, 1994) 254.

[9]   For discussion of Wikileaks' association with the *Guardian* newspaper see David Leigh and Luke Harding, *Wikileaks: Inside Julian Assange's War on Secrecy* (Guardian, 2011) 90. See also Heather Brooke, *The Revolution will be Digitised: Dispatches from the Information War* (William Hienemann, 2011) 56.

[10]   For example, Edward Snowden chose to make disclosures to the *Guardian* newspaper (UK) rather than to approach a newspaper based in the United States.

[11]   For example, South Tyneside Council faced considerable difficulty in trying to obtain an order for source disclosure after becoming aware of various allegations made by an employee on a blog. The blog was based on a server in the United States, prompting the Council to apply for the court order in the United States. Josh Halliday, 'Twitter anonymous user battle', *Guardian*, 29 May 2011; for the related court documents see San Mateo Court website, www.san mateocourt.org/midx/strip.php?kase=jp5w3.

provide an additional layer of protection for the source, particularly where the conduit is based outside of the legal jurisdiction.[12] However, where information has been provided by a conduit, the risk to both the journalist and recipient audience arguably increases. Journalists need to test for accuracy, a task made more difficult if they do not have direct access to the source.[13] The audience is reliant upon the journalist to ensure that the information they read is true.[14] Whereas print newspapers may once have quoted from the leaked documents, there is now an increasing trend for traditional media outlets to publish official documents on their websites. This will often require accompanying explanations to highlight their significance.[15] In deciding whether to publish these documents, editors are effectively required to make decisions about whether the information they have in their possession will cause harm if published. This arguably presents an increased risk of investigatory tactics and prosecution. It also presents an unquantifiable risk to national security.[16]

---

[12] For example, Wikileaks uses a system called 'Tor'. The system utilises a network of computer servers and multi-layered encryption in order to route anonymous information via other computers using the Tor system, the result being that the origin of the information cannot be identified: Leigh and Harding, above n. 9, 52. For an alternative view note that prior to the official launch of Wikileaks, Ben Laurie, commenting on the levels of protection Wikileaks intended to provide to whistleblowers, suggested that he 'would not trust his life or even his liberty to Tor'. See further Paul Marks, 'How to Leak a Secret and Not Get Caught', *New Scientist*, 12 January 2007.

[13] Jamie Matthews, 'Journalists and their Sources: The Twin Challenges of Diversity and Verification' in Karen Fowler-Watt and Stuart Allen (eds), *Journalism: New Challenges* (Centre for Journalism and Communication Research, 2013).

[14] Dean distinguishes three classes of the recipient audience, suggesting that 'those who believe through the judgements of others' are placed at the most risk. Jodi Dean, 'Publicity's Secret' (2009) 29(5) *Political Theory* 646. Neocleous bolsters this position by identifying that society is placed at a 'serious technical and organisational disadvantage' when it comes to secret information. Society may lack the ability to determine whether the information disclosed is true, Mark Neocleous, 'Privacy, Secrecy, Idiocy' (2002) 69(1) *Social Research* 87.

[15] Bok suggests that unless the information disclosed is accompanied by 'indications of how the information can be checked' the value of the communicated message is diminished. Bok, above n. 1, 223.

[16] For example, both current and former intelligence officials have claimed that the Snowden leaks have caused irreparable damage to intelligence gathering capabilities. The harm is arguably unquantifiable because of the difficulty of providing a causal link between the number of terrorist attacks that can no longer

The threats to media freedom have also changed. Whereas a UK newspaper may have been subject to a court order to reveal their source or police searches of premises (both of which are subject to codified protections to safeguard the media), the Snowden revelations have identified that GCHQ and intelligence partners have extensive capabilities to obtain communications data.[17] The intelligence agencies are faced with a nigh on impossible task, to prevent terror attacks and to curtail increasingly co-ordinated networks of extremists.[18] However, these blanket methods, which appear to have been lawfully authorised, make it impossible for agencies to effectively separate terrorist actors, ordinary citizens, Members of Parliament in communication with their constituents, and the subject of this analysis: journalists and their sources.[19]

This chapter will provide an assessment of the various threats to the protection of journalistic sources as well as an analysis of the legal protections available. It will start by considering the key principles set out by the European Court of Human Rights (ECtHR) before proceeding to identify whether or not the United Kingdom is meeting these standards.[20]

---

be stopped and the leaks, and further unquantifiable because society lacks the capacity to test the accuracy of these claims. Moreover, the security and intelligence services are reluctant to provide detailed information because of the secret nature of their work.

[17] For detailed discussion see Glenn Greenwald, *No Place to Hide: Edward Snowden and the Surveillance State* (Hamish Hamilton, 2014).

[18] According to the Director General of the Security Service, Andrew Parker, Lord Mayor's Defence and Security Lecture, 28 October 2015, available at www.mi5.gov.uk/home/about-us/who-we-are/staff-and-management/director-general/speeches-by-the-director-general/a-modern-mi5.html.

[19] For decisions regarding communications between MPs and their constituents see *Lucas and others* v. *Security Service and others* [2015] IPT/14/79/CH, IPT/14/80/CH, IPT/14/172/CH; and *Davis, Watson, Brice and Lewis* v. *Secretary of State for the Home Department* [2015] EWHC 2092.

[20] The chapter does not purport to provide detailed discussion on domestic development of the protection of journalistic sources. For discussion, see generally Helen Fenwick and Gavin Phillipson, *Media Freedom under the Human Rights Act* (Oxford, 2006); for discussion with comparative examples, see Janice Brabyn, 'Protecton Against Judicially Compelled Disclosure of the Identity of News Gathers' Confidential Sources in Common Law Jurisdictions' (2006) 69(6) *Modern Law Review* 895.

I ECTHR SAFEGUARDS

In *Goodwin* v. *United Kingdom*,[21] the ECtHR set a particularly high standard for the protection of journalistic sources. The Court held that the protection of sources is 'one of the basic conditions for press freedom': if sources are not protected individuals may be deterred from coming forward with information on matters of public interest, the watchdog role with be undermined, leading to a chilling effect which cannot be justified unless there is 'an overriding requirement in the public interest'.[22] The Court identified that with regard to the proportionality test, national authorities 'enjoy a certain margin of appreciation' in order to determine whether there is a 'pressing social need for the restriction'.[23] Yet, with regard to the protection of journalistic sources, the 'national margin of appreciation' is 'circumscribed by the interest of democratic society in ensuring and maintaining a free press'.[24] Limitations imposed on the confidentiality of journalistic sources therefore require the most careful judicial scrutiny.[25] The reasoning in *Goodwin* has been followed in several decisions. In *Voskuil* v. *The Netherlands*, the Court found that the detention of a journalist for two weeks in an attempt to force the disclosure of documents which could reveal sources was in breach of Article 10 of the European Convention on Human Rights (ECHR).[26] In *Financial Times* v. *United Kingdom*, the Court found that the future risk of repetition and the motivation to obtain damages for breach of confidence was not sufficient to outweigh protection of the source. In *Sanoma Uitgever BV* v. *The Netherlands*, the Court held that journalists could not be compelled to hand over material which could reveal sources without independent judicial authorisation. Similarly, in *Telegraaf Media Nederland Landelijke Media BV and others* v. *The Netherlands*, the Court held that journalists could not be compelled to hand over secret documents concerning the Dutch intelligence service. In addition, the Court held that there was a breach of Article 8 on the basis that the journalists had been subjected to surveillance activities.[27]

---

[21] *Goodwin* v. *United Kingdom*, above n. 3.
[22] *Ibid.* [39].
[23] *Ibid.* [40].
[24] *Ibid.* [40].
[25] *Ibid.* [40].
[26] *Voskuil* v. *The Netherlands*, Application No. 64752/01 (ECtHR, 22 November 2000).
[27] *Telegraaf Media Nederland Landelijke Media BV and others* v. *The Netherlands*, Application No. 39315/06 (ECtHR, 22 November 2013).

Where a journalist has been seen to overstep the mark they may struggle to obtain protection. Whilst the following cases do not have a direct impact on the protection of journalistic sources they are of relevance as they concern the actions taken against journalists who report on information provided by confidential sources. In *Pederson and Baadsgaard* v. *Denmark*, the ECtHR identified that the enhanced level of protection afforded to journalists carries with it duties and responsibilities, and as a consequence they should act 'in good faith and on an accurate factual basis and provide reliable and precise information in accordance with the ethics of journalism'.[28] The journalists had failed to verify information obtained from a witness regarding an alleged miscarriage of justice. In *Stoll* v. *Switzerland*, the Grand Chamber held that the publication of classified documents which revealed strategies to repay Holocaust victims money held in Swiss bank accounts was not sufficient to obtain protection.[29] The judgment focussed heavily on the conduct of the journalist, the Court finding that the story had been reported on in a 'sensationalist style'[30] and that the chief intention had been to make the disclosed report the 'subject of needless scandal'.[31]

II SOURCE PROTECTION

In contrast to countries like Sweden, the United Kingdom does not have a stand-alone journalistic shield law.[32] Instead, the United Kingdom has adopted a piecemeal approach with safeguards added to legislation which may impact on journalistic source protection. The first protection concerns court orders compelling journalists to reveal their sources.[33] The second concerns the special procedures that the police must adopt in obtaining a warrant to search and seize journalistic material. The third concerns Human Rights Act 1998, section 6, which requires public authorities, including the police, intelligence agencies and the courts to

---

[28] *Pederson and Baadsgaard* v. *Denmark,* Application No. 49017/99 (ECtHR, 17 December 2003) [78].
[29] *Stoll* v. *Switzerland*, Application No. 6968/01 (ECtHR, 10 December 2007).
[30] *Ibid.* [140].
[31] *Ibid.* [151].
[32] Freedom of the Press Act 1949 (Sweden).
[33] Contempt of Court Act 1981, s.10.

act compatibly with the Convention, meaning that they must acknowledge the high level of protection Article 10 affords to journalistic sources.[34]

III ORDERS FOR SOURCE DISCLOSURE

An aggrieved party can apply to the court for a *Norwich Pharmacal* order.[35] The orders are often made without notice requiring a judge to make a decision based on representations from the applicant without hearing justifications from the recipient party as to why the order should not be made. If the party refuses to disclose the identity of the wrongdoer, they may be subject to prosecution for contempt of court. Contempt of Court Act 1981, section 10, contains the journalistic safeguard:

> No court may require a person to disclose, nor is any person guilty of contempt of court for refusing to disclose, the source of information contained in any publication for which he is responsible, unless it be established to the satisfaction of the court that disclosure is necessary in the interests of justice or national security or for the prevention of disorder or crime.[36]

The four exceptions to section 10 rest upon the central idea of 'necessity'. The element of necessity is deemed as a crucial justification for courts' use of the contempt power.[37] Its meaning has been stated as 'more than merely relevant or desirable, useful or expedient'.[38] Although it is based upon a question of fact,[39] judgment will also be dependent upon

---

[34]   In addition, Human Rights Act (HRA) 1998 s.12 places an obligation on courts to have particular regard to the importance of freedom of expression in considering whether or not to make an order.

[35]   *Norwich Pharmacal Co. and others* v. *Customs and Excise Commissioners* [1974] AC 133.

[36]   For a comparative example see Evidence Act 2006 (New Zealand), s.68. The section protects journalists from having to reveal the identity of sources or produce documents in any civil or criminal proceedings. The section is subject to limitations contained in s.68(2) where a High Court judge may order disclosure if the public interest in disclosure outweighs the public interest in non-disclosure.

[37]   See Ronald Goldfarb, *The Contempt Power* (Columbia University Press, 1963) 22.

[38]   See *Maxwell* v. *Pressdram Ltd* [1987] 1 All ER 656, CA and *X* v. *Y* [1998] 2 All ER 648. See also N. Lowe and B. Sufrin, *Borrie and Lowe: The Law of Contempt* (3rd edn, Butterworths, 1996).

[39]   [1988] AC 660, 704.

the extent of enquiries made by the person requiring the order of disclosure.[40] It is also expected that the person requesting the order will give specific reasons for doing so.[41] Section 10 covers 'any speech, writing or other communication in whatever form, which is addressed to the public at large or any section of the public'.[42]

Contempt of Court Act 1981, section 10, which pre-dates the Human Rights Act (HRA) 1998, must be read and given effect to by the courts, so far as it is possible to do so, in a way which is compatible with Article 10 ECHR under HRA 1998, section 3(1). The term 'interests of justice' does not appear in Article 10(2) ECHR and is open to wide interpretation. In order to be compliant with Article 10(2), the term 'necessary' must now be interpreted as 'necessary in a democratic society'.[43] However, despite the clear determination regarding the application of proportionality in *Goodwin*, the domestic courts have failed to get the balance right, consistently favouring applicants for disclosure orders. Furthermore, domestic courts have wrongly placed emphasis on the 'malevolent motive' of sources. In *Interbrew SA* v. *Financial Times Ltd*, focus on the motive of a person who leaked documents to the newspaper was sufficient to satisfy the Court of Appeal that an order was necessary in the interests of justice.[44] The *Financial Times* applied to the ECtHR, where the Court held that the domestic legal proceedings had determined the source's motive without the opportunity of hearing full evidence on the matter.[45] Without compelling evidence, courts could not assume that the source was 'acting in bad faith'.[46] This factor is most important because it identifies the different approach needed to proportionality balancing in matters concerning journalistic source cases, in contrast with whistleblowing cases where the identity of the individual is known. In applications for *Norwich Pharmacal* orders, the motivation of the source must not be a significant part of the balancing exercise, whereas in

---

[40] *Broadmoor Hospital* v. *Hyde, Independent*, 4 March 1994.

[41] *Attorney General* v. *Guardian* [1985] AC 339, [346] per Lord Diplock, [360] per Lord Fraser, [364] per Lord Scarman, [368] per Lord Roskilland, [372] per Lord Bridge.

[42] Contempt of Court Act 1981, ss.2(1), 19.

[43] *Interbrew SA* v. *Financial Times Ltd* [2002] EWCA Civ 274, para. 53.

[44] *Ibid.*

[45] *Financial Times Ltd* v. *United Kingdom*, Application No. 821/03 (ECtHR, 15 December 2009).

[46] *Ibid.* [63].

whistleblowing cases, the motivation of the source becomes most important in determining whether the individual had made the disclosure in good faith.[47]

Impact Post Manning and Snowden

In *Financial Times* v. *United Kingdom*, the ECtHR held that the domestic courts had failed to consider whether the matter could be dealt with by use of an injunction rather than an order for disclosure.[48] An injunction could arguably prevent UK newspapers from reporting on information obtained as a result of an unauthorised disclosure. However, where information has been provided by a person acting as a conduit, the threat of any enforcement action is unlikely to restrict publication or prevent further leaks. Both the Manning and Snowden leaks identify that disclosures of large quantities of documents are possible and that these disclosures may take place over a period of time to maximise press and public interest.

The ECtHR has made clear that a disclosure order may be justified in exceptional circumstances where there is a risk of repetition on two clear grounds: first, where it was clear that there were no alternative or less invasive means available; and secondly, where the risk threatened is 'sufficiently serious and defined' to render the disclosure order necessary within the meaning of Article 10(2).[49] If an injunction is not possible or is unlikely to succeed, this is likely to satisfy the first limb. Where the information at issue concerns national security, it is likely to satisfy the second limb, namely, that the circumstances are sufficiently serious to require a disclosure order to protect national security or to prevent disorder or crime.

If the information concerned contains personal information, an additional complication will arise. In the Manning disclosures, many of the files contained information which would engage Article 8 ECHR. In *Ashworth Hospital Authority* v. *MGN Ltd*, the House of Lords upheld a *Norwich Pharmacal* order to determine the identity of an individual who disclosed patient records.[50] The domestic court would therefore be required to undertake the new methodology test set out in *Re S*, to

---

[47] Applying the reasoning in *Guja* v. *Moldova*. Application No. 14277/04 (ECtHR, 12 February 2008).

[48] *Financial Times Ltd* v. *United Kingdom*, above n. 45, [69].

[49] *Ibid.* [69].

[50] *Ashworth Hospital Authority* v. *MGN Ltd* [2002] UKHL 29.

determine whether or not the confidentiality rights protected by Article 8 outweighs the public interest value of the information protected by Article 10.

All of the above factors place the domestic courts in a quandary. If an application is made to obtain an order against a journalist based in the United Kingdom, an injunction could restrict publication but is unlikely to mitigate against the risk of repetition. Based on this aforementioned reasoning, a *Norwich Pharmacal* order could still be made against a UK journalist. Where the information has been provided by a conduit, the journalist may not have any knowledge of the identity of the source but is unlikely to have an opportunity to convince a court of this prior to the making of the order given that application is likely to be made *ex parte*. If the *Norwich Pharmacal* order is made against a conduit based outside of the jurisdiction, it will be extremely difficult to enforce.[51] The next section will consider the interception of communications information which can reveal the identity of sources. It will identify that the methods discussed circumvent the need to obtain a traditional court order for source disclosure.

IV INTERCEPTION OF COMMUNICATIONS

The Snowden revelations have identified the extent to which the United States and its partners to the 'Five Eyes' agreement are engaged in the surveillance and interception of communications over the Internet.[52] The Snowden leaks identified that the United States National Security Agency (NSA) had been obtaining communications data via US Internet companies under a program codenamed PRISM.[53] Snowden alleged that the

---

[51] For consideration of *Norwich Pharmacal* orders against individuals based in the United States, see *Louis Bacon* v. *(1) Automattic Inc. (2) Wikimedia Foundation (3) Denver Post Inc.* [2011] EWHC 1072. See also *Re Request for Assistance from Ministry of Legal Affairs of Trinidad and Tobago* 848 F.2d 1151 (1988) concerning a request for assistance in criminal proceedings.

[52] See generally Greenwald, above n. 17; Luke Harding, *The Snowden Files: The Inside Story of the World's Most Wanted Man* (Guardian, 2014). For discussion regarding the impact of the Snowden leaks on state surveillance see Maria Helen Murphy, 'The Pendulum Effect: Comparisons between the Snowden Revelations and the Church Committee: What are the Potential Implications for Europe?' (2014) 23(2) *Information and Communications Technology Law* 192 and David Lyon, 'The Snowden Stakes: Challenges for Understanding Surveillance Today' (2015) 13(2) *Surveillance and Society* 139.

[53] See generally Harding, above n. 52.

UK intelligence organisation tasked with electronic surveillance, Government Communications Headquarters (GCHQ), were illegally accessing communications data under the PRISM program. PRISM takes its legal basis from the US Foreign Intelligence Surveillance Act (FISA) 1978. Authorisations under the Act require approval from the FISA Court, which holds proceedings in secret.[54] Further to these activities, Snowden disclosed information regarding joint projects between the NSA and GCHQ. The TEMPORA program concerns the interception of underwater fibre-optic cables.[55] The MUSCULAR program concerns the interception of data from fibre-optic cables.[56]

The Intelligence Services Act 1994 placed GCHQ (and also the Secret Intelligence Service, MI6) on a statutory footing.[57] The general power to obtain information from an intelligence partner is contained in section 7 which concerns the authorisation for acts done abroad. Effectively, this prevents individuals from being subject to liability provided that an authorisation has been signed by a Secretary of State. Section 7(4) has particularly broad application, identifying that the authorisation 'may relate to a particular act or acts, to acts of a description specified in the authorisation or to acts undertaken in the course of an operation so specified'. Authorisations may also be provided by a senior official in 'urgent cases', however no definition of this is provided.[58]

The general power to conduct surveillance and obtain data is taken from Regulation of Investigatory Powers Act (RIPA) 2000, Part I, which is split into two chapters.[59] Chapter I, sections 1–20 covers the obtaining of content data. Chapter 2, comprising of sections 21–25, covers the acquisition and disclosure of communications data. The intelligence services can conduct targeted interception whereby the focus of the

---

[54] For detailed information on the work of the FISA Court and legislation see the excellent resource provided by the Federation of American Scientists, Secrecy News Blog, http://fas.org/irp/agency/doj/fisa/.

[55] Ewan MacAskill *et al.*, 'GCHQ taps fibre-optic cables for secret access to world's communications', *Guardian*, 21 June 2013, available at www.the guardian.com/uk/2013/jun/21/gchq-cables-secret-world-communications-nsa.

[56] Dominic Rushe *et al.*, 'Reports that NSA taps into Google and Yahoo data hubs infuriate tech giants', *Guardian*, 31 October 2013, available at www.the guardian.com/technology/2013/oct/30/google-reports-nsa-secretly-intercepts-data-links.

[57] Security Services Act 1989.

[58] Intelligence Services Act 1994, s.7(5)(b).

[59] It should be noted that at the time of writing the government announced that a new Bill would be published to reform the regime.

intelligence gathering is on known individuals. They can also conduct bulk interception, whereby intelligence is gathered from information sent or received outside of the United Kingdom, and obtain bulk personal datasets by receiving data from communications service providers, intercepting data by tapping into transatlantic fibre-optic cables or obtaining the data from overseas partners.[60] The agencies can also obtain communications data in this way.

In order to conduct targeted interception, the intelligence services must obtain authorisation under RIPA 2000 from the relevant Secretary of State.[61] An exception to this process is provided in urgent cases, whereby a senior official may sign the warrant provided that it has been expressly authorised by the Secretary of State or by a senior civil servant in cases where there has been a request for assistance made under an international mutual assistance agreement by an agency based outside of the United Kingdom and the individual who is the subject of the interception is outside of the United Kingdom or the interception relates to premises outside of the United Kingdom.[62] RIPA 2000, section 8 details two types of interception warrant: a section 8(1) warrant, under which the agency must specify a person or premises in relation to which the interception will take place (referred to as a 'targeted warrant' by the Investigatory Powers Tribunal), and an 'untargeted' section 8(4) warrant.[63] In contrast to section 8(1) warrants, section 8(4) warrants do not have to include a schedule identifying what communications are to be intercepted.

The section 8(4) warrants are capable of wide application. Whilst they are limited to external communications, this in effect means communications entering and exiting the United Kingdom from another jurisdiction. It therefore provides scope for the obtaining of communications data from UK citizens and from abroad. The warrants are subject to safeguards contained in RIPA 2000, sections 15 and 16. Section 15(3) requires the information and any relevant communications data to be

---

[60]   The full capabilities were explained in the report from the Intelligence and Security Committee, *Privacy and Security: A Modern and Transparent Legal Framework*, HC-1075 (2015).

[61]   The security service seeks authorisation from the Home Secretary whilst GCHQ and the Secret Intelligence Service obtain authorisation from the Foreign Secretary. RIPA 2000, s.7, details this process. In addition, for a detailed explanation of the warrant application process see Interception of Communications Commissioner, *Annual Report*, HC-1184 (2004) 5.

[62]   RIPA 2000, s.7(2)(b).

[63]   *Liberty and others* v. *Government Communications and others* [2014] UKIPTrib 13_77-H, [65].

destroyed when it is no longer necessary and proportionate to retain it. Section 16 limits what information may be examined to the extent to which it has been certified. Moreover, the information must not be examined where the individual is known to be in the British Islands.[64] However, section 16(3) allows examination of an individual known to be in the United Kingdom where it is certified as necessary by the Secretary of State on the basis of national security, serious crime or economic wellbeing. Section 16(5) will apply where the agencies believed an individual to be abroad when in fact they had entered the United Kingdom, in which case a senior official may provide the authorisation. Put simply, the agencies can lawfully obtain a vast amount of data which is entering and exiting the United Kingdom but can only lawfully examine it if the information does not relate to an individual known to be in the British Islands, unless the Secretary of State certifies it is necessary to do so, or a senior official so certifies in limited circumstances.

In authorising the warrant and certification, the Secretary of State must conduct a 'triple test' to ensure compliance with the ECHR. In obtaining bulk datasets from intelligence partners, the agencies conduct the same test.[65] First, the action must be 'for a lawful purpose' meaning that it is in the interests of national security, to safeguard the economic wellbeing of the state or for the prevention and detection of serious crime. Second, the action must be necessary for one or more of the aforementioned purposes.[66] Third, it must be proportionate, meaning that 'the action must be no more intrusive than is justified for the purpose of the investigation, and must not unnecessarily intrude on the privacy of innocent people'. It should therefore be considered whether the information can be obtained by less obtrusive means.[67]

The Intelligence and Security Committee (ISC) provides a helpful distinction between the different types of data which may be obtained. The ISC distinguishes between 'Communications Data' which identifies the 'who, when and where', and 'Communications Data Plus' which would provide more detail, identifying web domains or locational tracking information; both types of information are considered communications data under RIPA 2000.[68] Both 'Content Derived Data' which

---

[64]   RIPA 2000, s.16(2)(b).
[65]   As discussed in the ISC Report, above n. 60, ch. 4.
[66]   *Ibid.*
[67]   *Ibid.*
[68]   *Ibid.*, 52.

requires analysis of the information and 'Content Data' are treated as 'Content' by RIPA 2000.[69]

The Intelligence and Security Committee held that Snowden's allegations were unfounded on the basis that GCHQ's activities had been lawfully authorised on the basis of the above legislation.[70] Where there was evidence of bulk interception or analysis of bulk datasets this was determined to be lawful and proportionate because the agencies do not actively read through the communications and browsing history of the populations but instead conduct a filtering process using predetermined trigger words to sift through the data. Moreover, the agencies did not have the resources to conduct full analysis of all data obtained. Whilst the ISC acknowledged that 'Communications Data Plus' could identify privacy sensitive information, the Committee was satisfied that it was not as intrusive as analysis of content data. The ISC did, however, call for a single law to update and consolidate the regime. In a separate report, the Interception of Communications Commissioner was also satisfied that the agencies' involvement with the NSA and data gathering activities were lawful.

Liberty, Amnesty International and a number of other organisations challenged the alleged activities before the Investigatory Powers Tribunal (IPT) on the basis that the agencies were in breach of Articles 8 and 10 ECHR. In a judgment handed down on 5 December 2014, the IPT made no findings of wrongdoing. These determinations were made on a series of assumed facts based on the Snowden leaks and the NSA admitting to the existence of PRISM and UPSTREAM.[71] In the second judgment handed down on 6 February 2015, the IPT then made a declaration that the obtaining, storage and transmission of PRISM and UPSTREAM data prior to 5 December 2014 contravened Articles 8 and 10, however, because information on the activities had been made public, the IPT were satisfied that the agencies were now compliant.[72] At the time of writing, this is the only finding the IPT has made against the security and intelligence services.

---

[69] *Ibid.*
[70] Intelligence and Security Committee, Statement on GCHQ's Alleged Interception of Communications under the US PRISM Programme (July 2013), available at http://isc.independent.gov.uk/committee-reports/special-reports.
[71] *Liberty* v. *Government Communications*, above n. 63, [4].
[72] *Ibid.*

It is clear that the IPT failed to afford sufficient regard to the Strasbourg decisions in *Sanoma Uitgevers BV* v. *The Netherlands*[73] and *Telegraaf Media Nederland* v. *The Netherlands*.[74] In *Sanoma*, a case concerning the search and seizure of journalistic material, the ECtHR held that the proportionality test must be independently undertaken by a body separate to the investigatory authority which have a clear and vested interest in obtaining the material sought.[75] Moreover, the independent body must be in a position to carry out the balancing act before any disclosures are actually made by the investigatory authority; the exercise of an independent review after the material capable of revealing a source has been handed over would undermine this protection. The Grand Chamber unanimously held that the absence of any procedure in domestic law which required an independent body to engage in an effective and adequate assessment of the proportionality of the interference made to the possible revelation of a journalistic source failed to satisfy the quality of law test.

In *Telegraaf Media*, the case concerned the unauthorised disclosure of classified documents appearing to originate from the Netherlands Security and Intelligence Service (AIVD). The journalists were ordered to surrender the documents to the authorities, were placed under surveillance and had their telephones tapped. The surveillance was authorised by a senior official. The Court found breaches of both Articles 8 and 10 and held that without prior review of the authorisation, the law could not provide sufficient safeguards to protect journalistic sources. Most importantly, it found that 'review *post factum*', be it by one of a number of oversight mechanisms, was not sufficient to 'restore the confidentiality of sources'.[76]

The IPT appeared to distinguish the targeted surveillance in *Telegraaf Media*, identifying that with regard to a 's.8(4) warrant, it is clearly impossible to anticipate a judicial pre-authorisation prior to the warrant limited to what might turn out to impact upon Article 10'.[77] In doing so, the Tribunal missed the point that any breach could not be rectified *post*

---

[73] *Sanoma Uitgevers BV* v. *The Netherlands*, Application No. 38224/03 (ECtHR, 14 September 2010). For commentary see Ashley Savage and Paul David Mora, 'Independent Judicial Oversight to Guarantee Proportionate Revelations of Journalistic Sources: The Grand Chamber's Decision in Sanoma Uitgevers B.V. v. The Netherlands' (2011) 22 *Entertainment Law Review* 1.

[74] *Telegraaf Media Nederland* v. *The Netherlands*, above n. 27.

[75] *Sanoma Uitgevers BV* v. *The Netherlands*, above n. 73, [91].

[76] *Ibid.* [100]–[102].

[77] *Telegraaf Media Nederland* v. *The Netherlands*, above n. 27, [151].

factum. Moreover, it is difficult to see how the untargeted bulk collection of communications data could not have a chilling effect on sources, deterring others from raising public interest concerns to the press for fear of detection. The chilling effect goes to the very heart of the ECtHR's motivation to protect sources. Whilst the filtering of the bulk data could be seen as a way of mitigating against the risk of identifying journalistic sources, it provides little guarantee because information has not been given to the public on the 'triggers' used as part of the analysis process. Also, based on the information provided in the official reports there appears to be no way of 'filtering' to restrict the obtaining of journalistic material, at source, to prevent its storage, however temporary.[78] Ultimately, one cannot trust the determination by the IPT that the agencies were complaint with Articles 8 and 10 where the judgement was based on assumed publically available information and limited disclosure by the respondents in the case.[79] At the time of writing, Big Brother Watch and others had applied to the ECtHR challenging the legality of the surveillance practices and the RIPA 2000 authorisation process.[80]

Data Retention

The Data Retention and Investigatory Powers Act 2014 was enacted following the European Court of Justice (ECJ)'s judgment in *Digital Rights Ireland* which found the EU Data Retention Directive 2006/24/EC to be invalid.[81] The impact of the decision meant that communications service providers could no longer be required to retain communications data. As a consequence, the Data Retention Investigatory Powers Act (DRIPA) 2014 was enacted. Section 1 gave the Secretary of State the power to issue a retention notice requiring a public telecommunications operator to retain data for a period specified, provided that the notice was necessary and proportionate for the purposes of RIPA 2000, section 22.

---

[78] The ISC Report, above n. 60, for example identifies that the communications data is deleted after the filtering process (note that this section is redacted in part).

[79] For a short critique of the decision see Ian Leigh, 'GCHQ datasharing with the NSA deemed unlawful—but don't expect things to change', *The Conversation*, 7 February 2015, available at https://theconversation.com/gchq-datasharing-with-the-nsa-deemed-unlawful-but-dont-expect-things-to-change-37309.

[80] *Big Brother Watch and others* v. *United Kingdom*, Application No. 58170/13 (ECtHR, lodged 4 September 2014).

[81] C-293/12 *Digital Rights Ireland* v. *Minister for Communications and others* (ECJ, 15 May 2014).

In *Davis, Watson, Brice and Lewis* v. *Secretary of State for the Home Department*,[82] the applicants successfully obtained a declaration that DRIPA 2014, section 1, was inconsistent with EU law on the basis that the section did not set out precise rules for the obtaining and use of communications data which was restricted for the purposes of preventing and detecting offences, and, crucially for the purposes of this analysis, access to the data was not dependent on prior review by a court or an independent administrative body to strictly limit the use of the data for the defined objective.[83]

On 27 January 2015, CBC News and The Intercept revealed, on the basis of documents provided by former US NSA employee and whistle-blower, Edward Snowden, that Canada's equivalent intelligence agency, the Communications Security Establishment (CSE) was conducting a surveillance program called LEVITATION. Similar to the activities of GCHQ and the NSA, the CSE was said to be intercepting Internet cables, 'analyzes records of up to 15 million downloads daily' and 'can monitor downloads in several countries across Europe, the Middle East, North Africa, and North America'.[84] The German Bundestag established a commission of inquiry to investigate the extent of the violation of the rights of German nationals by the US NSA's surveillance programs,[85] as well as the involvement of its intelligence partner GCHQ.[86] An investigation conducted by former Federal Court Judge Kurt Graulich found that the NSA had sent the German Federal Intelligence Service (Bundes-nachrichtendienst (BND)) a list of selector words to be used to search BND databases.[87] Graulich found that the NSA were in breach of a memorandum of understanding signed by the BND and the NSA by

---

[82] [2015] EWHC 2092.

[83] *Ibid.* [64].

[84] Ryan Gallagher and Glenn Greenwald, 'Canada casts global surveillance dragnet over file downloads', *The Intercept*, 28 January 2015, available at https://firstlook.org/theintercept/2015/01/28/canada-cse-levitation-mass-surveillance/; 'CSE tracks millions of downloads daily: Snowden documents', CBC News, 27 January 2015, available at www.cbc.ca/news/canada/cse-tracks-millions-of-down loads-daily-snowden-documents-1.2930120.

[85] Derek Scally, 'NSA whistleblowers' testimony electrifies Bundestag committee', *Irish Times*, 2 July 2014, available at www.irishtimes.com/news/world/europe/nsa-whistleblowers-testimony-electrifies-bundestag-committee-1.1855972.

[86] 'German Parliament confirms NSA inquiry, to start in April', Deutsche Welle, 20 March 2014, available at www.dw.com/en/german-parliament-confirms-nsa-inquiry-to-start-in-april/a-17511518.

[87] Maik Baumgärtner and Martin Knobbe, 'Sonderermittler spricht von klarem Vertragsbruch der NSA', *Der Spiegel*, 30 October 2015, available at

failing to strip out the identities of German nationals from the database. Further, the report alleged complicity in the spying on embassies and government bodies.

Police Activities

The Interception of Communications Commissioner's Office (IOCCO) conducted an inquiry into police use of Part I of RIPA 2000 to obtain communications data of journalists in order to reveal their sources.[88] The press had alleged that the police had abused their powers during investigations into the 'Plebgate affair' and the trial of former Minister Chris Huhne and Vicky Price for perverting the course of justice.[89] In addition to this, police were also requesting data as part of the Operation Elvedon inquiry into the payment of public officials in return for stories.[90] The IOCCO found that whilst the correct authorisations had been given, the police had failed to give sufficient regard to necessity and proportionality in the decision-making process, and that the Home Office Code of Practice did not contain sufficient safeguards. As an interim measure, the IOCCO placed a new requirement on public authorities that judicial authorisation should be sought where data concerning journalistic activities is required.[91] The IOCCO's recommendation further compounds the need for legislation which effectively safeguards the protection of journalistic sources. Judicial authorisation is needed to ensure that the competing interests of preventing crime and or national security and the need to protect sources are rigorously balanced by an independent

---

www.spiegel.de/politik/deutschland/nsa-selektorenliste-kurt-graulich-spricht-von-klarem-vertragsbruch-a-1060280.html.

[88]   Interception of Communications Commissioner's Office, *Inquiry into the Use of Chapter 2 of Part 1 of the Regulation of Investigatory Powers Act (RIPA) to Identify Journalistic Sources* (4 February 2015).

[89]   The 'plebgate' affair involved several leaks of information concerning the actions of a government Minister, Andrew Mitchell, and police officers guarding the Downing Street gates. See generally, 'Plebgate row: timeline', BBC News, 27 November 2014, available at www.bbc.co.uk/news/uk-24548645; 'Chris Huhne admits perverting the course of justice', BBC News, 4 November 2013, available at www.bbc.co.uk/news/uk-21320992.

[90]   Ella Pickover, 'Operation Elveden: Arrests made in police payment probe', *Independent*, 28 January 2012.

[91]   IOCCO, above n. 88. This led to the provision of secondary legislation: Regulation of Investigatory Powers (Acquisition and Disclosure of Communications Data: Code of Practice) Order 2015.

judge. The next section will now consider other methods which may be used to obtain the identity of sources, entry, search and seizure.

V REFORM OF SURVEILLANCE POWERS

The aforementioned surveillance activities present two main challenges to the effective protection of journalistic sources: targeted/directed activities against journalists and/or the source, and the 'chilling effect' caused by the obtaining and storage of bulk data for analysis. Both the UN Special Rapporteur on the Promotion and Protection of Human Rights while Countering Terrorism and the UN Special Rapporteur on the Promotion and Protection of the Right to Freedom of Opinion and Expression have expressed concerns that the surveillance activities of the United Kingdom, United States and others impact on the expression and privacy rights of citizens.[92] Both Special Rapporteurs argue that there is a need for reform and that surveillance powers should be subject to prior judicial authorisation.[93] The following analysis will consider the possibility of reform with reference to the Investigatory Powers Bill which was introduced in November 2015.

Authorisation: By Politician or Judge?

The Intelligence and Security Committee determined in its report that Ministers are best placed to make these decisions as they are politically accountable – but as they identify, this is reliant on transparency.[94] This is problematic for two reasons. First, the above analysis of the Strasbourg case law identifies that decisions which impact on the protection of journalistic sources should be made by a judge. Second, it is arguable that the current system lacks a strong regime to oversee the system and RIPA 2000, section 19, adds considerable secrecy to the process.[95] The Home Affairs Committee conducted an inquiry on counter-terrorism which focussed on matters arising from the Snowden revelations. The

---

[92] UN Special Rapporteur on the Promotion and Protection of Human Rights while Countering Terrorism, Seventieth Session: Item 73B (A/70/361 2015) [62]; UN Special Rapporteur on the Promotion and Protection of Human Rights while Countering Terrorism, Sixty-ninth Session: Item 68A (A/69/397) [46].

[93] *Ibid.*

[94] ISC Report, above n. 60, [GG].

[95] For further analysis see Chapter 6.

Committee was highly critical of the oversight regime, questioning the effectiveness of the Commissioners who oversee the warrant process and oversight as a whole.[96] David Anderson QC, the Independent Advisor on Counter-Terrorism Legislation, argued that warrants should be approved by a judge.[97] The Royal United Services Institute (RUSI) argued for a mixed approach: where a warrant concerns the detection or prevention of serious and organised crime, RUSI suggested that this should be approved by a judicial commissioner. In cases involving national security, the warrant should be authorised by the Secretary of State but with a review by a Judicial Commissioner prior to the authorisation. This could be bypassed in urgent cases but the Commissioner would have to be notified and a review taken *ex post facto*.[98]

Clause 16 of the Investigatory Powers Bill would require a 'designated senior officer' to apply to the Judicial Commissioner where the warrant is requested in relation to 'communications data for the purpose of identifying or confirming a source of journalistic information'. The term 'source of journalistic information' is defined to include 'individual who provides material intending the recipient to use it for the purposes of journalism or knowing that it is likely to be so used'. A Judicial Commissioner would be able to make an order to quash the application if they considered it not to be made on reasonable grounds. Gavin Millar QC has argued that the clause 16 process does not provide a sufficient safeguard for journalistic sources.[99] This is because the Judicial Commissioner's role would be to review whether the authorisation is reasonable rather than to provide judicial authorisation. Millar also suggested that the police did not need to apply the Strasbourg principles on source protection.[100] There are two further issues with the proposals. First, the designated person does not need to seek authorisation 'where it is not necessary because of an imminent threat to life'. This is potentially capable of wide interpretation; arguably, an argument could be made to

---

[96]   Home Affairs Select Committee, *Counter-Terrorism*, HC-231 (2013–14) ch. 6.

[97]   David Anderson QC, *A Question of Trust: Report of the Investigatory Powers Review* (2015) ch. 14.

[98]   Royal United Services Institute, *A Democratic Licence to Operate: Report of the Independent Surveillance Review* (July 2015).

[99]   William Turville, 'Media law QC warns police could use Investigatory Powers Bill to "routinely" identify journalistic sources', *Press Gazette*, 5 November 2015, available at www.pressgazette.co.uk/media-law-qc-warns-police-could-use-investigatory-powers-bill-routinely-identify-secret-journalistic.

[100]   *Ibid.*

suggest that an unauthorised disclosure of national security information could meet this exception. Second, as will be identified in the *Miranda* case below, the court in that case was satisfied that Miranda was not a journalistic source and so did not require protection.[101] The drafting of the section is not sufficiently robust to protect individuals who would be in a similar position to Miranda.

The 'chilling effect' on journalistic expression and on prospective journalistic sources is set to continue because of the proposal in the Bill to require Internet Service Providers to retain Internet connection records for 12 months.[102] This would provide the authorities with a new capability to obtain information on the websites that citizens visit but not the pages viewed on the website. However, if an individual were to go on the Wikileaks website or to research investigative journalists, it may still be possible to identify journalistic sources. Whilst it may be argued that these processes could be circumvented by using a secure communications platform such as 'Tor' this would require a degree of technical expertise and access to download Tor or a secure web-browser, which would require an individual to have the technical expertise to use the services as well as a means of going online to download the services without accessing a website which will identify they have used the services. Moreover, the bulk interception and obtaining of bulk personal datasets is retained and reinforced under the proposed Bill.[103] Whilst these activities would require a warrant for access, it is suggested that the safeguards and oversight regime will not be sufficient to mitigate against the harm caused to the protection of journalistic sources and the chilling effect which may dissuade individuals from raising concerns.

Enhanced Oversight

If intelligence is to be continued to be shared between international partners there is a need to consider ways to improve the capabilities of accountability and oversight bodies in the jurisdictions involved. There is a need therefore to facilitate the sharing of best practice between these organisations and a need to share information regarding concerns.

---

[101] *Miranda* v. *Secretary of State for the Home Department* [2014] EWHC 255.

[102] Investigatory Powers Bill, Part 4. In contrast the Telecommunications (Interception and Access) Amendment (Data Retention) Act 2015 (Australia) requires providers to hold data for two years.

[103] Investigatory Powers Bill, Parts 6 and 7.

The Intelligence and Security Committee, for example, took the unprecedented step of engaging with the United States Senate Intelligence Committee as part of their enquiries following the Snowden revelations.[104] Whilst the purpose of this chapter is to focus on the protection of journalistic sources, oversight has an impact on the protection of sources, because without effective oversight there is an increased risk that intelligence agencies and policing bodies will utilise the technology available to obtain the identities of sources. The Geneva Centre for the Democratic Oversight of Armed Forces who recently produced guidance for oversight of international intelligence co-operation also identified that: 'in the absence of cooperation, the effectiveness of any investigation is dependent on whistle-blowers and the work of NGOs and investigative journalists'.[105] The Investigatory Powers Bill does not contain legislative provision to support collaboration of oversight bodies and, arguably, does not sufficiently deal with the issue of oversight of the intelligence agencies when engaging with agencies from other jurisdictions. Intelligence Services Act 1994, section 7, still provides wide scope for the intelligence services to conduct activities abroad, whilst the Justice and Security Act 2013 limits the oversight powers of the Intelligence and Security Committee to consider operational matters.[106]

Protection for Whistleblowers

Consideration must also be given to the employment protection employees may receive if they choose to raise concerns. Police officers, employees in SOCA and HMRC would receive protection for raising concerns under the Public Interest Disclosure Act (PIDA) 1998, provided that they do not break the law in doing so. The Information Commissioner is currently included as a 'prescribed person' designated to receive whistleblowing concerns. At present, the Interception of Communications Commissioner is not designated for this purpose, meaning that it would be more difficult for individuals to receive protection for raising concerns to the Commissioner because the evidential requirements are harder to

---

[104]   ISC Statement, above n. 70.
[105]   Geneva Centre for the Democratic Oversight of Armed Forces (DCAF), *Making Intelligence Accountable* (2015) 76, available at www.dcaf.ch/Publications/Making-International-Intelligence-Cooperation-Accountable.
[106]   For full discussion see Chapter 6.

satisfy. Employees of the security and intelligence services currently do not have access to PIDA 1998, thus reducing the incentive to raise concerns.

VI ENTRY SEARCH AND SEIZURE

In criminal proceedings, the Police and Criminal Evidence Act (PACE) 1984 contains safeguards for the protection of journalistic material. Section 9 identifies such material to be excluded from the ordinary process of police officers obtaining search warrants. PACE 1984, section 13, defines the meaning of journalistic material as 'only if it is in the possession of a person who acquired or created it for the purposes of journalism'. PACE 1984, section 13(3) also covers persons who receive material from someone who 'intends that the recipient shall use it for the purposes of journalism'. The police must apply for an order from the court for disclosure under the special procedures contained in section 1 of the Act. The officer must identify that there are reasonable grounds that an indictable offence has been committed, that the material is likely to be of substantial value to the investigation and relevant, and that it is in the public interest to order disclosure. Most importantly, the Act provides for the police to satisfy the court that other methods of obtaining the material have been tried without success or have not been tried because it appeared that they were bound to fail. If the application for the order is successful the journalist must produce the information to a police constable for him to take away or give him access to it.

Despite the aforementioned safeguard, the police have used the Terrorism Act 2000 to detain an individual and search and seize journalistic material. In *Miranda* v. *Secretary of State for the Home Department*,[107] the partner of Glenn Greenwald, the journalist who was primarily responsible for publication of stories on the Snowden leaks, was detained under Terrorism Act 2000, Schedule 7, paragraph 2(b). Section 53, which gives effect to Schedule 7 to the Act, gives a constable the power to stop and search a person in a port or border area to determine whether the individual is 'concerned in the commission, preparation or instigation of acts of terrorism'. David Miranda was detained by police at Heathrow Airport for the maximum period of nine hours and a number of encrypted storage devices containing documents provided by Snowden were taken

---

[107]   *Miranda* v. *Secretary of State for the Home Department* [2014] EWHC 255, note that at the time of writing David Miranda was awaiting determination of an appeal of the decision.

from him. After the police first questioned the request to stop Miranda on terrorist grounds, the security service argued that Miranda was carrying information 'the disclosure or threat of disclosure was designed to influence a government and is made for the purposes of promoting a political or ideological cause'.[108] Whilst use of Schedule 7, paragraph 2(b) is subject to the ordinary obligations that police have under Human Rights Act 1998, section 6, its use is more advantageous for orders for disclosure under Terrorism Act 2000, Schedule 5, which requires a court order subject to safeguards protecting journalistic material.

Miranda later applied for a judicial review to challenge the legality of the police conduct. Miranda's application failed. Lord Justice Laws did not think it necessary to place any reliance on Strasbourg jurisprudence and suggested that the domestic common law was a 'sufficient area for the debate'.[109] This was despite the domestic common law failing to afford adequate weight to the public interest value of the communication and the protection of sources. Laws LJ first placed emphasis on *Attorney General* v. *Guardian* and *Verrall*, both cases pre-dating the coming into force of the Human Rights Act 1998.[110] Later in the judgment, Laws LJ placed very little emphasis on the Strasbourg jurisprudence on source protection, primarily because he did not see it as an issue in the case, proclaiming 'the source is no secret: Mr Snowden stole the material, and the claimant (however indirectly) got it from Mr Snowden'.[111] In doing so, he failed to consider the public interest value of the documents held by Miranda: 'the claimant was not a journalist; the stolen GCHQ intelligence material he was carrying was not "journalistic material", or if it was, only in the weakest sense'.[112] Laws LJ failed to recognise that the documents in question concerned information detailing extensive and intrusive surveillance methods being used by the security and intelligence services. Snowden had alleged that GCHQ's involvement did not have legal authorisation. The information concerned had a wide-scale impact following publication by Mr Greenwald. It is therefore difficult to identify why Laws LJ refused to consider the value of the information at issue in the case. In order to be fully compliant with the court's obligations under Human Rights Act 1998, sections 2 and 6, Laws LJ should have given full consideration to the *Sanoma* and *Telegraaf*

---

[108]   *Ibid.* [12].
[109]   *Ibid.* [41].
[110]   *Ibid.* See also *Attorney General* v. *Guardian Newspapers (No. 2)* [1990] 1 AC 109; *Verrall* v. *Great Yarmouth Borough Council* [1981] 1 QB 202.
[111]   *Miranda* v. *Secretary of State*, above n. 107, [48].
[112]   *Ibid.* [72].

judgments. Laws LJ was convinced by the argument made by the respondents that the ECtHR had not imposed an absolute role of independent judicial authorisation, and in any case it was within the state's margin of appreciation to disregard this, particularly as the powers exercised under the Terrorism Act 2000 were subject to test of proportionality.

The *Miranda* episode sets a worrying precedent that laws which have been drafted to combat terrorism can be used to detain and search individuals who are involved in journalistic activity. It also highlights the inherent weakness in the United Kingdom's journalistic source protection law. Since *Miranda*, in 2015 police successfully applied for a court order to obtain a laptop belonging to Secunder Kermani, a journalist for the BBC current affairs programme *Newsnight*, using the Terrorism Act 2000.[113] Kermani had been reporting on stories involving young Jihadis in the United Kingdom and as a result had engaged in dialogue with an individual who claimed to be part of the terrorist group known as 'ISIL'. The police officers reportedly wanted to identify the man.

Seizure Beyond Scope of the Order

A breach of Article 10 ECHR may occur when an order to produce the material results in the seizure of other material not intended in the original order. Criminal Justice and Police Act 2001, section 50, provides that a police officer who is lawfully on the premises and has the authorisation to seize items, may also seize items he is not entitled to if the material sought is contained within them and it is not reasonably practicable to separate it. An example of such an item could be a CD-ROM, a computer or a USB memory stick. In applying this reasoning to the circumstances surrounding the Wikileaks disclosures, journalists and intermediaries were provided with USB memory sticks containing thousands of documents. Section 50 is therefore likely to be used where such searches take place. The difficulty with modern technological devices is that the information required for the investigation may be contained in the same device where other information is stored. Thus, an investigation of the unauthorised disclosure of one document by one individual may expose the identities of other sources, with the likely consequence that prospective sources will be deterred from providing information. Following the *Sanoma* judgment, it is submitted that section

---

[113] Nicola Harley, 'Police use terror powers to seize laptop of *Newsnight* reporter', *Telegraph*, 28 October 2015).

50 should be amended to incorporate safeguards for the protection of journalistic sources, as this provision appears to be in breach of Article 10.

With regard to the unauthorised disclosure of information pertaining to national security, various longstanding provisions contained in the Official Secrets Acts provide scope for search and seizure without the need to seek judicial authority. Official Secrets Act 1920, section 6, as amended by Official Secrets Act 1939, sections 1 and 2, gives a wide provision for a chief of police, where he is satisfied that there are reasonable grounds for suspecting that an offence under Official Secrets Act 1911, section 1, has been committed (which essentially concerns espionage and the penalties for spying) and that a person can furnish information, then the officer can apply to the Home Secretary for permission to require a person to divulge the information; failure to do so will result in the commission of an offence. If there are reasonable grounds to believe that there is a 'great emergency' and that in the 'interest of the state' immediate action is necessary, he may demand the information without needing the consent of the Home Secretary.[114] While the Official Secrets Act 1989 made the provision of search warrants obtained under section 9(1) of the 1911 Act subject to the 'special procedures' in PACE 1984, the Act also made it a criminal offence to impart information resulting from an unauthorised disclosure[115] and to fail to comply with an order to return the information.[116]

VII OFFENCES

A journalist based in the domestic jurisdiction may incur personal liability under the Official Secrets Acts. The offence of receipt of information that formerly applied under section 2 of the 1911 Act has now been repealed, but journalists may still be liable under section 5 of the 1989 Act which allows for prosecution of persons who publish information which is in contravention of other sections contained in the Act 'without lawful authority'. A notable example of this is the threat

---

[114] Official Secrets Act 1920, s.6(2).
[115] Official Secrets Act 1911, s.5.
[116] Note also, provisions contained in Terrorism Act 2000, Sch. 5, which allow for a police officer to apply for search warrants for the obtaining of material likely to be of substantial value for the purposes of a terrorist investigation, including 'excluded' or 'special procedure' material as defined in PACE 1984.

made by Attorney-General Lord Goldsmith to prosecute newspapers under section 5 if they published the contents of a document which allegedly related to a dispute between Tony Blair and George Bush over the conduct of military operations in Iraq.[117] The authorities are likely to encounter difficulties in carrying out this threat where the journalistic organisation is based outside of the jurisdiction.[118]

The threat to prosecute journalists can be used as to obtain information on a journalistic source and can serve to discourage further co-operation between sources and journalists. The ECtHR considered the prosecution of journalists in *Stoll* v. *Switzerland*.[119] The applicant had been prosecuted for publishing a document containing discussion of deliberations between the World Jewish Congress and Swiss banks concerning compensation due to Holocaust victims for unclaimed assets deposited in Swiss bank accounts. The Court reiterated that notwithstanding the vital role the press plays in a democratic society, journalists cannot be released from their duty to obey the ordinary criminal law on the basis that Article 10 ECHR affords them protection.[120] The Court held that the safeguard afforded by Article 10 to journalists is subject to the proviso that in publishing the information they do so in good faith, that the information is accurate, and that they have provided 'reliable and precise' information 'in accordance with the ethics of journalism'.[121]

The ECtHR identified that the conviction of a journalist for disclosing information considered to be confidential or secret may discourage those working in the media from informing the public on matters of public interest, thus impacting on the role of the press as public watchdog.[122] In order to determine whether the interference with Article 10 ECHR rights was proportionate, the Court held that it must have regard to the following factors: the nature of the interests at stake; the conduct of the applicant; and whether or not the fine imposed was proportionate.[123] With regard to the interests at stake, the ECTHR attached importance to the government's argument that the publishing of a report classified as 'confidential' or 'secret' would both have an 'adverse and paralysing' effect on a country's foreign policy and make the official's position

---

[117] See Richard Norton-Taylor, 'Legal gag on Bush–Blair war row', *Guardian*, 23 November 2005.
[118] Considered in Chapter 2.
[119] *Stoll* v. *Switzerland*, above n. 29.
[120] *Ibid.* [102].
[121] *Ibid.* [103].
[122] *Ibid.* [110].
[123] *Ibid.* [112].

untenable – in this case the Court noted that the official was forced to resign.[124] It followed the reasoning in *Hadjianastassiou*, assessing that the disclosure of the report and the articles were at the time of publication capable of causing considerable damage.[125] The court hearing the criminal case must determine in advance whether the 'secret' classification appears justified in the light of the purpose and content of the documents disclosed.[126]

With regard to the conduct of the applicant, the ECtHR drew a distinction between the manner in which the applicant obtained the report and the content of the articles in question.[127] The Court held that the manner in which a person obtains information considered to be confidential or secret may be of relevance to balancing interests in the context of Article 10(2). The Court noted that the journalist could not claim in good faith to be unaware he was committing a criminal offence.[128] It found that the way in which the paper was edited, the sensationalist headlines and the inaccuracy of the articles were likely to mislead the reader.[129]

VIII   REFORMS TO ENHANCE THE PROTECTION OF JOURNALISTIC SOURCES

This chapter has identified that the United Kingdom's domestic source protection laws are not sufficiently robust to safeguard journalistic sources. This has arguably led to failings by the courts, police and the intelligence services to have sufficient regard to the strong protections that the ECtHR has afforded to sources. It is suggested that part of this failure is due to the Human Rights Act 1998. Whilst section 6 places obligations on the courts, police and intelligence services to have regard to Convention rights, the law does not expressly require the public authorities to follow Strasbourg jurisprudence. Where there are legal protections in place, these are focussed primarily on orders for source disclosure and warrant applications for searches where journalists may be affected. These protections do not reflect current investigatory practices under which police and the security and intelligence services have the

---

[124]   *Ibid.* [129].
[125]   *Hadjianastassiou* v. *Greece,* Application No. 12945/87 (ECtHR, 16 December 1992) [45].
[126]   *Ibid.* [138].
[127]   *Stoll* v. *Switzerland,* above n. 29, [140].
[128]   *Ibid.* [141].
[129]   *Ibid.* [149].

scope to use anti-terror laws and surveillance powers to obtain information regarding journalistic sources rather than making applications for authorisation before a court. The ECtHR has made clear in cases such as *Sanoma* that independent authorisation is required. Given that the United Kingdom is currently debating whether to replace the Human Rights Act 1998 with a British 'Bill of Rights', it is suggested that it is now timely to consider the introduction of a freedom of the press law or to consider enshrining these rights as part of the suggested Bill.[130]

The Freedom of the Press Act 1949 (Sweden) provides protection for both journalistic sources and journalists. Sweden was reportedly once chosen by Wikileaks to base its operations there due to the strength of the law.[131] Chapter 3, article 1 of the Act in particular protects the anonymity of journalistic sources. The law also attempts to counterbalance this right against national security. For example, Chapter 3, article 3(3) contains exceptions regarding 'high treason', the 'wrongful release of an official document', and Chapter 7, article 4(4) concerns an exception for the unauthorised trafficking of secret information. In Contrast, Norway does not have a Freedom of the Press Act but does have strong protections contained in its civil and criminal law provisions. Civil Procedure Act (Norway), section 22–11, allows journalists and media staff to refuse orders to disclose sources. Criminal Procedure Act (Norway), section 125, offers protection in criminal proceedings. In addition, section 197 of the Act provides safeguards for the search of journalists' premises. Despite the availability of this protection, in 2014 the Norwegian Data Protection Authority identified that the Armed Forces Intelligence Service had conducted illegal surveillance of nine journalists in order to determine the identity of a source.[132] In other jurisdictions, journalists have attempted to assert their right to protect sources under a general constitutional right to freedom of speech. The following examples

---

[130] At the time of writing a Bill had been suggested but not published. Leaks surrounding the proposals appeared to suggest that the United Kingdom would remain signatories to the ECHR but would have certain powers to disregard Strasbourg jurisprudence: 'British Bill of Rights to be fast-tracked into law next summer', *Independent*, 17 October 2015, available at www.independent.co.uk/news/uk/politics/british-bill-of-rights-to-be-fast-tracked-into-law-by-next-summer-a6698261.html.

[131] 'Sweden plays key role in Wikileaks operations', *Swedishwire*, 29 July 2010, available at www.swedishwire.com/politics/5586-sweden-plays-key-role-in-wikileaks-operations.

[132] 'OSCE representative lauds ruling that finds illegal monitoring of journalists in Norway', OSCE, 30 September 2014, available at www.osce.org/fom/124587.

identify that whilst courts are prepared to recognise this right, they do not consider it to be absolute. In Canada, the Supreme Court held that the constitutional right to protect journalistic sources could be overruled in the public interest to support a criminal investigation.[133] In Australia, the Supreme Court of New South Wales held that the constitutional right to protect sources was not absolute where it was alleged that the sources had provided information leading to defamatory articles.[134] All of the aforementioned examples identify that the protection of journalistic sources may not be absolute. Circumstances may arise where it is necessary for the identity of a source to be revealed on the grounds of national security, to prevent crime or to allow for action to be taken in defamation whereby the conduct of the source is at issue. These restrictions on expression may be justified under Article 10(2) ECHR, however the identity of the source may only be revealed where it can be justified in the narrowest of circumstances. In order to ensure compliance with Article 10 and the extensive Strasbourg jurisprudence in this area, it is suggested that any law which places limits on the protection of sources must allow for rigorous balancing of the competing interests subject to judicial determination.

IX CONCLUSION

The aforementioned analysis has identified that domestic courts have failed to apply the high standard of protection the ECtHR affords to journalistic sources. The use of an online outlet such as Wikileaks can provide an alternative to the traditional journalist and source relationship. However, the Snowden revelations identify that security and intelligence agencies have the extensive capability to intercept and store data. Those without sufficient technical knowledge to bypass the surveillance tech-niques may be placed at risk of being identified as a source if they attempt to leak information online. Those who wish to make disclosures to journalists also risk being discovered because of the surveillance activities. This places a disproportionate chilling effect on the right to freedom of expression and may discourage individuals from making disclosures to journalists where they would otherwise be protected by law

---

[133]   *R* v. *National Post* [2010] 1 SCR 477.
[134]   *Liu* v. *The Age Company Ltd* [2012] NSWSC 12. See also the decision concerning Judith Miller in the United States. Miller refused to testify before a grand jury to identify the source of a story naming Valerie Plame Wilson as an undercover CIA operative, *Miller* v. *United States* 125 S Ct 2977 (2005).

for doing so. Without effective source protection laws, those faced with ineffective authorised whistleblowing mechanisms may simply decide not to raise important public interest concerns at all.

4. Legal protections for raising concerns

Whistleblowers in the United Kingdom enjoy the protection of the Public Interest Disclosure Act (PIDA) 1998. Despite being heralded as 'model in this field of legislation as far as Europe is concerned',[1] the Act has since faced mounting criticism from groups such as Whistleblowers UK, a non-profit organisation offering support to whistleblowers.[2] Part of the difficulty is that the Act only provides protection 'post-detriment' or 'post-dismissal', thus requiring workers to bring a claim after mistreatment.[3] PIDA 1998 does not require workers to exhaust internal procedures before choosing to go outside of their organisation. Organisations are under no obligation to follow a baseline standard of procedures in handling whistleblowing concerns, in fact they need not provide any whistleblowing procedures at all.[4] The absence of procedural hurdles for workers has allowed UK whistleblowers greater flexibility in how they may raise concerns and to whom. However, this flexibility, combined with the absence of agreed base-line standards, has inevitably led to a myriad of different approaches between organisations.[5] If things go

---

[1] See further, Council of Europe, *The Protection of Whistle-blowers*, Doc. 12006 (14 September 2009).

[2] See Whistleblowers UK organisation website, www.wbuk.org/index.html. Also see critique from academics such as David Lewis, 'Ten Years of Public Interest Disclosure Act 1998 Claims: What Can We Learn from the Statistics and Recent Research?' (2010) 38(3) *Industrial Law Journal* 325; Jeanette Ashton, '15 Years of Whistleblowing Protection Under the Public Interest Disclosure Act: Are We Still Shooting the Messenger' (2015) 44(1) *Industrial Law Journal* 29; Kelly Bouloy, 'The Public Interest Disclosure Act 1998: Nothing More Than a 'Cardboard Shield' (2012) 1 *Manchester Review of Law, Crime and Ethics* 1.

[3] Subject to interim relief.

[4] In contrast, Protected Disclosures Act (PDA) 2014 (Ireland), s.21, requires all public bodies to establish procedures.

[5] A situation not helped (in the context of Civil Service departments) by a lack of central co-ordination from government as concluded by the Public Accounts Committee. See further Public Accounts Committee, *Whistleblowing, Ninth Report*, HC-593 (2014) 7.

wrong, claimants, at times unaided, must make a claim before an employment tribunal. PIDA 1998 can require claimants to mount often complex legal arguments without having the requisite expertise to do so.[6] The whistleblowing charity, Public Concern at Work, established a Commission which suggested a number of reforms to PIDA 1998.[7] The National Audit Office have published reports on the handling of concerns by regulators and the whistleblowing policies and arrangements available to civil servants.[8] The Public Accounts Committee has also conducted its own inquiry, expressing concern at the way that whistleblowers were being treated and inconsistency in the handling of concerns across government.[9] The Department of Business, Innovation and Skills commenced a public consultation in 2014, the outcome of which has led to a number reforms, of which many fall short of the numerous recommendations proposed.[10]

This chapter is split into two sections. The first section will identify the standards set by the European Court of Human Rights (ECtHR) which relate to freedom of expression. It will discuss the notion of contractual waiver of expression rights before proceeding to provide analysis of how the Strasbourg Court has handled cases involving whistleblowing. The second section will discuss PIDA 1998; it will consider the impact of the new overarching public interest requirement and will provide reference to public interest jurisprudence of particular value to Crown servants. The

---

[6] In a response to a freedom of information request made by the author (received 8 May 2015), HM Courts and Tribunals Service provided the following information on the number of claimants recorded as unaided (without representation): 2010–11: 505; 2011–12: 611; 2012–13: 761; 2013–14: 927; March to December 2014: 355. Note that claimants representing themselves are not required to inform the tribunal of this fact. The numbers recorded are where no representative was made known to the tribunal. It is not clear whether this number accounts for representatives such as Mckenzie Friends and union representatives.

[7] Public Concern at Work, *The Whistleblowing Commission, Report on the Effectiveness of Existing Arrangements for Workplace Whistleblowing in the UK* (2013), available at www.pcaw.org.uk/whistleblowing-commission-public-consultation.

[8] National Audit Office, *Government Whistleblowing Policies* (2014), available at www.nao.org.uk/report/government-whistleblowing-policies/.

[9] See further, Public Accounts Committee Report, above n. 5.

[10] See further Department for Business, Innovation and Skills (DBIS), *The Whistleblowing Framework: Call for Evidence,* Ref: BIS/13/953 (2014) and DBIS, *The Whistleblowing Framework: Call for Evidence—Government Response,* Ref: BIS/14/914 (2014). The reforms will be considered in further detail later in this chapter.

chapter will undertake an analysis of how PIDA 1998 and Article 10 of the European Convention on Human Rights (ECHR) fit together in the light of these changes, questioning compatibility with the Convention. The chapter will conclude with an assessment of the current standard of whistleblowing protection law in the United Kingdom and will provide suggestions for reform, with reference to comparative examples from other jurisdictions.

I ECTHR STANDARDS

Crown servants work for public authorities who are subject to Human Rights Act 1998, section 6. Section 6(1) provides that it is unlawful for a public authority to act in a way which is incompatible with a Convention right. Crown servants, by the nature of their employment with a public authority should, therefore, benefit from a degree of protection when exercising their Article 10 ECHR right to freedom of expression. Section 6 further extends to courts and tribunals who must exercise particular care when Convention rights are engaged.[11] The right to freedom of expression is not absolute. Civil servants are required to agree to restrict their rights upon entering employment. Moreover, not all forms of expression attract equal value; the level of protection is diminished when outweighed by a countervailing argument to restrict expression because it is necessary in a democratic society to do so. It is questionable whether public authorities and, in turn, courts and tribunals are getting the balance right.[12] This section will provide analysis of the standards set by the ECtHR and the limitations applied to public servants.

---

[11]   Human Rights Act 1998, s.6(3)(a).

[12]   An enquiry made more difficult by the accessibility of employment tribunal judgments. Whilst decisions of the Employment Appeals Tribunal and higher courts are published promptly and made freely available online, employment tribunal judgments must be obtained from the HM Courts and Tribunals service for a fee, making tracking and analysis of tribunal decisions difficult. Moreover, there is a closed register of employment tribunal claims. Whilst this register is aimed at facilitating settlement between the parties, it arguably serves as a barrier to the identification of concerns raised, a point argued by the charity Public Concern at Work. Whilst the charity was successful in bringing a judicial review claim, the register currently remains inaccessible. See further *R* v. *Secretary for Central Office of Employment Tribunals, ex parte Public Concern at Work* [2000] IRLR 658 HC, and Public Concern at Work website, www.pcaw. org.uk/open-justice.

Article 10 ECHR provides:

1. Everyone has the right to freedom of expression. This right shall include freedom to hold opinions and to receive and impart information and ideas without interference by public authority and regardless of frontiers. This article shall not prevent States from requiring the licensing of broadcasting, television or cinema enterprises.
2. The exercise of these freedoms, since it carries with it duties and responsibilities, may be subject to such formalities, conditions, restrictions or penalties as are prescribed by law and are necessary in a democratic society, in the interests of national security, territorial integrity or public safety, for the prevention of disorder or crime, for the protection of health or morals, for the protection of the reputation or rights of others, for preventing the disclosure of information received in confidence, or for maintaining the authority and impartiality of the judiciary.

The protection of the right to freedom of expression constitutes one of the 'essential foundations of a democratic society'.[13] Subject to the aforementioned limitations identified in Article 10(2), it is applicable 'not only to information or ideas that are favourably received or regarded as inoffensive or as a matter of indifference, but also to those that offend, shock or disturb the State or any sector of the population'.[14] The following sections will identify the well-established Strasbourg jurisprudence relating to the types of expression acknowledged as being subject to the protection of Article 10. Whilst it is acknowledged that some of the cases discussed concentrate on the role of the press, the standards are often cited and are generally applicable to all applicants bringing cases before the Court. The focus will then narrow to consider how the Court has handled cases concerning whistleblowers.

General Political Expression

Political expression is afforded a high degree of protection by the ECtHR, particularly where the information concerned is considered to be of a high value to the public interest.[15] In *Sunday Times* v. *United*

---

[13] *Handyside* v. *United Kingdom* [1976] ECHR 5, para. 49.
[14] *Ibid.*
[15] For general consideration of freedom of expression and Convention rights in the workplace (some with reference to whistleblowing) see further Dirk Voorhof and Patrick Humblet, 'The Right to Freedom of Expression in the Workplace under Article 10 ECHR' in Filip Dorssemont, Klaus Lörcher and Isabelle Schömann (eds), *The European Convention on Human Rights and the*

Kingdom, the case concerned a contempt of court action brought in respect of an article it published which detailed the risks posed by the use of the drug Thalidomide by pregnant mothers and criticisms against a company involved in ongoing litigation at the time.[16] In focussing on the role of the press, the Court held that Article 10 ECHR guarantees not only their right to inform the public but also the right of the public to be informed.[17] In *Jersild v. Denmark*, the Court held that whilst the press must not overstep the boundaries set (identified in Article 10(2) above) it is incumbent on journalists to 'impart information in the public interest'.[18] If the press were restricted from doing so they would be unable to exercise their vital role as 'public watchdog'.[19]

Allegations Against Collective Authority

The following cases provide examples of where the Court has protected the applicant's right to freedom of expression when criticising authority, whether it be general criticism of authority as a whole or individual political figures. Such protection draws strong parallels with the theoretical justifications from truth and from democracy. With regard to criticism of authority as a whole, in *Thorgeirson v. Iceland*, a journalist had been prosecuted for writing newspaper articles detailing allegations of police brutality.[20] The Court noted that the journalist had not made allegations against particular officers but had written with the 'sole

---

Employment Relation (Hart, 2013) ch. 10; Lucy Vickers, 'The Protection of Freedom of Political Opinion in Employment' (2002) 4 *EHRLR* 468; Valya Filipova, 'Standards of Protection of Freedom of Expression and the Margin of Appreciation in the Jurisprudence of the European Court of Human Rights' (2012) 17(2) *Coventry Law Journal* 64.

[16] (1979–80) 2 EHRR 245.

[17] *Ibid.* para. 66.

[18] *Jersild v. Denmark*, Application No. 15890/89 (ECtHR, 23 September 1994) [30]. In *Stoll v. Switzerland*, Application No. 696981/01 (ECtHR, 10 December 2004), the applicant was held to have overstepped the bounds. The applicant had disclosed information regarding negotiations between the Swiss government and the World Jewish Congress on the repayment of assets of Holocaust victims held in Swiss banks. Whilst the information was considered to be in the public interest, the manner in which the applicant had reported on the information and the confidential nature of the documents outweighed the need to protect the applicant.

[19] *Ibid.*

[20] *Thorgeirson v. Iceland*, Application No. 13778/88 (ECtHR, 25 June 1992).

purpose' that the Minister of Justice would establish an independent body to investigate.[21]

The Court held that the articles were about a matter of 'serious concern'.[22] The journalist's conviction and sentence were therefore deemed capable of discouraging open discussion of those matters.[23] The ECtHR later identified in *Castells* v. *Spain* that in a democratic society, 'the actions or omissions of the government must be subject to close scrutiny not only of the legislative authorities but also of the press and public opinion'.[24]

Individual Political Figures

With regard to criticism of individual political figures, in *Lingens* v. *Austria* the Court identified that freedom of expression constitutes one of the essential foundations of a democratic society and one of the basic conditions for its process and for each individual's self-fulfilment.[25] Central to this, 'freedom of political debate' is at the 'very core of the concept of a democratic society which prevails throughout the convention'.[26] The Court recognised that freedom of the press 'affords the public one of the best means of discovering and forming an opinion of the ideas and attitudes of political leaders'.[27] It noted that a politician who was himself 'accustomed to attacking his opponents had to expect fiercer criticism than other people'.[28] Unlike private individuals, politicians knowingly lay themselves 'open to close scrutiny' of their 'every word and deeds' both by 'journalists and the public at large'. As a consequence they must display a greater degree of tolerance to criticism.[29]

Most importantly, in *Lingens* the Court identified that the matter at issue was not 'his right to disseminate information but his freedom of opinion and his right to impart ideas' subject to the restrictions in Article 10(2) ECHR.[30] The protection of political speech must therefore extend

---

[21] *Ibid.* [66].
[22] *Ibid.* [67].
[23] *Ibid.* [68].
[24] *Castells* v. *Spain*, Application No. 11798/85 (ECtHR, 23 April 1992) [36].
[25] *Lingens* v. *Austria*, Application No. 9815/82 (ECtHR, 8 July 1986) [41]. See further below.
[26] *Ibid.* [42].
[27] *Ibid.* [42].
[28] *Ibid.* [37].
[29] *Ibid.* [42].
[30] *Ibid.* [45].

beyond the communication of pure factual information to include protection of expressions of opinion. *Lingens* therefore supports, in principle, instances of 'protest whistleblowing' whereby individuals may express concerns with regard to matters of public policy because in their opinion a proposed course of action is wrong.

Challenges Against the Personal Conduct of Public Officials

Whilst the aforementioned cases identify that Article 10 may confer strong protection for free expression rights, it should be noted that where such expression extends to criticism of an individual politician's conduct of a personal relationship, the individual may not be protected. For example, in *Tammer* v. *Estonia* criminal penalties imposed in respect of reporting of a sexual relationship between the Prime Minister and a political aid did not constitute a violation of Article 10 ECHR.[31]

The right to freedom of expression may justifiably provide a strong trump right, however, all rights under the qualification are qualified, not absolute. The right may be subject to other conflicting rights such as the right to privacy, contained in Article 8 ECHR. The Council of Europe has identified that the right to privacy afforded by Article 8 should 'not only protect an individual against interference by public authorities but also against interference by private persons or institutions, including the media'.[32]

Contractual Limitation of the Right to Freedom of Expression

The Commission has stated that an individual may contract to limit their expression rights and, as a consequence, enforcement of the agreed restriction will not amount to an interference with Article 10(1) ECHR rights.[33] Allen, Crasnow and Beale argue that an employer and employee could agree to limitation of freedom of expression, provided there was no improper coercion of either party, the employer must show that such a waiver is made in full awareness of the right and the restriction does not interfere with other legal obiligations.[34] It is submitted that this reasoning

---

[31] *Tammer* v. *Estonia*, Application No. 41205/98 (ECtHR, 6 February 2001).
[32] Council of Europe Resolution 1165 of 1998.
[33] *Vereniging Rechtswinkels Utrecht* v. *The Netherlands*, Application No.11308/84 (ECtHR, 13 March 1986).
[34] Robin Allen, Rachel Crasnow and Anna Beale, *Employment Law and Human Rights* (2nd edn, OUP, 2007) 265.

is consistent with the approach taken by the Strasbourg Court in a number of decided cases.

The ECtHR has indicated that appointment as a civil servant does not deprive the individual of the protection of Article 10 ECHR[35] however; whilst the Court and the Commission have observed that a person's employment will not affect their freedom of expression, the existence of contractual obligations has indicated that limitations are evident in certain circumstances. In *Rommelfanger* v. *Germany*,[36] a doctor working at a Catholic hospital had his contract of employment terminated after signing a letter criticising the Church's stance on abortion. The Commission accepted that by entering into contractual obligations with his employer, the applicant had accepted a 'duty of loyalty' towards the Catholic Church which 'limited his freedom of expression to a certain extent'.[37]

In *Vogt* v. *Germany*,[38] the case involved the dismissal of a teacher who was a member of the German Communist Party. The Court accepted that the dismissal was sufficient to constitute an interference with the right to freedom of expression. The cases of *Rommelfanger* and *Vogt* can be distinguished. In *Rommelfanger*, the employee of the hospital effectively gave a public display of disloyalty, whereas in *Vogt,* membership of the German Communist Party constituted a personal expression of a differing viewpoint.

In *Ahmed* v. *United Kingdom*, the Court held that regulations designed to prevent local government officers from engaging in political expression would be a proportionate restriction of Article 10 rights, particularly

---

[35] *Glasenapp* v. *Germany*, Application No. 9228/80 (ECtHR, 26 August 1986) [49]–[50]. The case involved a school teacher appointed with the status of a probationary civil servant. In undertaking the role she agreed (as required by German law) to uphold the free democratic constitutional system. It was later discovered after inquiries were made by the authority that she was not capable of upholding the principles she had agreed to and her employment at the school was terminated. Whilst the court agreed that there was not a right of recruitment to the Civil Service, it did however believe that members of the Civil Service maintained their right to freedom of expression, basing their opinion on Arts 1 and 14 ECHR which stipulate that 'everyone within the jurisdiction of the Contracting States must enjoy the rights and freedoms in Section 1 "without prejudice on any ground"'.

[36] *Rommelfanger* v. *Germany*, Application No. 12242/86 (ECtHR, 6 September 1989).

[37] *Ibid.* [53].

[38] *Vogt* v. *Germany*, Application No. 17851/91 (ECtHR, 29 September 1995).

where the system of government in question is historically based upon the need for politically impartial advisers.[39] The Court identified that the restriction would be within the domestic authorities' margin of appreciation.[40] The local government system was reliant upon a relationship of trust between council members and their officers. Central to this reasoning, it suggested that members of the public:

> have a right to expect that those whom they voted into office will 'discharge their mandate in accordance with the commitments they made during an electoral campaign and that the pursuit of that mandate will not founder on the political opposition of their members' own advisers. It is also to be noted that members of the public are equally entitled to expect that in their own dealings with local government departments they will be advised by politically neutral officers who are detached from the political fray.[41]

The reasoning in *Ahmed* v. *United Kingdom* may be transposed to the position of civil servants working in Whitehall. Crown servants have obligations to be politically impartial; such obligations may inhibit the rights of those individuals to be active participants in democracy.[42] A Crown servant who makes an unauthorised disclosure of a government policy document, for example, may face accusations that his or her actions are politically motivated and disloyal.[43]

By becoming a Crown servant involved in national security matters, the individual will agree to a number of undertakings which limit the right to freedom of expression, at least in the context of disclosing information obtained during employment.[44] This was illustrated in a

---

[39] *Ahmed* v. *United Kingdom*, Application No. 8160/78 (ECtHR, 12 March 1981) 63.

[40] *Ibid.* [61].

[41] *Ibid.* [53].

[42] Under the Civil Service Code, see further www.gov.uk/government/publications/civil-service-code/the-civil-service-code.

[43] Considered further in Chapter 5.

[44] As a Crown servant the worker will be subject to the Official Secrets Acts 1911 and 1989. If the worker is an employee of the security and intelligence services they will be subject to a life-long ban on communication of their employment activities (under Official Secrets Act 1989, s.1). Crown servants are often required to 'sign' the Official Secrets Acts, a symbolic gesture which provides evidence of this contractual limitation. Civil servants are required to adhere to the Civil Service Code, a contractual agreement between the civil servant and the Crown where they are instructed not to disclose information without authority. Crown servants may also be required to sign confidentiality

slightly different scenario to that of the 'whistleblower'. In *Hajian-astassiou* v. *Greece*,[45] the ECtHR considered the case of a Greek Air Force officer who had originally written a missile assessment for the Airforce, classified 'secret'. Later, he wrote an assessment of another missile for a private defence contractor. He was convicted and sentenced to five months' imprisonment for unlawfully disclosing military secrets, despite arguing that the information was already published in widely available scientific publications and that the second assessment contained no information derived from the first. The ECtHR stated that the conviction was justified under Article 10(2) ECHR as 'necessary in a democratic society', regardless of the fact that the information had already been pubished in the public domain in scientific journals. The information concerned and nature of disclosure in question was irrelevant in this case. The Strasbourg Court has since taken a more progressive stance in cases concerning whistleblowers.[46] Despite the aforementioned contractual limits on expression, the obligations to protect the political impartiality of public services and loyalty to the employer will be discharged where the high public interest value in the content of the speech outweighs any countervailing duties. This analysis will now turn to consider specific Strasburg jurisprudence relating to whistleblowing.

Whistleblowing and Article 10 ECHR

The question of whether 'whistleblowing' speech will be protected by Article 10 ECHR has been considered in recent decisions at Strasbourg. *Guja* v. *Moldova*[47] concerned the unauthorised disclosure of two letters to the press by the head of the Moldovan Prosecutor General's Office. The letters contained information suggesting that the Moldovan Parliament had asserted pressure on the Prosecutor General to discontinue criminal proceedings against four police officers. The applicant was dismissed and sought reinstatement before applying to the ECtHR. In referring to the *Vogt* and *Ahmed* cases, the Court noted that civil servants have a duty of loyalty and discretion to their employer and because of the nature of their position will be exposed to information which the

---

agreements, many of which are incorporated into the Official Secrets Acts agreement.

45   [2002] EWCA Civ 214.

46   Including when the employee was involved in national security matters, see *Bucur and Toma* v. *Romania*, Application No. 40238/02 (ECtHR, 8 January 2013) discussed further below.

47   *Guja* v. *Moldova*, Application No. 14277/04 (ECtHR, 12 February 2008).

government would have legitimate reasons for keeping confidential or secret.[48] The Court recognised, however, that circumstances may arise where the civil servant is the only person or 'part of a small category' who becomes aware of wrongdoing and is therefore 'best placed to act in the public interest by alerting the employer or the public at large'.[49] In recognising that this was the first time the Court had determined a whistleblowing case, it developed a new framework for dealing with Article 10 claims involving whistleblowing. The next section will now consider the *Guja* framework.

Whether the applicant had alternative channels for making the disclosure
First, it was suggested that a court must ask whether the applicant had 'alternative channels for making the disclosure'. Disclosure should therefore be made, in the first instance, to the person's superior or other competent authority or body. Public disclosure will only be justified 'as a last resort' where it would be 'clearly impractical' to raise concerns using the aforementioned methods.[50] In conducting the proportionality test, the court must have regard to whether there were 'any other effective means of remedying the wrongdoing' which the individual intended to uncover.[51]

Based upon the aforementioned reasoning, a court in conducting the proportionality analysis must place significant emphasis, not only on the existence of internal procedures, but also the effectiveness of those procedures. In *R* v. *Shayler*, which pre-dates the decision in *Guja*, the House of Lords identified that Shayler had a number of authorised channels available to raise his concerns but did not seek to test the effectiveness of those channels.[52]

Public interest in the disclosed information
The court must have regard to the public interest involved in the disclosed information. The damage suffered by the public authority must be weighed against the interest of the public in having the information revealed. The Court identified that, in a democratic society, 'acts or omissions must be subject to close scrutiny' not only of the legislative

---

[48]   *Ibid.* [70] and [71].
[49]   *Ibid.* [72].
[50]   *Ibid.*
[51]   *Ibid.*
[52]   Detailed discussion of the *Shayler* decision is provided in Chapters 2 and 6.

and judicial authorities but also of the media and public.[53] The interest of the public in the information concerned may therefore be 'so strong as to override even a legally imposed duty of confidence'.[54] The ECtHR did not develop further what types of information may be considered in the public interest.

Authenticity of the disclosed information

The Court identified that the authenticity of the information disclosed will be relevant to the balancing exercise. The Court suggested that it was open to the competent state authorities to 'react appropriately and without excess to defamatory accusations devoid of foundation or formulated in bad faith'.[55] Ultimately, the individual who chooses to disclose the information must 'carefully verify' its contents 'to the extent permitted by the circumstances' to 'determine whether it is accurate and reliable'.[56]

Detriment to the employer

The Court identified that it must then weigh the damage suffered as a result of the disclosure in question and then must assess whether the 'damage outweighed the interest of the public of having the information revealed'.[57] The Court identified that the 'subject matter of the disclosure' and the 'nature of the administrative authority' concerned may be relevant in this process.[58]

Whether the applicant acted in good faith

The Court found that it was important to establish that in making the disclosure 'the individual acted in good faith and in the belief that the information was true and in the public interest to disclose it'.[59] If the disclosure was motivated by a personal grievance or an expectation of personal advantage this would not justify a strong level of protection. Moreover, the Court held that it must consider whether 'no other, more discreet means of remedying the wrongdoing' were available.[60]

---

53   *Guja* v. *Moldova*, above n. 47, [74].
54   *Ibid.*
55   *Ibid.* [75].
56   *Ibid.*
57   *Ibid.* [77].
58   *Ibid.*
59   *Ibid.*
60   *Ibid.*

Severity of the sanction
Finally, the Court must consider the severity of the sanction imposed on the applicant for making the disclosure.[61]

Application of the framework
The Court found in favour of the applicant. Guja's motivation for disclosing the letters had been to help combat corruption in Moldova. It noted that the President of Moldova had campaigned against political interference with the criminal justice system. The letters were genuine and their disclosure shed considerable light on an issue which the public had a legitimate interest in being informed.[62] The Court found that the decision to dismiss the applicant was a 'very harsh measure'.[63] The decision could also have a 'serious chilling effect' on other civil servants and employees raising concerns in the future.[64] Most importantly, the ECtHR found that the applicant did not have access to an effective alternative channel to make the disclosure.

Subsequent Influence

Bucur and Toma v. Romania
The first applicant in *Bucur and Toma* v. *Romania* worked in a military unit of the Romanian Intelligence Service (RIS) tasked with the interception of telephone communications.[65] Bucur became aware of a number of irregularities, concerning incomplete records written in pencil, leaving the justification and authorisation of the interception unclear. The most serious concern was that the telephones of a large number of politicians, journalists and businessmen were being tapped. Bucur raised his concerns with colleagues and the head of the organisation without success. He then approached a Member of Parliament on the parliamentary committee tasked with oversight of the organisation, who informed him that approaching the committee would be ineffective as the committee chairman had links to the Director of the RIS. The MP suggested that Bucur should hold a press conference. He made his concerns public, supported by audio cassettes containing recordings of several journalists and politicians. Bucur argued that the information did not consist of state

---

61   *Ibid.*
62   *Ibid.* [87].
63   *Ibid.* [95].
64   *Ibid.*
65   *Bucur and Toma* v. *Romania*, above n. 46.

secrets but rather proof that the RIS was engaged in political activities during an election year.

The ECtHR applied the *Guja* v. *Moldova* framework. First, with regard to whether the applicant had had alternative means to make the disclosure, the Court found that the SRI lacked internal procedures for the raising of concerns.[66] The Court was further satisfied that the parliamentary committee with oversight of the RIS were unlikely to be effective.[67] Due to the aforementioned circumstances, public disclosure could therefore be justified. Second, the information was found to be of value to the public interest. The allegations related to abuses committed by high-ranking officials and thus affected the democratic foundations of the state. Third, the information was considered to be authentic. The Court noted that the Romanian government had not supplied justifications as to why the information disclosed required a 'top secret' classification.[68] Fourth, in considering the damage caused to the RIS by the disclosure, the Court held that the disclosure of information concerning illegal activities within the RIS was so important that it outweighed the countervailing interest in maintaining public confidence in the organisation. Fifth and finally, in considering the applicant's good faith, the Court noted that he had approached the parliamentary commission responsible for oversight of the RIS rather than approach the press directly in the first instance.[69] The Court unanimously found in favour of the applicant.

Heinisch v. Germany

The *Guja* v. *Moldova* test was also adopted in *Heinisch* v. *Germany*.[70] In *Heinisch*, the applicant worked in a home for the elderly. She had regularly attempted to raise concerns to management that they were short staffed and that this had had an impact on the level of care provided. After falling ill, the applicant made a criminal complaint via her lawyer prompting the public prosecutor to investigate. Heinisch was later dismissed, the employer citing her repeated illness as a justification.

The ECtHR identified that in conducting the proportionality test it must weigh up the employee's right to freedom of expression 'by signalling illegal conduct' or wrongdoing on the part of the employer,

---

66   *Ibid.* [96].
67   *Ibid.* [98].
68   *Ibid.* [112].
69   *Ibid.* [118].
70   *Heinisch* v. *Germany*, Application No. 28274/08 (ECtHR, 21 July 2011).

against the latter's interests.[71] The nature and extent of the duty of loyalty owed by an employee to their employer in a particular case will impact upon the weighing of those conflicting interests.

The Court reiterated that as a consequence, concerns should first be raised to a person's superior or other competent authority or body. It is only where this is clearly impractical that the information could be disclosed directly to the public.[72] In the instant case, the Court held that the no other, more discreet means of remedying the situation were available to her. Upholding her complaint, the Court held that the public interest in receiving information regarding the poor provision of care for the elderly by a state-owned company was 'so important in a democratic society that it outweighs the interest in protecting the employer's business reputation and interests'.[73]

Rubins v. Latvia

In *Rubins* v. *Latvia*, the applicant was professor and head of department in a university department. He had sent various emails critical of plans to merge his department with another.[74] During the course of email exchanges he also alleged mismanagement of university finances. Matters came to a head when the applicant sent a letter proposing a settlement agreement which aimed to rectify his employment situation as well as suggesting that if the Rector chose to adopt a decision favourable to himself, rather than the applicant, Rubins would appeal, making every-thing public beforehand. The Rector did not agree to the demands and after a further unsuccessful attempt to get the merger annulled at a meeting the following day, the national news agency published the applicants views alleging shortcoming of the university management. Rubins was later dismissed and sought relief via the domestic labour court. The domestic courts found that Rubins had made inappropriate demands in the settlement letter and the suggestion that he would make allegations public amounted to a threat.

In considering the applicant's motives, the Court did not consider the case to be one of whistleblowing.[75] Focus was then placed on the applicant's right to freedom of expression in the context of a labour dispute. Whilst the Court conducted a proportionality analysis focussing upon some of the elements contained in the aforementioned framework,

---

71 *Ibid.* [65].
72 *Ibid.*
73 *Ibid.* [90].
74 *Rubins* v. *Latvia*, Application No. 79040/12 (ECtHR, 13 January 2015).
75 *Ibid.* [87].

the principles of *Guja* and *Heinisch* were not fully considered. The ECtHR did, however, acknowledge that the applicant worked for a public organisation and the issues raised by the applicant were of some public interest.[76] It was evident that the university did not seek to challenge the truthfulness of the allegations. Finding in favour of the applicant, the ECtHR held that the domestic courts had failed to assess both the public interest and the truthfulness of the information.

Analysis of the ECTHR's Approach to Whistleblowing

The proportionality framework developed for whistleblowing cases is consistent with the political expression cases outlined above. Communication of matters of 'serious concern' directly to the public will be justified, as previously identified in *Thorgierson* v. *Iceland* and *Sunday Times* v. *United Kingdom*. The position is less clear, however, when considering the communication of opinions or ideas, as per the justifications identified in *Lingens* v. *Austria*. The communication of a policy decision which does not identify wrongdoing or illegality but is nevertheless a decision to which an employee does not agree, would be justified under the principles underlined in *Lingens* v. *Austria* but may not be justified using the framework provided in *Guja* v. *Moldova*. This is because the communication of such information may not be of a sufficiently high value to outweigh the competing interests of the employer.

Vickers draws a distinction between 'Watchdog Whistleblowing' and 'Protest Whistleblowing'.[77] 'Watchdog whistleblowing' requires the individual to disclose misconduct or wrongdoing whereas 'protest whistleblowing' allows for the disclosure of information relating to lawful policies, on the basis that the individual raising the issues has the necessary experience to provide an opinion that the policy complained of is the wrong course of action.

The difficulty with 'protest whistleblowing' is that it may lead to accusations that the individual concerned is engaging in an overtly political act.[78] Employees of the UK Civil Service are required to be 'a-political' dependent upon their requisite level of employment. Those involved in 'industrial' and 'non-office' grades are identified as 'politically free' individuals, whereas those working in the politically contentious offices of Whitehall must follow the restrictions imposed by the

---

[76] *Ibid.* [85].
[77] Vickers, above n. 15, 8.
[78] Considered further in Chapter 5.

Civil Service Management Code. Most importantly, for the purposes of this analysis, paragraph 4.4 requires civil servants not to 'speak in public on matters of national political controversy; expressing views on such matters in letters to the press, or in books, articles or leaflets'.[79] Similarly, paragraph 14 of the Civil Service Code requires civil servants to be 'politically impartial'. The restrictions are arguably consistent with the principles established in the *Vogt* and *Rommelfanger* decisions, in that civil servants upon entering employment must agree to a restriction, at least in part, of their Article 10 ECHR rights.[80]

In discussing political speech, Vickers suggests that 'in order to serve its purpose of contributing to the democratic process' the communication 'requires publicity', therefore, the 'only suitable channel for communication of the ideas will be external to the employer'.[81] The expression of protest whistleblowing may not be justified under the framework provided in *Guja* v. *Moldova*, as the applicant is expected to use internal channels and only to communicate the information to the public directly 'as a last resort'. The Court will inevitably question whether the individual who disagreed with a policy position attempted to make his misgivings heard by colleagues or superiors before raising the concerns externally.

It is perhaps most telling that the court in *Rubins* v. *Latvia* chose not to adopt the principles established in *Guja* and *Heinisch* in their entirety. Rubins' concern was primarily about the decision to merge two academic faculties and the impact that it would have on academic administration and service delivery. This type of concern lends itself to an act of 'protest whistleblowing' or 'protest expression'. Indeed, the court identified that this was not considered to be a case of whistleblowing at all. It is not suggested, however, that Rubins is indicative of how future 'protest whistleblowing' cases may be handled by the ECtHR. The facts of the case weighed heavily towards a private employment dispute rather than an act of whistleblowing. The government had argued that Rubins had sought to blackmail the Rector in order to reaffirm his employment position. Focus was therefore centred on a letter used to obtain settlement. The Court noted that Rubins had identified assessment irregularities and other concerns; these matters could be characterised as 'watchdog whistleblowing' but in this case did not appear to be the primary focus of the letter or the applicant's motivation. Where principles

---

[79]   The Code is available at www.civilservice.gov.uk/about/resources/civil-service-management-code.

[80]   See also *Ahmed* v. *United Kingdom*, above n. 39, [63].

[81]   Vickers, above n. 15, [56].

from the *Guja* and *Heinisch* cases were referenced, focus was placed upon principles relating to the duty owed by an employee to an employer.

The ECtHR does not expressly differentiate between acts of 'watchdog' and 'protest' whistleblowing. The aforementioned cases identify that the expression of both fact and opinion can qualify for protection under Article 10. In the proportionality analysis, the countervailing interests of the state, namely, the harm caused by an act of expression to the organisation, are more likely to outweigh protest speech than watchdog speech. The Court's reasoning in a number of well-established cases identifies that public employees do not have the right to openly express views to the wider public *carte blanche* because they voluntarily accept a degree of limitation of their speech upon entering employment. The *Guja* framework may be seen as a continuation of this approach and it sets a relatively high threshold for applicants to overcome before protection may be obtained. By providing for assessment of whether the applicant had sought to address their concerns through internal channels and the viability of those channels, it seeks to determine whether the applicant has discharged his or her loyalties to the intramural community. Extramural community interests are considered in the determination of whether the speech has a public interest value. Extramural community interests are therefore pitted directly against the interests of the intramural community as a direct consequence of the proportionality analysis conducted by the Court.

Extramural community interests will most likely triumph where it is clear that the information concerned is of such value to the public that it outweighs any obligation or consideration owed to the intramural community. The circumstances in *Burcur* v. *Romania* provide an example where the countervailing interests of the intramural community were at the highest level. Disclosures of intelligence material and information concerning intelligence gathering activities were likely to cause 'considerable damage' to the Romanian Intelligence Service.[82] Despite this, the court held that the public interest in knowing that RIS was involved in illegal activities outweighed any interest in maintaining confidence in the institution.[83] The interests of the extramural community trumped the interests of the intramural community in a case where it was evident that the intramural community was unlikely to be able to rectify the alleged illegal activity. Contrast to acts of so-called 'protest whistleblowing' and it is clear that the information is unlikely to outweigh such strong

---

[82] See above n. 65, [144]
[83] *Bucur and Toma* v. *Romania*, above n. 46, [115].

countervailing interests unless the applicant can convince the court that the matter complained of has an overriding detrimental impact on the state and the organisation which the public has a right to know about.

It is axiomatic that in both protest and watchdog whistleblowing cases, the success of an applicant's claim will be dependent on two predominant factors: first, the strength of the public interest value of the information, and, second, the strength of the countervailing duty of loyalty owed to the organisation and the harm caused to that organisation by the disclosure. It is here that the different intramural communities identified in the first chapter are exposed. An applicant working in a Civil Service department will have a higher chance of success in arguing their concern is in the public interest in comparison to an employee of the security and intelligence services. As the countervailing interest in the intramural community increases, so must the public interest value in the information concerned. Applicants from the security and intelligence services as well as service personnel in the armed forces are likely to fail unless they can show that their expression has considerable public interest value and that the official procedures that were available were likely to be ineffective in rectifying the activity complained of. This chapter will now proceed to consider how the United Kingdom protects whistleblowers.

II PUBLIC INTEREST DISCLOSURE ACT 1998

The Public Interest Disclosure Act (PIDA) 1998 was initially introduced as a Private Member's Bill by Richard Shepherd MP.[84] Whereas some legal jurisdictions have 'sector specific' whistleblowing laws to protect public servants,[85] others have enacted laws which cover workers in all sectors.[86] PIDA 1998 is applicable to both the public and private sectors.

---

[84] For background, see generally, Richard Calland and Guy Dehn, *Whistleblowing Around the World: Law Culture and Practice* (ODAC, 2004); David Lewis, *Whistleblowing at Work* (Athalone Press, 2001) and Lucy Vickers, *Freedom of Speech and Employment* (OUP, 2002).

[85] The Civil Service Reform Act (amended by the Whistleblower Protection Act and later the Whistleblower Protection (Enhancement) Act) (USA); Public Servants Disclosure Protection Act 2005 (Canada); Public Interest Disclosure Act 2013 (Australia) provide such examples.

[86] Examples include the Protected Disclosures Act 2014 (Ireland); Protected Disclosures Act 2000 (South Africa); Whistleblower Protection Act 2004 (Japan); and Protected Disclosures Act 2000 (New Zealand). It is indicative that the legislators of many of the aforementioned cross-sector provisions have been influenced, at least in part, by the UK PIDA 1998.

In contrast to whistleblower protections which require the worker to follow prescribed routes to obtain protection,[87] PIDA 1998 provides three 'steps' which allow for the worker to decide to whom the disclosure may be made without precondition.[88] The first step allows for concerns to be raised internally to an employer, line manager or person designated by a policy to receive a concern.[89] The second step allows for disclosures to be made externally to a prescribed person.[90] The third allows for disclosures to be made to anyone else, thus agencies or bodies who are not prescribed, the police, the media and members of the public.[91] Unlike some comparative jurisdictions,[92] employees working in the security and intelligence services, those exempted by ministerial certificate and service personnel in the UK Armed Forces, do not have access to whistleblower protection.[93]

Unauthorised disclosures concerning wrongdoing can be protected, however, an individual who commits a criminal offence in making the disclosure will lose protection. Workers who are arrested for any offence relating to the disclosure must therefore wait for proceedings to conclude before bringing a PIDA 1998 claim. The Act does not protect individuals from criminal prosecution if they commit an offence (for example, under the Official Secrets Acts or misconduct in public office) nor does it protect from civil actions for breach of confidence and defamation. By providing scope to protect disclosures to the media and wider public without providing protection against criminal and civil action, the legislators deliberately left these matters to be rectified by existing common

---

[87] For example, Protected Disclosures Act 2000 (New Zealand) and Public Servants Disclosure Protection Act 2005 (Canada); see further Ashley Savage, 'Legislative Flexibility versus Procedural Rigidity: A Comparison of the UK and Canadian Approaches to Public Service Whistleblowing Protection', paper delivered to the 40th World Congress of the International Institute of Sociology, New Delhi, India, 2012.

[88] Also referred to as 'tiers' of protection, see further John Bowers, Martin Fodder, Jeremy Lewis and Jack Mitchell, *Whistleblowing: Law and Practice* (2nd edn, OUP, 2012) Part I.

[89] Employment Rights Act 1996, s.43C, as inserted by PIDA 1998.

[90] *Ibid.* s.43F, as inserted by PIDA 1998.

[91] *Ibid.* s.43G, as inserted by PIDA 1998.

[92] For example, the United States (Intelligence Community Whistleblower Protection Act 1998, Military Whistleblower Protection Enhancement Act 2013); Republic of Ireland (Protected Disclosures Act 2014).

[93] Employment Relations Act 1998, Sch.8(1) (replacing Employment Rights Act 1996, s.193). See above n. 82. Employment Rights Act 1996, s.192, as inserted by PIDA 1998, exempts Armed Forces personnel.

law principles. Whilst the stepped disclosure regime provides flexibility and potential employment protection, the consequences of the making of unauthorised disclosures remain uncodified and therefore perilously uncertain. The following sections will provide a critical overview of the regime.

Scope of Protection

In order to obtain protection under PIDA 1998, the person must first make a 'qualifying disclosure'. Section 43B defines 'a qualifying disclosure' as:

> any disclosure of information which, in the reasonable belief of the worker making the disclosure, is made in the public interest and tends to show one or more of the following:
>
> (a) that a criminal offence has been committed, is being committed or is likely to be committed,
> (b) that a person has failed, is failing or is likely to fail to comply with any legal obligation to which he is subject, that a miscarriage of justice has occurred, is occurring or is likely to occur,
> (d) that the health and safety of any individual has been, is being or is likely to be endangered,
> (e) that the environment has been, is being or is likely to be damaged, or
> (f) that information tending to show any matter falling within any one of the preceding paragraphs has been, is being or is likely to be deliberately concealed.

Despite many unauthorised disclosures in the United Kingdom being prompted by matters of public policy or government action rather than wrongdoing, these disclosures are unlikely to be protected, unless the disclosures indicate wrongdoing as outlined in the aforementioned categories.[94] There are a number of jurisdictions which provide a broader range of categories than PIDA 1998, however, these stop short of expressly allowing protest-type disclosures. For example, the sector-specific Public Servants Disclosure Protection Act 2005 (Canada) allows for disclosures relating to 'a misuse of public funds or a public asset' and 'a gross mismanagement in the public sector'.[95] Similarly, in addition to the 'unlawful or otherwise improper use of funds or resources of a public body', the cross-sector Protected Disclosures Act 2014 (Republic of Ireland) includes acts which are 'oppressive, discriminatory

---

[94]   For examples, see Nicholas Jones, *Trading Information* (Politicos, 2006).
[95]   Public Servants Disclosure Protection Act 2005 (Canada), s.8(a) and (b).

or grossly negligent or which constitute gross mismanagement'.[96] The Public Interest Disclosures Act 2013 available to Australian Commonwealth public servants protects disclosures relating to 'maladministration', 'misuse of public money' and 'abuse of public trust'.[97] However, the Act expressly disallows disclosures which only relate to disagreements with Commonwealth government policy.[98]

UK PIDA 1998, section 43B(b), potentially widens the scope of protection, provided that the claimant can show that there was a legal obligation in place. A breach of a legal obligation can, therefore, include a breach of contract. Civil servants are subject to the Civil Service Code which is a contractual obligation between the civil servant and the Civil Service.[99] Consequentially, the Code read in conjunction with section 43B(b) would allow a civil servant to raise concerns regarding matters under the Code.[100] The following section will consider the impact of the overarching public interest test and how it relates to the categories qualifying for protection.

Public Interest Test

A claimant faces two main hurdles. The first is to identify that they reasonably believed their disclosure was in the public interest; the second, that their disclosure meets one or more of the prescribed categories. The 'public interest' requirement was inserted by Enterprise and Regulatory Reform Act 2013, section 17. The measure was intended to reverse the effect of *Parkins* v. *Sodexho*,[101] where the claimant successfully argued that a private employment concern qualified for protection as a breach of a legal obligation under section 43B.

On paper, inclusion of the public interest requirement makes it more difficult for a claimant to obtain protection. Whereas previously the individual would have needed to meet one of the aforementioned categories, they must first argue that they thought their disclosure was in the public interest. In the absence of any further legislative direction in section 17, this raises the possibility that a disclosure may meet one of

---

[96]   Protected Disclosures Act 2014 (Ireland), s.5.
[97]   Public Interest Disclosure Act 2013 (Australia).
[98]   *Ibid.* s.13.
[99]   The raising of concerns under the Civil Service Code and issues of compliance are discussed further in Chapter 5.
[100]   HM Government, Civil Service Code (March 2015), available at www.gov.uk/government/publications/civil-service-code/the-civil-service-code.
[101]   [2001] UKEAT 1239_00_2206.

the categories in section 43B but the claimant may fail to convince the tribunal that they had a reasonable belief that the concern was in the public interest. The reform therefore creates a paradoxical situation. It is axiomatic that the aforementioned categories were drafted with the public interest in mind. Rather than deletion of the list of prescribed categories in favour of a general public interest test, or amending the category relating to legal obligations only, the drafters have effectively narrowed the scope of protection.

It may be observed that a civil servant would be unable to obtain PIDA 1998 protection on the grounds that a government policy would be detrimental to a large cross-section of the population. Such information could meet a public interest test but would be unlikely be the covered by one of the categories of information. At present, Human Rights Act 1998, section 6, makes it unlawful for a public authority to act in a way which is incompatible with a Convention right. Employment tribunals are obliged to consider the jurisprudence of the Strasbourg Court, which includes the decision and framework developed in *Guja* v. *Moldova*.[102] It should be noted that although domestic courts are afforded a margin of appreciation when considering the jurisprudence of the ECtHR, in *R (Ullah)* v. *Special Adjudicator*, it was held that although 'not strictly binding', in the 'absence of special circumstances' domestic courts should apply the case principles. Where Convention rights are engaged, a tribunal must conduct a proportionality analysis.[103] Whilst the ECtHR in *Guja* endorsed the protection of civil servants in the making of disclosures of illegal conduct or wrongdoing in certain circumstances, it did not limit itself to defined categories or characteristics of wrongdoing when it conducted the proportionality analysis.[104]

A public interest test interpreted narrowly and read in conjunction with the aforementioned categories contained within section 42B may render PIDA 1998 incompatible with Article 10 ECHR. Human Rights Act 1998, section 3, identifies that 'so far as it is possible to do so, primary legislation and subordinate legislation must be read and given effect in a way which is compatible with the Convention rights'. It is difficult to envisage how, without effectively redrafting section 43B to widen its scope, a tribunal might achieve this aim. Where a tribunal is unable to make the legislation compatible with the Convention rights the only option is to make a declaration of compatibility, however this does

---

[102]   Human Rights Act 1998, s.2.
[103]   See generally *Smith and Grady* v. *United Kingdom*, Applications Nos. 33985/96 and 33986/96 (ECtHR, 1999).
[104]   *Guja* v. *Moldova*, above n. 47, [73].

not impact on the instant case and moreover is only available in higher courts and not the employment tribunal.[105] As Lewis identifies, workers who are unable to obtain PIDA 1998 protection could still bring an 'ordinary' unfair dismissal claim.[106] However, the claimant would need to have obtained the qualifying period of a year's employment before they could being such a claim. Unlike PIDA 1998, damages for ordinary unfair dismissal are also capped.[107] As Ashton identifies (in providing a situation pre-PIDA 1998) claimants encountered considerable difficulties in using ordinary unfair dismissal to obtain protection for whistleblowing.

The case of *Chesterton Global Ltd* v. *Nurmohamed* suggests that the Employment Appeal Tribunal, at least at present, is prepared to apply the public interest test liberally.[108] The claimant had raised three concerns alleging that the appellant had deliberately misstated costs and liabilities and that this impacted on the earnings of 100 senior managers including Chesterton himself. Counsel for the appellant had sought to argue, first, that the 100 managers was an insufficient group of the public to amount to the matter being in the public interest, and, secondly, that the tribunal was obliged to consider objectively whether or not the disclosures were of real public interest.[109] Supperstone J held that section 43B(1) did not require the tribunal to determine the 'public interest' in the concern raised but instead it required an objective assessment that the individual had a reasonable belief that the disclosure was made in the public interest.[110] Applying *Babula* v. *Waltham Forest College*,[111] Supperstone J agreed with counsel for the respondent that the public interest test can be satisfied 'where the disclosure is wrong and/or there was no public interest in the disclosure' provided that the 'worker's belief that the disclosure was made in the public interest was objectively reasonable'.[112]

Supperstone J relied upon *Pepper* v. *Hart* to seek clarification from parliamentary debates as to the aim of the public interest requirement,

---

[105] PIDA 1998, s.4(5) lists the courts who may make a declaration of incompatibility.

[106] David Lewis, 'Is the Public Interest Test for Workplace Whistleblowing in Society's Interest?' (2015) 57(2) *IJLMA* 152.

[107] Jeanette Ashton, '15 Years of Whistleblowing Protection Under the Public Interest Disclosure Act 1998: Are We Still Shooting the Messenger?' (2015) 44(1) *ILJ* 29.

[108] [2015] Appeal No. UKEAT/0335/14/DM.

[109] *Ibid.* [20].

[110] *Ibid.* [28].

[111] *Babula* v. *Waltham Forest College* [2007] ICR 1026.

[112] *Chesterton Global Ltd* v. *Nurmohamed*, above n.108, [36].

identifying that the Minister had said insertion of the 'public interest' was to prevent claimants from relying on breaches of their own employment contract for private purposes and that 'the clause in no way takes away rights from those who seek to raise matters in the public interest'.[113] The rule established by Lord Browne-Wilkinson allows for consideration of a ministerial statement which introduced the legislation at issue where the wording of the law is 'ambiguous or obscure or the literal meaning of which leads to an absurdity'.[114] It is unclear from the judgment in *Chesterton* why Supperstone J believed that the modification in section 43B met this test. Moreover, if the motivation was to close the lacuna so evident in *Parkins* v. *Sodexho*, *Chesterton* still leaves considerable scope for an applicant to convince a tribunal that they believed their concern had a sufficient public interest value even if they are later proved to be wrong.

The use of an objective test to determine a claimant's reasonable belief that their concern was in the public interest represents a significant departure from established common law principles in breach of confidence cases and *Norwich Pharmacal* applications in particular, whereby a court would be required to assess the public interest value in the information at issue. Indeed, where the courts have erred in the past, it has been because the court, in conducting the public interest test, has sought to determine the motive of the communicator. The application of *Chesterton* would arguably make it easier for claimants to obtain protection; this in itself would not suggest, in principle, that Supperstone J's construction of section 43B is incompatible with Article 10 ECHR values. However, determination of the claimant's reasonable belief without any determination of the public interest value of the disclosed information is inconsistent with the approach taken by the ECtHR in whistleblowing cases, and indeed all cases where Article 10 is an issue. In conducting the proportionality analysis, the court will most likely test the applicant's motives for raising the concern but it will also test whether the information itself is authentic. If the information disclosed is false, the opportunity to successfully obtain Article 10 protection is likely to diminish significantly. Determination of the public interest value of the information concerned has always been central to cases concerning Article 10.

---

[113]   *Ibid.* [19].
[114]   *Pepper* v. *Hart* [1993] AC 593, 634, HL.

Stepped Disclosure Regime

Internal disclosures

At the lowest tier a worker is protected by section 43C for making an internal disclosure such as to a person in the line management chain, nominated officer or his employer. Section 43C(2) allows disclosures to be made to persons (other than the employer) who are designated under the employer's policy. This would cover disclosures to the Civil Service Commission, who whilst independent of the management structure are designated to receive concerns under the Civil Service Code. The worker is required to show that they had the reasonable belief that the failure relates solely or mainly to the conduct of a person other than his employer or any other matter to which a person other than his employer has a legal responsibility.[115] The Court of Appeal provided clarity on the requirements of reasonable belief in *Babula* v. *Waltham Forest College*.[116] Courts should conduct an assessment as to whether the claimant had the belief that the concerns raised fit within the categories prescribed in section 43B (a subjective assessment) and then objectively consider whether the belief held was reasonable. At the internal disclosure level, the worker need not be right about their concern provided that they have a 'reasonable belief' which is determined in all of the circumstances of the case.[117] Whilst it will become evident from discussions of the other 'steps in the regime' that section 43C presents the easiest way to obtain protection, the worker will still clearly be at risk of retaliation. Section 43C may present an 'indirect' deterrent effect, i.e. employers may resist retaliatory practices for fear that they may be the subject of legal proceedings, but there are no express provisions which provide protection pre-detriment or dismissal. The Protected Disclosures Act 2000 (New Zealand) is much stronger on this aspect. Section 18 which provides immunity for criminal and civil action also identifies that 'no person will be liable for a disciplinary proceeding' as a result of the raising of a concern.[118] The Public Interest Disclosures Act 2013 (Australia) takes a much stronger approach by making retaliation against whistleblowers a criminal offence subject to two years' imprisonment. Whilst it is acknowledged that legal provisions can only deter rather than prevent retaliatory

---

[115] PIDA 1998, s.43C. The various internal reporting mechanisms of the Civil Service are considered below.

[116] [2007] EWCA Civ 174.

[117] *Darnton* v. *University of Surrey* [2003] Appeal No. EAT/882/01, [29] and [33].

[118] Protected Disclosures Act 2000 (NZ), s.18 (1)(b).

action, the aforementioned sections act as an additional safeguard. In the United Kingdom, if the deterrent effects of PIDA are unsuccessful, claimants face a legal battle which on average can take approximately 40 weeks for the claim to be disposed of.

Disclosure to a government Minister

Section 43E allows workers in government appointed bodies to raise concerns with a Minister of the Crown. It provides for a protected disclosure to be made to a Minister of the Crown if it is made by a Crown servant and if it is made in good faith. Whilst section 43E may be seen as a welcome addition to PIDA 1998, one must ask if it is best suited to situations where a civil servant wishes to raise a concern about another civil servant or issues in his department. The Minister may be unlikely to address matters regarding their own conduct and the civil servant may not have the confidence to directly criticise the Minister. Disclosures at all three steps under PIDA 1998 do not require the recipients of the concerns to take action. Disclosures using section 43E are, however, particularly advantageous to civil servants working for organisations with a sponsoring department. Thus, circumstances may arise where the civil servant does not feel able to go to the chief executive of the organisation but could still raise the concern with the Minister with ultimate responsibility for the host department and all sponsored agencies. Section 43E also does not stipulate that the worker must approach the Minister of the sponsoring department, section 43E(b) requires that a disclosure is made to a Minister of the Crown. Technically, a civil servant could, therefore, approach another Minister (including Ministers without responsibility for the organisation in question); whilst this may be a way to allow the civil servant to obtain protection, they may struggle to get the concern addressed. Following Acts to devolve matters to the Scottish Parliament, members of the Scottish Executive were added to section 43, allowing individuals working on devolved matters to raise concerns.[119] With regard to devolved matters in Wales, the various legislative provisions which codified the Welsh devolution settlement did not include an amendment to section 43E.[120]

---

[119] Scotland Act 1998 (Consequential Modifications) Order 2000, SI 2000/2040, art. 19.

[120] Therefore, civil servants working for organisations on Welsh devolved matters are restricted to raising concerns to the First Minister for Wales who is appointed by the Monarch.

External disclosures to a prescribed person
The next level of the stepped disclosure regime allows protection if a disclosure is made to a 'prescribed person'. There is a noticeable difference between the evidential requirements for internal disclosures made under section 43C and external disclosures under section 43F. Under section 43F, the employee must have a reasonable belief that the relevant failure falls within any description of matters in respect of which that person is so prescribed and that the allegations contained in it are substantially true.[121] This requirement is in contrast to section 43C where the employee does not have to show that the allegation is substantially true but rather that he held the reasonable belief that it was true. Lord Borrie identified that the rationale of section 43F was to 'provide something of a halfway house in that it recognises the particular role of regulatory authorities which are charged to oversee and investigate malpractice within organisations'.[122]

The status of 'prescribed person' does not currently confer any requirements on the prescribed organisation to handle a concern or a whistleblower in any particular way. An inevitable consequence of this is that there are considerable differences in the way in which prescribed persons handle whistleblowing concerns.[123] For example, some regulators may decline to receive a concern where the individual wishes to remain anonymous, thus potentially encouraging the worker to make a wider unauthorised disclosure. Whilst the handling of a whistleblowing concern may not be of direct relevance to the legal protection a whistleblower later receives under PIDA 1998, it can inadvertently have an impact on the employment position of the individual. The likelihood of a worker suffering detriment and or dismissal will increase where a regulator fails to take proper care in investigating a concern raised in confidence. Information can be disclosed inadvertently to the organisation which, in turn leads, to the identification of the whistleblower.[124]

The worker may lose protection if they disclose a concern to a prescribed person which is outside of their remit.[125] Failure to disclose to

---

[121] Public Interest Disclosure Act 1998, s.43F(b).
[122] Hansard, HL Deb., vol. 589, col. 890, 11 May 1998.
[123] Ashley Savage and Richard Hyde, 'The Response to Whistleblowing by Regulators: A Practical Perspective' (2015) 35(3) *Legal Studies* 408.
[124] *Ibid.*
[125] In *Dudin* v. *Sailsbury District Council* (2003) ET 31022631/03, a local employee of the council made a disclosure about a health and safety issue to the council's own scrutiny panel, rather than to the proper authority, the HSE. The disclosure was held to be within s.43G, rather than s.43F. As the claimant could

the correct regulator may also prevent the worker from relying upon a public interest defence in a breach of confidence claim.[126] This is in direct contrast to the position in New Zealand where Protected Disclosures Act 2012, section 16, contains a provision to allow one appropriate authority to refer whistleblowing concerns to another where it is determined that it would be more appropriate for the concern to be investigated by the other authority.

Civil servants are instructed under the Civil Service Code to report evidence of 'criminal or unlawful activity' to regulatory authorities.[127] Following amendments contained in the Public Interest Disclosure (Prescribed Persons) (Amendment) Order 2014, SI 2014/2418, workers can now receive protection for raising concerns to Members of Parliament, provided that the matters complained of fit within the prescribed remit of the other prescribed persons on the list. Whilst this is a welcome addition in that it widens the scope for protection, it is potentially problematical for the civil servant as whistleblower. First, several parts of the Code contain specific restrictions aimed at maintaining the political impartiality of civil servants. Introduction of MPs into the process brings civil servants into the political sphere and could lead to a civil servant being subject to disciplinary action for breaching certain areas of the Code.[128] Secondly, the reform only includes Westminster MPs. Therefore, civil servants based in Wales or Scotland would be unable to raise concerns on devolved matters (for example, healthcare or education) to Members of the Scottish Parliament or the Welsh Assembly. This is a considerable oversight and, if left unrectified, is likely to deteriorate further due to moves to increase devolved powers and responsibility following the Scottish referendum in 2015. Moreover, if a civil servant makes the disclosure to a Westminster MP, following the decision in *Dudin*, the worker may lose protection under section 43F meaning that they must meet the evidential requirements in section 43G.

External 'wider' disclosures

The strongest feature of PIDA 1998 is the ability for workers to raise concerns outside of their organisation without having to exhaust internal

---

not meet the evidential standards under s.43G the claim failed as the employee had not made a protected disclosure.
[126]   *Re a Company* [1983] 2 All ER 36.
[127]   As well as the police. See further 'Rights and Responsibilities', Civil Service Code, above n. 100.
[128]   Considered further in Chapter 5.

procedures. Section 43G[129] concerns 'disclosures in other cases' whilst section 43H[130] concerns disclosures of an 'exceptionally serious failure'. Not surprisingly, both sections 43G and 43H are subject to the most stringent evidential requirements in the Act.

With regard to disclosures under section 43G, in order for the disclosure to be qualifying, the employee must reasonably believe that the information disclosed and any allegations are substantially true and that the disclosure was not made for personal gain. Additionally, the employee must meet one of the conditions contained in section 43G(2). For ease of reference this is quoted in full:

(a) that, at the time he makes the disclosure, the worker reasonably believes that he will be subjected to a detriment by his employer if he makes a disclosure to his employer or in accordance with s.43F,

(b) that in a case where no person is prescribed for the purposes of section 43F in relation to the relevant failure, the worker reasonably believes that it is likely that evidence relating to the relevant failure will be concealed or destroyed if he makes a disclosure to his employer, or

(c) that the worker has previously made a disclosure of substantially the same information:
  (i) to his employer, or
  (ii) in accordance with s.43F.

Most importantly, even if the relevant conditions above are met, there is a further requirement provided by section 43G(e). In all circumstances of the case it must be reasonable for the employee to make the disclosure. This is determined by a series of considerations prescribed in section 43G(3) which the employment tribunal must consider, including the identity of the person to whom the disclosure is made; the seriousness of the relevant failure; whether the relevant failure is continuing or is likely to occur in the future; and whether the disclosure is made in breach of a duty of confidentiality to any other person. Additionally, if the employee has reported the concern to his employer or a regulator the tribunal will have regard to any action which was taken by the employer or might have reasonably been expected to be taken as a result of reporting the

---

[129] Employment Rights Act 1996, s.43G, as inserted by the Public Interest Disclosure Act 1998.

[130] Employment Rights Act 1996, s.43H, as inserted by the Public Interest Disclosure Act 1998.

concern.[131] Section 43G(2)(C) presents a challenge to claimants. First, it places the emphasis on employers and regulators to handle concerns effectively despite there being no minimum standards for the handling of concerns.[132] The employer or regulator could be relatively effective at dealing with the concern but could be ineffective in communicating these actions to the whistleblower. The result of this non-communication or poor communication could prompt the whistleblower to decide to make a wider disclosure, causing them to lose the protection of either section 43C or 43F, thus making it more difficult to obtain protection under section 43G. As the author identifies in Chapter 5, many Civil Service departments fail to track and monitor concerns across the organisation, particularly where those concerns have been raised informally to line managers; this inevitably makes it difficult either to feed information back to the whistleblower, or to be able to utilise the intelligence to identify any trends or wide-spread problems across the organisation. Research by Hyde and Savage has also identified that prescribed persons at a local, national and international level are also failing to adequately track and monitor whistleblowing concerns. Secondly, the afore-mentioned research has also identified that both Civil Service depart-ments and prescribed persons are receiving whistleblowing concerns from workers who choose to be anonymous. Whilst anonymous whistle-blowing may allow concerns to be raised and add a degree of protection for the whistleblower,[133] section 43G (and the other provisions of PIDA 1998 which place emphasis on disclosures made to recipients and the actions taken thereunder) places considerable importance on the whistle-blower being able to prove that it was they who raised the concern – anonymity makes this a very difficult task.

Smith v. *Ministry of Defence and others* identified that in considering section 43G, a tribunal will consider whether or not the claimants

---

[131]   PIDA 1998, s.43G(4), provides a natural extension to the external disclosure of the information if the disclosure is about the employer's failure to take action as a result of reporting the concern.

[132]   Where workers are seeking the protection of s.43G(2)(c) it may well be advantageous for the recipient to be ineffective, so that the worker can enjoy the protection. However, this neither addresses the concern nor does it strengthen the worker's employment position.

[133]   By reducing the risk of the identity of the whistleblower being known to the organisation. However, the worker could still become known to the organ-isation where the information raised contains specific identifiers which could only have come from the worker in question.

attempted to use their organisation's whistleblowing policy before making the disclosure.[134] The case concerned a security guard who had received a caution for indecent assault on a child. After the guard was allowed to return to work, seven members of staff expressed concerns about the decision, claiming that as a nursery school was situated 50 yards away from their workplace this could pose a risk to the children. The seven staff members gave an interview to the media expressing their concerns and also contacted their local MP. The claimants brought a PIDA 1998 claim. The tribunal held that their actions did not constitute a qualifying disclosure. The claimants did not hold a reasonable belief, nor was the claim made in good faith. The tribunal identified that the claimants had not attempted to use their departmental whistleblowing policy and held that their act of disclosure to the media was therefore unreasonable.[135]

It is acknowledged that the case was prior to the removal of the good faith element from section 43G, yet the emphasis that the tribunal placed on the existence of a whistleblowing policy and the applicants' failure to use it is significant. Section 43G(2)(a) allows claimants to hold the reasonable belief that they will be subjected to a detriment by their employer if they make a disclosure. Section 43G(2)(b) further widens its scope to circumstances where the worker believes that evidence will be concealed and destroyed if they raise their concern with the employer. What the section does not take into account is whether, despite the existence of a policy or whistleblowing procedures, the claimant believed that the concern would not be handled effectively. The compatibility of PIDA 1998 with Article 10 ECHR may again be questioned here. The ECtHR in *Guja* held that in conducting the proportionality analysis the court must take into account whether there were 'any other effective means of remedying the wrongdoing' (other than the making of an unauthorised disclosure to the media).[136] The effectiveness of available official channels to raise concerns weighed heavily in the proportionality analyses in both the *Bucur* and *Guja* judgments. It is suggested that in the light of the aforementioned judgments, the employment tribunals, as per their obligations under Human Rights Act 1998, section 2, should consider the effectiveness of the available provisions. Where they fail to consider the existence of a whistleblowing policy or procedures as a

---

[134]   (2005) ET 1401537/04.
[135]   For commentary see also J. Bowers, M. Fodder, J. Lewis and J.Mitchell, *Whistleblowing Law and Practice* (OUP, 2007) [4.32].
[136]   *Guja* v. *Moldova*, above n. 47, [73].

predominant factor, this is likely to render the tribunal in breach of their obligations under Human Rights Act 1998, section 6.

The high evidential threshold identified in section 43G also exposes problems in relation to a number of organisations performing a regulatory function who are not currently prescribed persons for the purposes of section 43F. For example, a civil servant who raises a concern about a security guard could do so with the Security Industry Authority (SIA), the appropriate body who regulates the conduct of security personnel. Despite this, the SIA is not prescribed for the purposes of raising concerns. Workers raising concerns on matters to persons with a regulatory function who are not prescribed for that purpose are therefore at a considerable disadvantage to those raising concerns with organisations who are prescribed. Disclosures to the police would also be subject to section 43G protection even if the worker believes that allegations regarding criminality would be best handled by the police rather than a person prescribed under PIDA 1998.

Section 43H provides the opportunity to obtain protection when raising 'exceptionally serious concerns'. The following section is quoted in full:

(1) A qualifying disclosure is made in accordance with this section if:
    (a) the worker makes the disclosure in good faith, [this subsection had been omitted by the Enterprise and Regulatory Reform Act 2013 and is not applicable to disclosures made on or after 25 June 2013],
    (b) he reasonably believes that the information disclosed, and any allegation contained in it, are substantially true,
    (c) he does not make the disclosure for purposes of personal gain,
    (d) the relevant failure is of an exceptionally serious nature, and
    (e) in all the circumstances of the case, it is reasonable for him to make the disclosure.
(2) In determining for the purposes of subsection (1)(e) whether it is reasonable for the worker to make the disclosure, regard shall be had, in particular, to the identity of the person to whom the disclosure is made.

The Act does not define 'exceptionally serious', instead this is left to the employment tribunal to make a determination based on the available evidence. As Bowers, Fodder, Lewis and Mitchell identify, Parliament intended the section to apply to a very narrow set of circumstances.[137] The case of *Collins* v. *National Trust* identifies the type of situation which have been considered by the employment tribunal to fit within the

---

[137] Bowers *et al.*, above n. 136, [4.42].

definition.[138] The claimant was an employee of the National Trust who had the responsibility for a stretch of coastline in Cornwall. Collins became concerned that a report detailing coastal erosion which identified the risk of a chemical leak from a nearby quarry had not been acted upon. Collins passed the report to a local newspaper and it ran a story quoting Collins as the source. Collins was dismissed and made a claim on the basis that his act amounted to raising a concern of an exceptionally serious failure under section 43H. The tribunal found that the risk of chemical contamination proved a risk to health and safety and children playing at the beach and was sufficient to meet the threshold.[139]

Collins is most relevant to consideration of the protection of Crown servants in the making of unauthorised disclosures. The 'exceptionally serious' requirement sets the threshold too high. Despite having a degree of judicial deference, the tribunal must still make their determination based upon the public interest test and the prescribed categories of information contained within section 43B. As identified above, the public interest is an extremely important factor in the proportionality analysis carried out by the ECtHR. Although the Court will weigh up the public interest value of the information against the harms caused to the employer, the Court would not otherwise confine itself to the narrowest of circumstances as identified in section 43H, as to do so would render it unable to adequately conduct rigorous proportionality balancing. Narrow application of the 'exceptionally serious' threshold is likely to render the section incompatible with Article 10 ECHR.

Despite the clear evidential hurdles identified in both sections 43G and 43H, workers based in the United Kingdom are in a better position than their counterparts based in New Zealand and Canada. The Protected Disclosures Act 2000 (New Zealand) does not allow for external 'wider disclosures' to the media. Moreover, the Canadian Public Servants Disclosure Protection Act 2005 only allows disclosures through strictly prescribed channels. The Protected Disclosures Act (PDA) 2014 (Ireland) is similar to the UK PIDA 1998 in that it allows for disclosures to be made where the wrongdoing is exceptionally serious in nature.

The difference between the PIDA 1998 (UK) and the PDA 2014 (Ireland) is that the Irish legislation offers immunity from criminal prosecution.[140] It also provides protection against civil action, save for

---

[138] (2006) ET 250725505. For an alternative example concerning the trafficking of women for the purposes of prostitution, see *Bolkovac v. Dyncorp Aerospace* (2002) ET 3102729/01.

[139] *Ibid.* [5.8].

[140] Protected Disclosures Act 2014 (Ireland), s.14.

defamation claims.[141] PIDA 1998 (UK), section 43J renders any agreement void in so far as it would preclude a worker from making a protected disclosure. The section therefore requires the claimant to satisfy the provisions in sections 43C–H in order to obtain protection. As identified, the categories of protected disclosure read in conjunction with the overarching public interest requirement make this provision of limited value. Where a Crown servant has made an unauthorised disclosure, they would need to meet the highest evidential thresholds in either section 43G or 43H. If subject to a civil action for a breach of confidence, they would be better advised to rely upon the common law to offer protection using a well-established public interest defence.[142] Crown servants may be subject to criminal prosecution for Official Secrets Acts offences or misconduct in public office, to which PIDA 1998 offers no protection.[143] Furthermore, any conviction for an offence in the making of a disclosure will mean that the worker will also lose the opportunity to bring a claim under PIDA 1998.

III CONCLUSION

The inclusion of an overarching public interest requirement is overly restrictive when read in conjunction with the 'protected disclosure' categories listed in section 43B. The approach taken in *Chesterton Global* identifies that currently the Employment Appeals Tribunal would be satisfied with the claimant's subjective assessment of what constitutes 'the public interest'. In this case it allowed the worker to obtain protection for what was effectively a private employment dispute, despite it having an impact on a number of workers employed by the organisation. This is precisely the type of scenario that the amendment was designed to prevent.[144] If the approach taken in *Chesterton* continues, claimants may be in an advantageous position where they can argue that their concern has a 'public interest' dimension, despite the otherwise

---

[141] *Ibid.*

[142] *Gartside* v. *Outram* (1857) 26 LJ Ch. (NS); *Lion Laboratories* v. *Evans* [1985] QB 526.

[143] It should be noted that the Official Secrets Acts do not provide a public interest defence and that the defence of duress of circumstances is only available in the narrowest of circumstances.

[144] See further UK Parliament, *Enterprise and Regulatory Reform Bill: Explanatory Notes*, available at www.publications.parliament.uk/pa/bills/cbill/ 2012-2013/0007/en/13007en.pdf.

private nature of the concern. It is suggested that public servants may be in a better position to argue this than their private sector counterparts. For example, a worker in a large Civil Service department could argue the treatment of staff amounts to a breach of a legal obligation and is in the public interest to disclose because of the nature of the organisation.[145] If the progression of future case law leads to a narrow application of the 'public interest' test, it is submitted that tribunals will become close to being in breach of Article 10 ECHR (the right to freedom of expression) and Article 13 (the right to an effective remedy), particularly where the claimant in question has not accrued a qualifying period of employment to bring a claim for 'ordinary' unfair dismissal. The 'public interest' requirement leaves little room for effective proportionality balancing. This places the emphasis on employment tribunals to ensure that as Article 10 is engaged, a full assessment using the well-established proportionality analysis is undertaken. It was evident in the *Chesterton* case, for example, that the tribunal were reluctant to consider their determinations under established public interest jurisprudence. There is a danger that information which would otherwise have been protected by the high standards the ECtHR applies to protect freedom of expression, does not meet either the subjective public interest requirement or that it fails to fit within the prescribed categories of information in section 43B. Where information does not fit within these categories of information, the tribunal are still obliged to consider whether the information merits protection under Article 10. This would be appropriate in so-called 'protest speech' cases.

It is submitted that a sensible approach would be to remove the overarching public interest requirement. It should then be considered whether it is necessary to replace the provision in order to rectify the effect of *Parkins v. Sodhexo*. Lewis suggests that it is unfair to add a 'public interest' requirement for 'internal' disclosures made under section 43C.[146] One possibility could be to add a new public interest requirement to sections 43G and 43H which concern wider disclosures of information. This would be a similar approach to Protected Disclosures Act 2000 (South Africa), section 9, which closely mirrors the wording of PIDA 1998 but adds 'public interest' as a factor which a court must consider. Alternatively, it should be considered, as Public Concern at

---

[145]   For discussion of the suggested implications of the amendment see further, Ashley Savage, 'The Public Interest in Public Interest Disclosure', *HR Review* (2012), available at www.hrreview.co.uk/blogs/blogs-employment-law/ashley-savage-the-public-interest-in-public-interest-disclosure/38668.

[146]   Lewis, above n. 106, 152.

Work suggested during the consultation process to the amendment, whether 'public interest' should be added to the 'breach of a legal obligation' prescribed disclosure category. Given that under the obligation in Human Rights Act 1998, section 6, tribunals should consider the public interest as part of the proportionality analysis, it is suggested that it would be appropriate to remove the public interest requirement altogether.

Beyond consideration of the domestic application of Convention jurisprudence, the protected disclosure categories contained within PIDA 1998, section s.43B, are restrictive in comparison with the recently enacted PDA 2014 (Ireland). It is suggested that new categories of 'misuse of public funds' and 'gross maladministration' could be included to expand the scope of protection. Inclusion of a 'gross maladministration' provision would be particularly beneficial to Crown servants wanting to raise concerns regarding decisions made by Ministers of the Crown or the chief executive of a government agency, for example. Whilst it is argued that this would move PIDA 1998 closer to protecting acts of protest whistleblowing, legislation in other jurisdictions have successfully incorporated 'maladministration' into their respective whistleblowing protections. It should be considered that maladministration would potentially draw a tribunal into making an assessment of the conduct of members of the executive. In judicial review cases, the courts have grappled with attempting to uphold the separation of powers doctrine whilst having to make determinations concerning executive action. However, if section 43B were to stay in its current form, the tribunal would only need to be satisfied that the claimant had the subjective belief that the concern raised constituted 'gross maladministration'.

Whilst UK whistleblowers are arguably in a better position than many in other jurisdictions, particularly where there are no whistleblower shield laws,[147] more recent legislation such as the PDA 2014 (Ireland) offers more comprehensive protection. For example, PIDA 1998 currently provides employment protection for workers to raise concerns outside of their organisation but does not offer immunity from civil or criminal action. Workers risk losing their right to bring a claim where they are convicted of an offence. A new section providing immunity from civil and criminal action in certain circumstances would strengthen the legislation considerably. Later chapters will further explore whether

---

[147] For example, Germany and Portugal do not currently have whistleblower protection laws.

employees of the security and intelligence services and Armed Forces personnel should be protected by PIDA 1998.[148]

During consideration of the Public Interest Disclosure Bill, Lord Nolan had praised the drafters of the legislation for 'skilfully achieving the essential but delicate balance between the public interest and the interest of employers'.[149] However, one must consider whether PIDA 1998 is achieving this aim. Workers can be placed at a considerable disadvantage when raising concerns if they need to wait a considerable time for their claim to be disposed of. This, in conjunction with the complex nature of the legislation in its current form, suggests that employers are placed strategically in a better position from the outset. The inclusion of some form of 'pre-detriment' protection would help to readdress this balance. A section which expressly outlaws disciplinary sanctions where workers have raised concerns would not end detrimental treatment towards whistleblowers but it would assist in deterring such action from taking place.[150]

---

[148] See further Chapter 6 and Chapter 7.
[149] Hansard, HL Deb., vol. 590, col. 614, 5 June 1998.
[150] Protected Disclosures Act 2000 (New Zealand), s.18(1) provides an example.

5.   Whistleblowing in the Civil Service

> The British Civil Service is a non-political and professional career service
> subject to a code of rules and disciplines. Civil servants are required to serve
> the duly constituted Government of the day, of whatever political
> complexion. It is of the first importance that civil servants should conduct
> themselves in such a way as to deserve and retain the confidence of
> Ministers, and to be able to establish the same relationship with those
> whom they may be required to serve in some future Administration.[1]

Written in 1985, the aforementioned quote, taken from a memo drafted
by Sir Robert Armstrong, neatly encapsulates the relationship between
civil servants and their political masters. The relationship is one of trust
and loyalty. Civil servants are responsible to Ministers who are reliant
upon them to action policies which may otherwise be in direct conflict
with their own political persuasions. In return, Ministers are answerable
to Parliament and to the electorate for any actions taken by their
department, ultimately being prepared to take personal responsibility for
the actions of civil servants.[2] The Armstrong Memorandum is of historical significance, drafted in response to the outcome of the Ponting trial;
it was aimed at reaffirming the duties that civil servants owed to the
Crown. Yet Ponting disclosed information on the location of the Argentinean Cruiser the General Belgrano because he felt that government
Ministers had failed to keep up their end of the bargain, by misleading
Parliament and the electorate. In those circumstances, the civil servant
believed that he had a duty to bring the matter to public attention.[3]

The relationship between Ministers and their civil servants remains a
delicate one to balance. It may be naive to suggest both actors are locked
in a constant power play reminiscent of something satirised in the 1980s
sitcom *Yes Minister*, but leaks of official information regularly occur and
may be just as likely to originate from Ministers for political gain as

---

[1]   Robert Armstrong, *The Duties and Responsibilities of Civil Servants in
Relation to Ministers, Memorandum from the Cabinet Secretary* (1985).
[2]   Cabinet Office, *Ministerial Code* (2010).
[3]   See generally Clive Ponting, *The Right to Know: The Inside Story of the
Belgrano Affair* (Sphere Books, 1985) 125.

their civil servants.[4] Whilst the spirit of the Armstrong Memorandum still holds true today, the relationship between Ministers and civil servants has undoubtedly changed. The introduction of 'next steps' agencies, a legacy of the Thatcher administration, meant that whilst Ministers of a host department ultimately remained in charge, Chief Executives would head the new organisations.[5] As a result, Ministers are increasingly likely to resist calls to resign, placing blame on executives or civil servants, in marked departure from the doctrine of ministerial responsibility.[6] In addition, Ministers are becoming increasingly reliant upon 'special advisers' who provide politically informed advice in contrast to the politically neutral Civil Service.[7]

Civil servants have access to the innermost workings of government and are likely to be the first to observe issues which may become subject to whistleblowing reports. Entrance into the Civil Service requires civil servants to agree to a restriction of expression rights in the context of their work. In contrast to special advisers, the need for civil servants to be politically neutral, a construct of the Northcote-Trevelyan Report, can serve as a barrier to the raising of whistleblowing concerns.[8] Civil servants can observe activities or policies which appear at odds with extramural community values or their own political views. Even where the information complained of appears not to concern political matters

---

[4] *Yes Minister*, BBC Television Sitcom 1986–1988. For example, Leon Britain ordered a civil servant to leak a memo during the Westland Affair to discredit Michael Heseltine; for further discussion see Colin Pilkington, *The Civil Service Today* (Manchester University Press, 1999) 57. In a more recent example, Alasdair Carmichael, then Scottish Secretary, ordered his special adviser to leak information aimed at discrediting First Minister of Scotland, Nicola Sturgeon, in the lead up to the Scottish referendum; see further Cabinet Office, 'Scotland Office Memorandum Leak: Cabinet Office Inquiry Statement', Press Release, 22 May 2015.

[5] Kate Jenkins, Karen Caines and Andrew Jackson, *Improving Management in Government: The Next Steps* (HMSO, 1988). For discussion see further Adam Tomkins, *The Constitution after Scott: Government Unwrapped* (Oxford University Press, 1998) 84.

[6] For example, Home Secretary, Theresa May refused to resign following a relaxation of border checks by the UK Border Agency; May argued that Chief Executive Brodie Clark must take responsibility for the matter, 'Theresa May: I won't resign over UK Border Agency row', BBC News, 8 November 2011.

[7] See generally Ben Yong and Robert Hazel, *Special Advisers: Who They Are and Why They Matter* (Hart, 2014).

[8] Stafford Northcote and Charles Trevelyan, *Report on the Organisation of the Permanent Civil Service* (HMSO, 1894).

per se, the nature of the individual's workplace and options for raising the concern can give rise to allegations of political bias.[9]

The reported experiences of several high profile whistleblowers suggest a number of institutional failings in the way in which departments and agencies handle concerns. In 2011, Osita Mba made disclosures to the National Audit Office and two Parliamentary Select Committees that his superior at Her Majesty's Revenue and Customs (HMRC) had agreed to waive a £10 million tax bill. Mba was later placed under investigation using the Regulation of Investigatory Powers Act 2000 resulting in the seizure of telephone records and a computer. Mba later settled his claim and left the organisation. In 2012, David Owen, employed by the Treasury, raised concerns that a policy which had previously been given ministerial support was changed by senior civil servants and that this contravened the Civil Service Code. Despite winning an employment tribunal claim using the Public Interest Disclosure Act (PIDA) 1998, the department refused to employ him resulting in a tribunal awarding damages of £140,000. The Public Accounts Committee's inquiry into whistleblowing called the treatment of some whistleblowers in the Civil Service 'shocking' and 'appalling'.[10]

It is suggested that civil servants may encounter different types of concern which broadly fall into four distinct yet potentially overlapping categories. First, there are standard 'watchdog whistleblowing' concerns. These matters may concern health and safety breaches, harm to the environment or criminal activities and may be the type of matters which are as likely to be observed by employees working for private organisations.[11] The second type of concern to arise and one which has been discussed elsewhere in this work is that of 'protest whistleblowing'. These disclosures of policy may not concern wrongdoing per se but are likely to be matters that the individual chooses to raise because they

---

[9] Information regarding a health and safety concern could be the subject of increased public interest and thus political interest (particularly from opposition MPs) because it involves a government department. Disclosures to a Member of Parliament from an opposing political party may give rise to disciplinary action for breaching the Civil Service Code. This chapter will later identify that the Civil Service Code is currently at odds with Public Interest Disclosure Act (PIDA) 1998, s.43F, which allows workers to raise concerns to Members of Parliament regarding prescribed matters.

[10] Public Accounts Committee, *Whistleblowing*, HC-593 (2014) 5.

[11] Whilst recognising the potentially heightened public interest value in concerns raised regarding activities conducted by official departments. It is suggested that matters concerned within this category will be generally covered by the categories of protected information contained in PIDA 1998, s.43B.

disagree with the contents of a policy and its potential consequences based upon their employment experience. The third category relates to 'political dissent'. Closely linked to 'protest whistleblowing' these disclosures are likely to arise where the civil servant disagrees with a policy or course of action based on their own and potentially conflicting political beliefs. The final category concerns 'Ministerial misconduct' which effectively relates to potential breaches of the Ministerial Code. This category is unique to Crown service and can encapsulate situations whereby a Minister has misled Parliament. It would also cover matters where the individual conduct of the Minister may result in a breach of the Code. The aforementioned categories will be referred to at various points of this analysis.

The purpose of this chapter is to provide detailed consideration of the position of civil servants as whistleblowers.[12] Section I will focus on the obligations civil servants owe as per the Civil Service Code and Civil Service Management Code and the scope that the Civil Service Code, in particular, provides to allow civil servants to raise concerns. Section II will consider how whistleblowing concerns are raised under the Code by drawing upon extensive data obtained by freedom of information requests from 71 departments and agencies. Section III will consider the contribution that civil servants can make to external accountability mechanisms, including the provision of evidence to Select Committees, public inquiries and Members of Parliament as prescribed persons.

I OBLIGATIONS

In entering the Civil Service as an intramural community, civil servants must undergo security clearance to at least the baseline personnel security standard level.[13] Aside from the statutory limitations on expression posed by the Official Secrets Acts, the common law offence of misconduct in public office and other contractual confidentiality agreements, all civil servants are subject to the Civil Service Code.[14] At its

---

[12] This chapter will consider the position of civil servants in England, Wales and Scotland but will not consider employees in Northern Ireland who are employed by the Northern Ireland Civil Service.

[13] Cabinet Office, HMG Baseline Personnel Security Standard, version 4.0 (2014). More security sensitive roles may require developed vetting, the highest level of clearance.

[14] This chapter focusses on the UK Civil Service Code; civil servants in Scotland (save for employees of the Scottish Court Service (SCS) and the Office

heart are four core values: 'integrity, honesty, objectivity and impartiality'. The Code itself is not enshrined in law. However, the Constitutional Reform and Governance Act 2010 made the provision of a Code a statutory requirement. Section 7 of the Act also set out the provision of minimum standards which must be included, namely, the four core values listed above and that civil servants must 'carry out their duties for the assistance of the administration ... whatever its political complexion'. The Code presents civil servants with an unavoidable conflict of loyalty: a duty owed to the intramural community to serve the government of the day and a duty owed to Parliament which civil servants must not knowingly mislead. The following sections will identify and discuss several restrictions on expression rights.

Restrictions on Political Expression

Similar to the position of public servants in New Zealand, Ireland, Canada and Australia, employees of the UK Civil Service have obligations to remain politically impartial in conducting their work.[15] Throughout the Code, several instructions have relevance to political impartiality and thus impact on any attempts at protest whistleblowing or political dissent.[16] For example, civil servants must not misuse their official position by using information acquired in the course of their duties to further the interests of themselves or others. They must not disclose information without authority. They must serve the government of the day 'whatever its political persuasion' and whatever their own political beliefs. They must act in a way which retains the confidence of Ministers and must comply with any restrictions aimed at restricting their political activities. Civil servants must not 'act in a way that is determined by party political considerations, or use official resources for party political purposes' or allow their own 'personal political views' to determine their actions.

---

of the Scottish Charity Regulator (OSCR)) follow a separate Code of Conduct, the Civil Service Code (Scottish Executive Version), SG/2010/247 (2010), however the standard of behaviour in both codes is identical.

[15]   State Services Commission, *Code of Conduct for the State Services'* (New Zealand); Standards in Public Office Commission, *Civil Service Code of Standards and Behaviour* (Republic of Ireland); Australian Public Service, *Values and Code of Conduct* (Australia); Treasury Board of Canada, *Values and Ethics Code for the Public Sector* (Canada).

[16]   UK Civil Service, *Civil Service Code*, revised version (March 2015).

The Civil Service Management Code contains extensive rules concerning the political activities of civil servants. Civil servants in industrial and non-office grades are placed in the 'politically free' category meaning that they are allowed to partake in any political activities.[17] As the civil servant's exposure to government policy increases so does the level of restriction. Civil servants who are members of the Senior Civil Service and at all levels immediately below and members of the Fast Stream promotions programme are not allowed to take part in national party political activities and must seek permission to take part in local political activities.[18]

Civil servants deemed not to be in the politically free category are subject to a number of instructions with regard to their everyday conduct. They must not allow their expressions of political views to appear to be so strong that they inhibit loyal service to Ministers.[19] They must take 'particular care' to express comment with moderation, especially regarding controversial matters involving their own Ministers and must avoid personal attacks.[20] They must take care to avoid embarrassment to Ministers or to their organisation which could bring themselves into party political controversy. In addition to this, civil servants must 'retain a proper reticence in matters of political controversy so that their impartiality is beyond question'.[21]

Special advisers hold the status of 'temporary civil servants' for the duration of their employment. Special advisers are subject to their own Code of Conduct which was introduced in 2010.[22] They are required to observe the Civil Service Code, but because of the nature of their work, which may include the giving of advice relevant to party political matters, they are exempt from the requirement to behave with 'impartiality' and 'objectivity'.[23] This key distinction means that special advisers are effectively less restricted to communicate their own political views as well as communicating whistleblowing concerns.

The Code of Conduct for Special Advisors outlines standards of conduct governing the relationship with permanent civil servants. In particular, the Code states that advisers must not 'ask civil servants to do

---

[17] *Civil Service Management Code* [4.4.2]. The groups to be included in the category are subject to approval by the Minister for the Civil Service.

[18] *Ibid.* [4.4.9].

[19] *Ibid.* [4.4.13].

[20] *Ibid.*

[21] *Ibid.* [4.4.15].

[22] Cabinet Office, *Code of Conduct for Special Advisers* (2010).

[23] *Ibid.* [4].

anything which is inconsistent with their obligations under the Civil Service Code'.[24] The Code later instructs that where a civil servant has concerns regarding any request from a special adviser they should discuss the concern 'with their line manager, the Minister's Principal Private Secretary, their Permanent Secretary or the departmental nominated officer(s), the Cabinet Secretary or the Civil Service Commissioners'.[25] The section is problematical for several reasons. It does not present the option of disclosures to prescribed persons or to the wider public, despite these options being available in the Public Interest Disclosure Act 1998.[26]

If a civil servant were to raise concerns regarding the conduct of a special adviser to a Member of Parliament, the wider public or the media, it is likely that they will be in breach of the Civil Service Code's requirement of political impartiality. This likelihood is arguably increased, first, due to the nature of the work of special advisers, and secondly, because opposition MPs, in particular, have traditionally sought to criticise the actions and appointment of special advisers.[27] Whilst the special adviser's Code states that the 'preparation or dissemination of inappropriate material or personal attacks has no part to play in public life' the alleged use of controversial tactics by some advisers, including the leaking of information to the media, is well known. Special advisers are in a favourable position as, whilst the Code states that their involvement in party politics is 'carefully limited',[28] the reality is that whilst their actions advance personal or party political interests there will be less motivation for Ministers to dismiss them. In contrast, a special adviser could be in a position to subject a civil servant to detrimental treatment. The Code states that special advisers 'should not be involved in matters affecting a permanent civil servant's career'.[29] However, in spite of this advisers can decide to allocate civil servants to provide support, allowing them the opportunity to potentially side-line individuals. Advisers may also provide their views in performance appraisals of civil servants, allowing for attacks on performance matters.

---

[24]   *Ibid.* [7].
[25]   *Ibid.* [8].
[26]   PIDA 1998, s.43F allows for disclosures to prescribed persons; s.43G allows for wider disclosures; s.43H allows for exceptionally serious disclosures.
[27]   For example, Damian McBride, Andrew Coulson and Alasdair Campbell have all come under fire from the opposition benches.
[28]   *Code of Conduct for Special Advisers* [6].
[29]   *Ibid.* [9].

Restriction on the Disclosure of Information

The Civil Service Code provides two guiding principles relevant to the unauthorised disclosure of information. Civil servants are instructed that they must not 'disclose official information without authority' a duty which applies after individuals have left the Civil Service. They also must not 'misuse' their official position. The Code provides the use of information acquired in the course of official duties to 'further private interests or those of others'. No further guidance is provided in the Code and unlike some paragraphs in the Code no reference is made to PIDA 1998.

The Civil Service Management Code contains instructions that departments and agencies must remind staff of their obligations, on appointment, resignation or retirement, that they are bound by the criminal law and by a duty of confidentiality.[30] They must not take part in activities which may involve the unauthorised disclosure of information, including drawing upon their experiences.[31] Furthermore, they must not frustrate the policies or decisions of Ministers by making disclosures of information outside of government.[32]

Restriction on Contact with the Media

The revised Civil Service Code, published in March 2015, introduces a new requirement for civil servants who 'must ensure that they have ministerial authorisation before any contact with the media'. Whilst the Code contains a footnote identifying that PIDA 1998 may 'also apply in some circumstances', the Code does not provide any further information and at the time of writing the Directory of Civil Service Guidance is yet to be updated to reflect the change.[33] The circumstances of when it may be appropriate to go to the media remain uncertain and civil servants would receive little clarity from the Directory on this point. The explanation of PIDA 1998 still refers to 'good faith' which is no longer an evidential requirement following the 2014 amendments to the legislation. Provided an individual could prove that they have made a protected disclosure for the purposes of the Act, PIDA 1998, section 43J may void

---

[30] *Civil Service Management Code* [4.2.1].
[31] *Ibid.* [4.4.2].
[32] *Ibid.* [4.2.6].
[33] Cabinet Office, *Directory of Civil Service Guidance* (2010).

the restriction in so far as it prevents civil servants from the making of a disclosure.[34]

In cases of external whistleblowing disclosures to the media, the requirement to obtain permission before going to the media is likely to be disproportionate with Article 10 of the European Convention on Human Rights (ECHR) where the information is of a high value to the public interest. In practical terms, the restriction is likely to dissuade civil servants from approaching the media with concerns when both PIDA 1998 and Article 10 ECHR offers protection for doing so. The requirement should therefore be removed, reformed or at the very least guidance should be issued to clearly articulate the circumstances in which disclosures to the media could be allowed.

Whistleblowing and the Code

The Civil Service Code does not use the term 'whistleblowing'. Instead, it instructs individuals that if they believe that they 'are being required to act in a way which conflicts with the Code' or 'become aware of others' who they believe 'are in conflict with the Code', their department or agency 'must consider the concern, and make sure that you are not penalised for raising it'.[35] Civil servants are instructed to first raise the concern with a line manager or someone else in the line management chain, or alternatively to seek advice from their nominated officer. They are instructed to report 'evidence of criminal of unlawful activity to the police or other appropriate regulatory authorities'.

Whilst the guidance in the Code makes reference to PIDA 1998, it is far from explicit as to the circumstances where the protection may apply. This uncertainty may act as an inhibitor to the raising of concerns. Whilst it is acknowledged that government departments and agencies have individual whistleblowing policies, the significance of the failure to make explicit reference to PIDA 1998 in the Code should not be overlooked. The categories of disclosure contained in section 43B extend much wider than the standards of behaviour in the Civil Service Code, including health and safety and harm to the environment; 'a breach of a legal obligation' can extend the reach of PIDA 1998 much further. It is not clear from the Code whether departments and agencies are still under an obligation to consider the complaint if it falls outside of the scope of a complaint brought under the Code. Moreover, it is not clear whether or

---

[34] The Civil Service Code is a contractual agreement.
[35] *Ibid.*

not the department will not penalise individuals if they raise matters which fall outside the scope of the Code but would ordinarily be protected by PIDA 1998.

The instruction to report evidence of criminal or unlawful activity to the police or regulatory authorities is unhelpful without further reference to PIDA 1998. As identified elsewhere in this text, it is easier to obtain protection under the law for individuals who raise concerns to a prescribed person using PIDA 1998, section 43F rather than making a disclosure under sections 43G or 43H, because of the increased level of evidential requirements for the making of 'wider disclosures'. Put simply, it will be easier for a civil servant to obtain protection if they raise their concern with a regulator who is prescribed (for example, the National Audit Office) rather than directly to the police. Use of the term 'report evidence' is also out of step with PIDA 1998. Whilst disclosures under sections 43F, 43G and 43H all require a reasonable belief that the matter complained of is 'substantially true', an individual need not provide evidence to prove a concern to authorities. The Code also provides access to the Civil Service Commission which would be covered by PIDA, section 43C(2).[36] This states:

> If you have raised a matter covered in paragraphs 16 to 18, in accordance with the relevant procedures, and do not receive what you consider to be a reasonable response, you may report the matter to the Civil Service Commission. The [C]ommission will also consider taking a complaint direct.

The aforementioned passage appears to suggest that civil servants should raise concerns and wait for the outcome before raising a concern to the Civil Service Commission. The option of making a direct approach to the Commission is identified, however it is not made particularly clear that an individual does not need to exhaust the procedures before going to the Civil Service Commission. Whilst this provision is not entirely inconsistent with PIDA 1998, the ambiguous wording suggests the existence of an unnecessary procedural requirement.

The Code instructs that 'If the matter cannot be resolved using the procedures set out above, and you feel you cannot carry out the instructions you have been given, you will have to resign from the Civil Service'. It places undue emphasis on the effectiveness of the available

---

[36] PIDA 1998, s.43C(2) provides as follows: 'A worker who, in accordance with a procedure whose use by him is authorized by his employer, makes a qualifying disclosure to a person other than his employer, is to be treated for the purposes of this Part as making the qualifying disclosure to his employer'.

procedures by requiring an individual to resign if the matter is not resolved. The Code therefore fails to take into account circumstances where the failure to resolve matters has been due to the ineffectiveness of procedures. The Code is further out of step with PIDA 1998 because it fails to indicate that disclosures may be made to prescribed persons, to Members of Parliament for concerns regarding prescribed matters, as well as to the media.

It is suggested that PIDA 1998, section 43J could be applicable to any of the aforementioned restrictions on expression. Section 43J identifies that 'any provision' in an agreement is 'void in so far as it purports to preclude the worker from making a protected disclosure'. Section 43J(2) identifies that the provision is applicable to any agreement, whether in a worker's contract or not. The Civil Service Code, as a contractual agreement between the civil servant and the Civil Service, will therefore engage the section. A worker could use section 43J to argue that they should not be subject to disciplinary action or dismissal where they have raised concerns. However, it should be noted that section 43J has received little attention before the courts thus far. If a department or agency failed to acknowledge the protection and the civil servant suffered a detriment or dismissal, they would then need to attempt to bring an employment tribunal claim. At the time of writing there is no available information to suggest that the section is being actively used by civil servants to protect against disciplinary action or detrimental treatment for breaching the Code.

Chapter 4 identified that the European Court of Human Rights (ECtHR) has considered restrictions on the expression rights of public servants to be proportionate under Article 10 ECHR. However, the Court made clear in *Guja* v. *Moldova* and subsequent cases that where a public servant communicates information regarding wrongdoing which out-weighs the detriment caused to the organisation, any restriction on expression will be disproportionate.[37] In such circumstances the rights of the extramural community will prevail. In light of the findings contained in the aforementioned analysis, the next section will now consider options for reform.

---

[37]   *Guja* v. *Moldova*, Application No. 14277/04 (ECtHR, 12 February 2008).

Scope for Reform

There is scope for significant and wide-ranging improvement to the Civil Service Code. First, the Code could be much more clearly aligned to the PIDA 1998. The Code should include the additional categories of information in section 43B to ensure that the whistleblowing mechanisms in government departments and agencies capture and address all concerns as protected by the Act. The Code should include all potential disclosure avenues which are protected by PIDA 1998. At present it is not sufficiently clear that civil servants can raise concerns to prescribed persons, non-prescribed regulators and the media in some circumstances. The wording of the Code should more clearly articulate that civil servants can make direct approaches to the Civil Service Commission without raising the matter internally first. The Code should also be more explicit on contact to the media.

Where references have been provided to the Civil Service Guidance, this guidance is out of date and currently pre-dates the legislative changes brought in by the Enterprise and Regulatory Reform Act 2014. Whilst it is acknowledged that departments and agencies across government will provide access to guidance documents as well as individual whistle-blowing policies, one should question whether it is appropriate to have several sources of information whilst providing little guidance in the Code itself. The Civil Service Code is considered as the core source of values to which civil servants agree upon entering employment, it therefore provides a guiding reference point. The author suggests that there are two possible options. First, the Code could be stripped back to a basic code of conduct and values with indicators to separate guidance accessible elsewhere. The New Zealand Code of Conduct for the State Services provides a deliberately concise one page document.[38] Secondly, the Code could be more explicit by providing more detailed explanations alongside the stated values and standards. The Republic Ireland Civil Service Code of Standards and Behaviour provides an example of this approach.[39] The Australian Public Service Code has a much clearer and more detailed section on whistleblowing.[40]

---

[38] State Services Commission, *Code of Conduct for the State Services* (New Zealand).

[39] Office Commission, *Civil Service Code of Standards and Behaviour* (Republic of Ireland).

[40] Australian Public Service, *Values and Code of Conduct* (Australia), note that at the time of writing the Code was due to be updated.

It is submitted that the Code should be much clearer on the protections afforded to whistleblowers who raise concerns. Recent reforms in policing have resulted in an amendment to the Police (Conduct) Regulations 2012, SI 2012/2632, which now state that 'the making of a protected disclosure by a police officer is not a breach of the Standards of Professional Behaviour'. A similar reform could be adopted in the context of the Civil Service. An amendment to the Civil Service Code backed by further amendments to the Civil Service Management Code would significantly enhance the protection available to civil servants by providing pre-detriment protection. This has the potential of reducing the need to bring a claim post-detriment using the employment tribunal, with the aim of repairing relations between the employee and employer before the relationship has broken down beyond repair.[41]

It should also be considered whether it would be appropriate to make the mistreatment of individuals who make a protected disclosure a breach of the Civil Service Code. There are a several policy considerations which would need to be fully explored before such a change could be adopted. The reform to the Police Regulations is very recent and it is too soon to determine how effective it will be in practice. In the light of the author's analysis in Chapter 4, consideration needs to be given as to whether restricting speech to protected disclosures is sufficient to ensure compliance with Article 10 ECHR. It is suggested that any amendment would require detailed instruction to departments and agencies, who in determining whether the civil servant had made a protected disclosure should also consider the individual's expression rights as they are required to do so in compliance with Human Rights Act 1998, section 6. Further to the aforementioned matters, departments and agencies may encounter difficulties where civil servants have made unauthorised disclosures to the media. A detailed assessment of whether the disclosure would constitute a protected disclosure under PIDA 1998, section 43G and/or 43H would need to be considered, as well as compliance with Article 10 ECHR. As a matter of policy, police officers are likely to be exposed to information which is as harmful as that handled by their counterparts in the Civil Service. In the context of policing the government's impact assessment favoured the amendment, thus identifying

---

[41]   An argument advanced by the author in the context of police officers and staff in Ashley Savage, 'Whistleblowing in the Police Service: Developments and Challenges' (2016) 22(1) *European Journal of Current Legal Issues* (forthcoming), and Ashley Savage, 'The Challenges to Implementing Effective Police Whistleblowing Mechanisms', paper delivered at Sheffield Hallam Public Law Conference, Sheffield, 2015.

confidence that the amendment will succeed.[42] The next section will proceed to consider how concerns are raised in the Civil Service.

II RAISING CONCERNS IN PRACTICE

This section aims to consider how concerns raised under the Civil Service Code are handled in practice. Research has been conducted into the policies by both Public Concern at Work and the National Audit Office. Some analysis has been conducted on the procedures and handling of disclosures in some departments by the National Audit Office, as well information obtained in evidence taken during the course of the Leaks and Whistleblowing in Whitehall inquiry undertaken by the Public Administration Select Committee (PASC) in 2010.[43] The aim of this part of the chapter is to advance this work further by providing a detailed picture of the status of concern handling across the Civil Service.

At the time of writing, the Public Accounts Committee had made a number of important recommendations, which the Government had undertaken to adopt. The amendments should improve the current status of whistleblowing in departments and agencies. However, this section will illustrate that there is significant variation in the way in which concerns are handled and that this must be overcome if the experiences of whistleblowers in the Civil Service are to improve. This variation is due, in part, to a lack of central co-ordination and standardisation in procedures used and the fact that the flexibility of PIDA 1998 has not required departments to follow any particular framework.[44]

---

[42] Home Office Impact Assessment, *Police Whistleblowing: Changes to Police (Conduct) Regulations 2012 and Home Office Guidance on Police Officer Misconduct*, HO-0175 (March 2015).

[43] Public Administration Select Committee, *Leaks and Whistleblowing in Whitehall*, HC-83 (2009).

[44] The position should be considered in contrast to how public service whistleblowing operates in Canada. The Public Servants Disclosure Protection Act 2005 provides a rigid structure for civil servants to follow, however it should be noted that the scheme has been the subject of criticism. See further, Ashley Savage, 'Legislative Flexibility versus Procedural Rigidity: A Comparison of the UK and Canadian Approaches to Public Service Whistleblowing Protection', paper delivered at 40th World Congress of the International Institute of Sociology, New Delhi, India, 2012.

Methodology

The author adopted a methodology previously developed and subsequently used by Savage and Hyde to conduct research into the handling of whistleblowing concerns by prescribed persons. The methodology utilises the Freedom of Information Act 1998, the Environmental Information Regulations 2004, SI 2004/3391 and the Freedom of Information (Scotland) Act to obtain empirical data on a large scale.[45] The author developed a standardised request asking organisations employing civil servants for information on how concerns raised regarding breaches of the Civil Service Code were handled, whether they were tracked/monitored/recorded, the arrangements regarding nominated officers, the nature of concerns raised and eventual outcomes. A standardised request was sent to 91 organisations which were part of the Civil Service People Survey.[46] In total 62 sets of responses were successfully received. In some instances, aggregated responses were received from the sponsoring department which incorporated responses from the agencies under the department's control.[47]

With regard to ethical considerations, public authorities are obliged to comply with the requirements of the Data Protection Act 1998 when formulating responses to freedom of information requests. The data may also be exempt where the information is held in confidence. The identities of individuals should not, therefore, be disclosed in responses thus negating any risk of harm to individuals. The author also developed a protocol to immediately inform the organisation of a breach of the requirements. This did not need to be implemented. As an additional

---

[45] For full details of the methodology see Ashley Savage and Richard Hyde, 'Using Freedom of Information Requests to Facilitate Research' (2014) 17(3) *International Journal of Social Research Methods* 303. For findings of the project, see further Ashley Savage and Richard Hyde, 'The Response to Whistleblowing by Regulators: A Practical Perspective' (2015) 35(3) *Legal Studies* 408.

[46] Cabinet Office, *Civil Service People Survey 2013* (February 2014). The survey was conducted across the UK Civil Service and thus provided a detailed list of organisations which employ civil servants.

[47] The Home Office included the Border Force and HM Passport Agency. The Ministry of Justice included the HM Courts and Tribunals Service, Legal Aid Agency, National Offender Management Service and Office of the Public Guardian. The Department of Transport provided an aggregated response which covered the department as well as the following agencies: Driver and Vehicle Standards Agency, Driver and Vehicle Licencing Agency, Highways Agency, Maritime and Coastguard Agency and Vehicle Certification Agency.

safeguard, the author has chosen to provide a general overview in the discussion of the concerns raised and will not discuss individual cases. It is acknowledged that as with all research methodologies, the information obtained and subsequently reported on must be viewed with a degree of caution. Due to the significant variances in the way in which departments and agencies handle and record information it is not feasible to make direct statistical comparisons of the number of concerns raised across the organisations. Further to this, some departments and agencies refused disclosure of information due to exemptions, particularly where response would likely go beyond the cost limit due to the way in which information was stored. In some cases, departments and agencies provided partial rather than full information.[48] Some departments requested clarification which would have resulted in significant departure from the standardised request.[49] It is also not possible to make allowances for individual error or variation in information due to individual respondents.

Disclosures to the Line Management Chain

Departments and agencies were asked whether disclosures to the line management chain were tracked/monitored and recorded. The recording of concerns is important; it can assist the whistleblower evidentially if they need to prove that they raised a concern. It can further assist the department or agency in identifying trends in intelligence, i.e. whether the concern raised by one individual is also being raised by others and can act as an indicator of systemic failings. The information should also be used for quality assurance. At the time responses were received there was a significant degree of variation in whether departments and agencies recorded concerns to line management and how this information was stored. In some agencies, the records are held by Human Resources.[50] In others the records are held by the sponsoring department.[51] The Ministry of Justice responded that it did not record the information within its

---

[48] Sixteen of the responses contained partial rather than full information.
[49] In such cases the information has not been included.
[50] Companies House, FOI response, received 23 December 2014; Debt Management Office, FOI response, received 8 December 2014; Wilton Park, FOI response, received 18 December 2014; Historic Scotland, FOI response, received 22 December 2014; Office of Rail Regulators, FOI response, received 16 December 2014; Competition Markets Authority, FOI response, received 6 January 2015.
[51] Insolvency Service, FOI response, received 8 January 2015; Disclosure Scotland, FOI response, received 30 December 2014.

management information system as there was a need for it to remain confidential, whereas Royal Parks and Ofsted hold the information on a secure system with restricted access.[52] One agency did not track or monitor concerns raised via the line management chain and did not hold a central record but records were held on the individual's personnel file.[53]

There were some positive indications of improvements to internal processes. Prior to February 2013, the Department for Environment, Food and Rural Affairs (DEFRA) did not track or monitor concerns but now record centrally and track to completion.[54] The Ministry of Defence (MOD) used to record concerns locally but since March 2014 record centrally.[55] HMRC provided a detailed response:

> Since March 2014 HMRC have introduced a mechanism for better tracking concerns raised under the Whistleblowing and Raising a Concern policy which are handled within management chains. Managers receiving a complaint must complete a template pro forma about the concerns and submit this to the Internal Governance department within HMRC, who collate statistics and information centrally for the department. Before, details were collated centrally for all cases which were referred to Internal Governance for investigation.[56]

The HMRC reporting mechanism should be considered as a possible exemplar of good practice. It is suggested that in order to provide consistent service delivery across the Civil Service, all departments and agencies need to centrally track and monitor concerns raised to line managers.

Disclosures to Nominated Officers

Nominated officers act as a focal point for individuals who want to raise a concern under the Civil Service Code. They can provide advice on interpretation of the Code; on steps which may be taken to resolve the

---

[52]   Ministry of Justice, FOI response, received 8 January 2015; Royal Parks, FOI response, received 17 December 2014; Ofsted, FOI response, received 7 January 2015.

[53]   UK Export Finance, FOI response, received 7 January 2015.

[54]   DEFRA, FOI response, received 8 January 15.

[55]   MOD, FOI response, received 9 January 2015.

[56]   HMRC, FOI response, received 29 January 2015.

concern; on how to take a concern forward using the available procedures; and how to complain to the Civil Service Commission.[57]
Thirty-seven responses provided information on their nominated officers.
All identified that the nominated officer role is performed in addition to
the person's usual role within the organisation.[58] These roles include
positions in Human Resources, team leaders, managers and directors and
governance and complaints roles. The Crown Prosecution Service identified that their nominated officers are part of an Internal Audit and
Assurance Team based in the Ministry of Justice.

All departments and agencies were asked to identify the nominated
officers' grade. In their report, *Leaks and Whistleblowing in Whitehall*,
the Public Administration Select Committee identified that nominated
officers could have an important role by providing a 'friendly face'
available to offer advice to staff without them necessarily raising a
complaint.[59] The report found that nominated officers were 'often senior
people' and that this could 'intimidate staff at lower grades'. The
Committee recommended that officers should be 'evenly spread' across
the grades and offices and be placed in pastoral type roles to 'make them
more approachable and to ensure consistency in advice'. Whilst it is clear
from the information provided above that nominated officers are being
placed in welfare roles, there does appear to be a variation across
departments as to the placement of the position. It is not possible to
determine from the information provided whether this has led to inconsistency in the advice received by civil servants, however, the
placement of an individual may impact on the consistency of the
approach taken across the Civil Service. For example, nominated officers
placed in compliance or complaint roles may have a vested interest in
encouraging the civil servant to raise the concern. From the majority of
responses received it is also clear that nominated officers still predominantly hold senior positions. Fifteen of the responses identified that the
nominated officers in their department or agency were 'senior civil
servants' or were at SCS (Senior Civil Service) grade. The remainder of
the responses received mostly identified that the officers were at grade 6

---

[57] Civil Service Commission, 'The Role of the Nominated Officer',
available at http://civilservicecommission.independent.gov.uk/information-for-
departments-civil-service-code/the-role-of-the-nominated-officer/.
[58] Note that Royal Parks answered that the organisation did not have a
nominated officer. It was not clear whether approaches could be made to a
sponsoring department: Royal Parks, FOI response, received 17 December 2014.
[59] PASC, above n. 43, [100].

or 7 level (or the departmental or agency equivalent) or provided their job titles, for example, 'head of division' or 'non-executive directors'.

Eighteen of the respondents identified that they had one nominated officer in their department. The remainder of the 37 respondents identified that they had more than one, thus identifying a missed opportunity to place other nominated officers in lower grades. For example, the Department for Environment, Food and Rural Affairs identified that it had three nominated officers, but these were all in the senior positions of Director General (SCS band 3), Deputy Director (band 1), and Chief Statistician (band 1).[60] National Savings & Investments (NS&I) were the exception. The organisation identified that it had four levels of nominated officer: Line Manager; HR Business Partner; Director; and Chief Executive.[61]

The size of the organisation did not necessarily correlate with the number of nominated officers. The Scottish Government response (which also included responses for Disclosure Scotland, Education Scotland, Student Awards Agency for Scotland, Transport Scotland, Accountant in Bankruptcy, Scottish Housing Regulator) identified that it only had one nominated officer.[62] This is of particular concern as civil servants, regardless of which agency they work for, only have access to the nominated officer based in the Scottish Government. Similarly, the Department for Education identified that it had one nominated officer, but it intended to recruit two further individuals in January 2015.[63] In contrast, UK Export Finance identified that it had 10 nominated officers.[64] HMRC identified that it had 11 nominated officers but that it intended to recruit individuals to obtain a total of 39 nominated officers across a range of grades in 2015.[65]

The data suggests that all departments and agencies need to re-evaluate the number of nominated officers placed within their organisation and the grading of those individuals. Whilst at first sight the NS&I approach identifies placement of nominated officers at a lower grade, this is also potentially problematical.[66] First, nominated officers should be individuals placed outside of the line management chain so that civil servants have access to a source of independent advice, as recommended by the British Standards Institution Code of Practice on Whistleblowing and the

---

[60]   DEFRA, FOI response, received 8 January 2015.
[61]   NS&I, FOI response, received 22 December 2014.
[62]   Scottish Government, FOI response, received 30 December 2014.
[63]   Department for Education, FOI response, received 5 January 2015.
[64]   UK Export Finance, FOI response, received 7 January 2015.
[65]   HMRC, FOI response, received 29 January 2015.
[66]   NS&I, FOI response, received 22 December 2014.

PASC report.[67] Secondly, line managers may be caught up in the concern itself and it therefore may be inappropriate to approach the individual. Thirdly, the civil servant may have a difficult working relationship with the line manager or concerns that approaching them may have an impact on appraisal and subsequent career progression. Fourthly and finally, the line manager would ordinarily be the first person to which a concern may be raised; where advice is sought rather than the wish immediately to raise a concern, the line manager may not be the most appropriate person for this purpose. The author recommends that all departments and agencies consider whether it would be appropriate to introduce a 'peer advice' scheme whereby civil servants who are not placed in senior positions could be trained to provide advice and guidance to civil servants. Alternatively, or in addition, where departments do not have such a provision in place it is suggested that consideration should be given to establishing an independent advice telephone line. Whilst it is acknowledged that independent advice sources are available, such as a union representative or organisations such as Public Concern at Work or Whistleblowers UK, not all workers are members of a union and this recommendation would provide organisation specific advice.[68] The need for independent advice is particularly important because of the risk of civil servants choosing to make an unauthorised disclosure or not raising the concern at all because they have not been made fully aware of the options to raise concerns and the possible consequences arising from them.

Tracking and Monitoring Concerns Raised to Nominated Officers

Departments and agencies were asked whether concerns were tracked/monitored/recorded by nominated officers. As with concerns recorded by line managers there is a need to record approaches made to nominated officers. Again, there was a significant variance in how concerns were being reported. UK Export Finance, for example, did not centrally record concerns but recorded information in individual's personnel files.[69] The Criminal Injuries Compensation Authority identified that

---

[67] British Standards Institution, *Code of Practice on Whistleblowing* (PAS 1998:2008) 21.

[68] The charity, Public Concern at Work, operates a free helpline to provide advice to whistleblowers: www.pcaw.org.uk. Whistleblowers UK is an organisation set up by whistleblowers to offer support and advice to others, www.wbuk.org/help.html.

[69] UK Export Finance, FOI response, received 7 January 2015.

it did not hold any information, as employees were required to raise concerns to a nominated officer based at the sponsoring department.[70] The Treasury Solicitor identified that the organisation recorded information and reported biennially to the Cabinet Office.[71] Most alarmingly, for the time period where information was obtained seven of the responses (one of which was an aggregated response) indicated that their department or agencies did not track or monitor concerns raised with nominated officers.[72] This is a significant oversight.

A key finding of the Public Accounts Committee report on whistleblowing was that departments were not using the intelligence obtained by whistleblowers effectively.[73] If records are kept on individual files but not tracked and monitored centrally it makes it more difficult for the organisation to build an accurate picture of the state of concern reporting arrangements in the organisation. Despite recording very few concerns, Ofsted appeared to be leading the way on central tracking of concerns. They identified that all concerns were tracked, monitored and recorded on a 'casework and advice spreadsheet on SharePoint' which had restricted access.[74] If they are not already doing so, all departments and agencies should consider the benefits of tracking and centrally recording all intelligence from whistleblowers. It was evident that some organisations were centrally recording concerns raised by whistleblowers to the nominated officers but were not centrally recording concerns raised to line managers. This will mean that, particularly in large organisations, nominated officers and other concern recipients may fail to identify that the concern raised has been raised by other colleagues before. The failure to track or monitor concerns is also a cause for concern, as unless files are individually updated it will not always be clear that a concern has been dealt with and that the matter has been resolved. This is significant, as the final paragraph of the Civil Service Code requires civil servants to leave if they have tried the avenues available and are unable to resolve a concern.

---

[70] Criminal Injuries Compensation Authority, FOI response, received 22 December 2014.

[71] Treasury Solicitor, FOI response, received 22 December 2014.

[72] HM Treasury, Serious Fraud Office, UK Trade and Investments, UK Export Finance, Scottish Housing Regulator, Ministry of Justice (and executive agencies).

[73] PAC, above n. 10.

[74] Ofsted, FOI response, received 7 January 2015.

Number of Concerns Raised and How They Were Received

Of the 17 organisations who stated that they had received one or more concerns raised under the Civil Service Code during the time period, 12 disclosed the number received. There is a distinct variation in the number of concerns received by departments.[75] With regard to central government departments, the Department for Work and Pensions (DWP) recorded 401 concerns and the Foreign and Commonwealth Office reported 136 concerns.[76] In contrast, the Department for Education and the Scottish Government reported less than five concerns.[77] With regard to non-ministerial departments, HMRC recorded 5,167 concerns in the time period whereas the Arbitration Conciliation and Arbitration Service and Serious Fraud Office reported less than five concerns.[78] The executive agencies who disclosed information, namely, the Animal Plant Health Agency, the Valuations Office Agency and the Intellectual Property Office, also identified that less than five concerns during the period had been raised.[79]

HMRC, which identified the highest number of concerns, also identified that they had a number of avenues in which concerns could be raised.[80] This included an anonymous reporting hotline, an in-confidence intranet reporting system, and other 'whistle-blower channels' which were not explained further.[81] Whilst the data provided must be viewed with a degree of caution, it is perhaps telling that the two organisations with the most number of concerns recorded, HMRC and DWP, both

---

[75] As an additional safeguard to avoid the disclosure of information which may impact on a whistleblower's position, the author has chosen to indicate where a department has received less than five concerns rather than provide an exact figure. The author will not provide specific information on any concerns raised.

[76] Department for Work and Pensions, FOI response, received 23 December 2014; Foreign and Commonwealth Office, FOI response, received 5 February 2015.

[77] Department for Education, FOI response, received 5 January 2015 and the Scottish Government, FOI response, received 30 December 2014.

[78] HMRC, FOI response, received 29 January 2015; Arbitration Conciliation and Arbitration Service, FOI response, received 10 December 2014; Serious Fraud Office, FOI response, received 5 January 2015.

[79] Animal Plant Health Agency, FOI response, received 2 January 2015; Valuation Office Agency, FOI response, received 5 January 2015; Intellectual Property Office, FOI response, received 7 January 2015.

[80] HMRC, FOI response, received 29 January 2015.

[81] *Ibid.*

operate whistleblower hotlines. Individuals may arguably feel better placed to contact a whistleblower hotline than approach a nominated officer in person. It is suggested that other departments and agencies that do not operate such a service should consider the value of implementing a hotline. There are, however, difficulties associated with anonymous whistleblowing concerns. It is difficult for whistleblowers to prove that it was they who raised the concern and then suffered detrimental treatment or dismissal if they cannot provide evidence of this.[82] Where possible, as an alternative option, some police forces in the United Kingdom have chosen to adopt a 'bad apple' reporting system to tackle anti-corruption and conduct issues.[83] The system allows the whistleblower to communicate with the recipient without disclosing their identity should they not wish to do so. Her Majesty's Inspectorate of Policing have found that the systems have led to whistleblowers feeling empowered to raise concerns on a confidential rather than anonymous basis after receiving assurances from the recipient.[84]

Types of Concern Received

The Department for Work and Pensions provided a general overview of the three main types of concern which relate to the alleged misuse of official information, official time or leave. The response identified that the remainder concerned a wide variety of issues regarding alleged irregularities, for example, the misuse of social media and improper use of computer systems. Similarly, HMRC provided a detailed response to this question identifying that 'attendance related matters, Confidentiality issues, Bullying and harassment, Tax irregularities, Internet or social

---

[82] The Department for Work and Pensions were unable to provide data on whether the concerns raised to the hotlines were on a self-identified, anonymous or confidential basis. All departments and agencies were asked whether the concerns they received were on a confidential, anonymous or self-identified basis, where departments did provide information the data provided identified no significant trends.

[83] Northamptonshire Police, *Confidential Reporting (Whistleblowing)* (Ref No. 13/12) 3; Derbyshire Constabulary, *Professional Standards Policy* (Ref: 7.06/045) 7.

[84] HMIC, *Integrity Matters: An Inspection of Arrangements to Ensure Integrity and to Provide the Capability to Tackle Corruption in Policing* (January 2015) 98, available at www.justiceinspectorates.gov.uk/hmic/wp-content/uploads/police-integrity-and-corruption-2015.pdf. For further discussion see Ashley Savage, 'Whistleblowing in the Police Service: Progress and Challenges' (2016) 22(1) *European Journal of Current Legal Issues* (forthcoming).

media issues, Abuse of official equipment or IT systems, Travel and subsistence related matters, recruitment process issues' were raised. In other departments and agencies, the concerns related to actions of a manager during a recruitment process, a potential breach of data security, honesty, integrity and objectivity and financial impropriety.[85]

Only four concerns raised were about department or agency policy; these would fall in the 'protest whistleblowing' category. The rest of the concerns appear to be acts of 'watchdog whistleblowing' which would be capable of PIDA 1998 protection.[86] There were no instances of concerns raised regarding ministerial conduct or the conduct of special advisers in the responses received.

Referrals to Another Body or Agency

There appears to be a lack of consistency across the organisations as to when a referral will be made and to whom. The Government Actuary's Department stated that they would not refer to another body unless there was a requirement to do so but did not provide further information.[87] There are differences in the way in which executive agencies handle concerns. Several executive agencies who responded identified that they may refer concerns to a sponsoring department but there were noticeable variances in when referrals would be made.[88] The Food and Environment Research Agency (FERA) identified that they will handle minor breaches of the Civil Service Code but that 'more serious breaches' would be handled under the agency's 'whistleblowing and raising a concern procedures'.[89] FERA indicated that the most serious breaches would be referred directly to the Civil Service Commission.

The Office for Standards in Education, Children's Services and Skills (Ofsted) identified that 'if all internal avenues have been explored or are not deemed to be appropriate for the particular concern' the matter can be raised with the Department for Education (Ofsted's sponsoring department).

---

[85] These singular examples have not been attributed to the department or agency as an additional safeguard to protect any individual who has raised a concern.

[86] Applying PIDA 1998, s. 43B.

[87] Government Actuary's Department, FOI response, received 5 January 2015.

[88] Criminal Injuries Compensation Authority, FOI response, received 22 December 2015; Scottish Government, FOI response, received 30 December 2014.

[89] FERA, FOI response, received 6 January 2015.

HMRC identified that if warranted a serious allegation may be referred to the Department for Business, Innovation and Skills. The Scottish Government identified that it would handle all concerns from executive agencies where they could not be resolved by the line management chain.[90]

In disclosing the outcomes of the concerns received, the Department for Work and Pensions identified that it had referred concerns to other government departments. The Foreign and Commonwealth Office identified that a small number of concerns were referred to the police.

It is not clear whether these concerns are being tracked further. As Savage and Hyde identify (in the context of disclosures to regulators) tracking the concern can assist organisations to update whistleblowers on what is happening.[91] An investigation may commence which may directly impact on the whistleblower's employment position, further evidence or information may be required by the investigators or the whistleblower themselves may need the information in evidence to support a future PIDA 1998 claim.

Subsequent Action

Due to the nature of the responses received it is not possible to provide an accurate picture of what action is taken to deal with concerns raised across the Civil Service.[92] One department identified that informal resolution had been used to resolve the concern, another example identified that the response resulted in dismissal and the issue of a letter of displeasure.[93] The Department for Work and Pensions were able to provide extensive data identifying that it takes a variety of different measures in dealing with concerns. The DWP disclosed that 15 concerns were handled immediately and 42 concerns had been referred to a different jurisdiction to consider further action.[94] A total of 169 concerns were referred to local managers to take action (including disciplinary action) and there were 96 concerns accepted for formal investigation by the internal investigations team. A total of 66 concerns were not deemed appropriate for further action and 13 were judged to be duplicate concerns. It is most significant that the DWP's

---

[90]   Scottish Government, FOI response, received 30 December 2014.

[91]   Savage and Hyde, above n. 45, 408.

[92]   Many respondents declined to provide the information on the basis that it would be over the cost limit in the Freedom of Information Act 2000 to do so. This is likely to be a reflection of the way in which the information is recorded.

[93]   Due to the small number of cases disclosed (less than five) the author has chosen not to disclose the names of these departments.

[94]   The DWP did not identify the jurisdictions in question.

system is able to identify and subsequently provide the number of duplicate concerns. Where departments and agencies are recording information locally the opportunity to identify that concerns have been raised before and by whom will be diminished. HMRC disclosed the outcomes of investigations handled by Internal Governance. Between the dates 1 January 2010 and 31 December 2013 there were 5,167 investigations resulting in 578 dismissals and 1,125 written warnings. It is submitted that where departments and agencies are not already doing so it would be useful for them to provide detailed information on their responses to concerns. Where individuals can identify that concerns will be taken seriously, they are more likely to be encouraged to utilise official channels. Departments and agencies should consider whether it would be appropriate to publish these statistics internally and, further, whether these statistics should be made publically available. As a workable example, public organisations in Canada proactively disclose information concerning investigations into wrongdoing.[95] It is suggested that departments and agencies should take care to remove and redact information which may identify a whistleblower.

Scope for Reform

The aforementioned analysis has identified that there is a distinct level of variation between departments and agencies as to how organisations handle concerns raised under the Civil Service Code. There is a variation in how concerns are recorded, whether concerns raised to line management are tracked and monitored centrally, and even whether concerns raised to nominated officers are tracked and monitored centrally. Following recommendations by the Public Accounts Committee, the Government agreed that departments should report on the effectiveness of whistleblowing arrangements in their governance statements in their Annual Report and Accounts.[96] If departments are to provide a full and accurate picture of effectiveness they must report, not only on approaches to nominated officers but also approaches made to line managers. This information should be tracked and monitored to its conclusion and should be kept centrally on a secure system so that analysis can be carried out, duplicate concerns can be identified, and so that whistleblowers can be kept up to date on subsequent action. It is suggested that this cannot be achieved by the provision of best practice alone. The Public Accounts

---

[95]   The Public Health Agency of Canada webpage provides an example: see www.phac-aspc.gc.ca/about_apropos/asd-dsv/id-di/index-eng.php.

[96]   HM Treasury, *Treasury Minutes*, Cm 8988 (2014).

Committee identified a lack of cross-governmental leadership and recommended that the Cabinet Office should 'set out how it will ensure whistleblowing policy and practices receive the strong leadership they need, so that there are consistent expectations across government and departments can be held to account'.[97] The Cabinet Office agreed to the recommendations, however, it is suggested that in order to maximise the availability and effectiveness of concern mechanisms sweeping changes are required across departments and agencies.

Central co-ordination and leadership of whistleblowing across the Civil Service must go much further than the provision of best practice. All departments and agencies should be required to centrally track and monitor concerns raised to line managers, nominated officers and other available mechanisms. The method of doing so should be consistent to ensure that an accurate picture of whistleblowing across the Civil Service can be achieved on an annual basis. Whilst it is recognised that departments and agencies will differ in size, this should not impact on the service delivery of whistleblowing concerns. It would make sense for every executive agency to have at least one nominated officer in order to provide a visible contact for civil servants to seek advice. The number of nominated officers appears to differ greatly between departments and agencies with no clear identifier as to why this is the case. For example, the Valuations Office Agency, an executive agency, reported that they had nine nominated officers, whereas the Scottish Government reported that they had one nominated officer, who covers six agencies as well as their own department.[98] It is submitted therefore that the Government needs to conduct a thorough assessment to determine the level of coverage needed to ensure that there is a sufficient number of nominated officers per staff depending on the size of the organisation. This benchmark figure should then be applied across the Civil Service to ensure that there is a minimum number of civil servants to cover a determined number of civil servants working within the organisation. Consistency can also be enhanced by the provision of regular training for nominated officers and line managers and regular checks on whether the schemes are operating in practice. This chapter will now proceed to consider the role of the Civil Service Commission who may investigate complaints after civil servants have attempted to raise matters internally, as well as taking on cases directly in some circumstances.

---

[97] *Ibid.*
[98] Disclosure Scotland, Education Scotland, Student Awards Agency for Scotland, Transport Scotland, Accountant in Bankruptcy, Scottish Housing Regulator.

Civil Service Commission

If a civil servant believes that a serious breach of the Civil Service Code has taken place, the Civil Service Code advises them to first attempt to raise the concern internally and if unsatisfied to raise it with the Civil Service Commission. The Commission is staffed by a Chief Executive, seven Commissioners and a Secretariat.[99] The Commissioners received the power to investigate appeals under the Civil Service Code in 1996. Constitutional Reform and Governance Act 2010, section 2, placed the Commission on a statutory footing. In response to a freedom of information request by the author, it can be identified that the total number of new approaches made by civil servants to the Commission making a complaint under the Code has remained low since it obtained the power to investigate.[100] Very few appeals are accepted for full investigation.[101] The Commission's latest report identifies that it dealt with four cases between March 2014 and April 2015. It would appear that part of the reason for the low number of cases accepted for investigation is due to the high number of cases it rejects on the basis that they fall outside of the organisation's remit because the concern involves HR matters which are excluded by the Code, or because the complainant is not a civil servant. Another possible explanation for the low number of complaints could be because the Civil Service Code and the Commissioner's own guidance deliberately steer prospective complainants towards internal departmental and agency complaint mechanisms.[102] Even for the provision of advice the guidance states that 'our

---

[99]   The provision of seven Commissioners is a statutory requirement contained in Constitutional Reform and Governance Act 2010, Sch. 1.

[100]   Civil Service Commission, FOI request, received 19 May 2011.

[101]   Between the years 1996 and 2009, the Commissioners investigated a total of 13 appeals, 10 were upheld or partially upheld and three were not upheld. In 2010–13 details were published in the Commissioner's Annual Report. Since 2013/14, the Commission has published the information on their website. The Commission dealt with 16 cases in 2011–12, 17 in 2012–13, 19 new cases in 2013–14 and four in 2013–14 (reports provide information from March to April the following year). All reports are accessible on the Commission's website: see http://civilservicecommission.independent.gov.uk/publications/annual-reports/.

[102]   *Civil Service Code* (2010). See also Civil Service Commission, *Guidance to Bringing a Complaint*, available at http://civilservicecommission. independent.gov.uk/wp-content/uploads/2012/04/Guide-to-bringing-a-complaint-to-the-Commissioners-Civil-Service-Code-March-20121.pdf.

staff will be happy to talk to you, but we would urge you to raise the matter internally if that is possible'.[103]

The circumstances in which a civil servant may raise a concern directly with the Commission are not identified in the Civil Service Code; guidance provided in a document accessible on the organisation's website does, however, identify possible circumstances where they may accept a complaint:

> Situations where the managers above the civil servant are involved in the matter of concern. Situations where the Permanent Secretary, or Chief Executive, are involved in the matter of concern. Situations in which the issue of concern is time-limited, urgent and serious. Situations where the Commission believed that the civil servant may have suffered a detriment as a result of raising a concern or is likely to suffer a detriment in future.[104]

It is submitted that this information could and should be made much more accessible to civil servants, particularly where a concern raised may result in detriment to the civil servant. Whilst the document is available on the Commission's website, the prospective whistleblower may not have sight or awareness of the information and will already need to navigate through the Civil Service Code, the Civil Service Management Code, as well as the departmental or agency whistleblowing policies. This strengthens the need for a more clearly defined and explicit Civil Service Code.

The guidance also identifies that 'the Commission do not encourage anonymous approaches'. The wording of the guidance could be much clearer on this point. A freedom of information response to the author identified that the Commission is 'unable to hear complaints if the complainant wishes to remain anonymous'. This is supported by cases published on the Commission's website which identify that the Commission has rejected concerns on the basis that they were anonymous. It is not suggested that anonymous approaches are the most appropriate way to get concerns addressed, yet there are circumstances whereby the severity allegation or the risk posed to a civil servant merits further investigation. Anonymity can be partially mitigated against when individuals are provided with a unique identifier to link the individual to the concern and there is a mechanism for a dialogue between the complainant and recipient. Further to this, the Commission is currently out of step with government departments and agencies who, as the aforementioned

---

[103]   *Ibid.* 9.
[104]   *Ibid.*

analysis has identified, are accepting and acting on anonymous concerns. If the Civil Service is effectively to provide an 'avenue of last resort' then the Commission must consider receiving anonymous concerns to ensure consistent service delivery. In terms of safeguarding national security it would be far better for a civil servant to make an anonymous disclosure to the Civil Service Commission in a secure environment than to make an uncontrolled anonymous disclosure to the media.

Investigations

Constitutional Reform and Governance Act 2010, section 6, identifies that the Civil Service management authorities, the complainant and any civil servant whose conduct is covered by the complainant must provide the Commission with any information 'it reasonably requires'; there is no provision contained within the section to deal with circumstances where there is a refusal to disclose information. In contrast, the Parliamentary Ombudsman's power to investigate government departments is far more comprehensive. The Ombudsman has the same powers as a court in respect of the attendance and examination of witnesses and the production of documents. Furthermore, departments cannot rely on secrecy or legal privilege as reasons not to disclose documents to investigators.[105] There are procedures in place for the handling of national security sensitive material. The Commission notes that in dealing with information marked 'Secret or above', the civil servant should advise the Commissioners beforehand so that provision can be made for appropriate handling of the information.[106] Further to this, the Commission confirmed to the author that staff working for the Commission sign the Official Secrets Acts.[107]

The Civil Service Commission identified in their 2014–2015 *Annual Report* that they aim to acknowledge complaints within three working days and to 'complete initial assessments on whether a case [is] "in scope" within 15 working days'.[108] In an age where documents can be self-published online, emailed to journalists or uploaded to an online disclosure outlet such as Wikileaks, one must consider whether three

---

[105] Parliamentary Commissioner for Administration Act 1967, s.8(3).
[106] See *Guide to the Civil Service Code*, available at www.civilservice commissioners.org/web-app/plugins/spaw2/uploads/files/Guide%20to%20the%20 Civil%20Service%20Code.pdf.
[107] Civil Service Commission, FOI response, received 23 April 2014.
[108] Civil Service Commission, *Annual Report and Accounts*, HC 251 (2014–15) 44.

days to receive an acknowledgement followed by a further 15 days to see whether an investigation will take place is an appropriate time to wait. As the Commission has expressed a desire to improve its complaints handling process, it is submitted that the process to determine whether complaints should be investigated must be improved.[109]

Following an investigation, the Commission will send a report of the findings to the individual and the department.[110] The Commission can make recommendations to the department subject to the complaint. The Commission identifies in its guidance that there is no 'specific obligation on a department to follow the Commission's recommendations' but suggests that if their recommendations are ignored there are 'levers of significant power' available to them.[111] It suggests that it may draw 'public and parliamentary attention' to the fact that their recommendations have not been actioned and would raise the matter with the Permanent Secretary or Agency Chief Executive concerned and, if judged necessary, with the Cabinet Secretary. It then indentifies that if the steps did not produce action then they would 'probably' draw the matter to the attention of other bodies such as the PASC or the Committee on Standards in Public Life.[112] In the absence of legal provisions to enforce findings of corrective action, these 'levers of power' place undue reliance on individuals and public and parliamentary pressure, all of which can be uncertain.

The Commission publishes the findings of investigations on its website. With regard to the publication of information the Commission's guidance states the following:

> The name of the department and the name of the civil servant who brought the complaint are not given in the Annual Report. Only a summary is given of the nature of the complaints.[113]

Whilst the published 'findings and recommendations' reports do not identify the name of the individual who raised the concern, they identify how the individual raised the concern and they identify the department running contrary to the aforementioned guidance. The reports also

---

[109] *Ibid.*
[110] Civil Service Commission, *Civil Service Code: A Guide to Bringing a Complaint to the Civil Service Commission* (2010), available at http://civilservicecommission.independent.gov.uk/civil-service-code/complaints-to-the-commission/.
[111] *Ibid.*
[112] *Ibid.* 20.
[113] *Ibid.* 21.

provide a degree of detail in the summaries which could potentially identify the individual who raised the concern. Given that the Commission will not accept anonymous approaches from individuals but will accept confidential reporting, this is likely to further discourage servants from coming forward with concerns. It is acknowledged that the reporting of investigations may encourage individuals to raise concerns by showing that the system is working but this should not include information which could still identify the whistleblower.

Scope for Improvement

The Civil Service Commission has, as it identified in its latest annual report, improved the availability of information on its website. However, it is timely for the guidance for civil servants, now over five years old, to be reviewed to ensure that the language used is reassuring and that, where possible, uncertainties are removed. The Commission should consider whether it would be appropriate to receive anonymous concerns. The Commission identified that their office has been the subject of cuts and 'resources are very limited'.[114] If the Commission are to present a viable alternative to the making of unauthorised disclosures, it is vitally important that the Commission receives the resources it needs, particularly where it is apparent that the time which it takes to accept complaints needs to be reduced. The Commission also has responsibility for handling recruitment complaints and it identified in its last Annual Report that complaints regarding recruitment and the Civil Service Code were increasing. It should therefore be considered whether, given the size of the Civil Service, it is appropriate to split the recruitment function and the Civil Service Code function to separate bodies and allocate sufficient resources to each. The Civil Service Commission would benefit from enhanced statutory powers. The Constitutional Reform and Governance Act 2010 represents a missed opportunity. A provision for dealing with situations where the department has failed to act on the recommendations of the Commission would formalise an important aspect of the Commission's functions and would reduce uncertainty. The discussion will now proceed to consider 'external disclosures': whilst disclosures to the Civil Service Commission technically represent an individual 'going outside' an organisation, the Civil Service Code makes it clear that civil servants can approach the Commission, thus disclosures may be subject to PIDA 1998, section 43C(2). The following 'external' disclosure routes are

---

[114]   *Ibid.* 15.

highly relevant to whistleblowers in the Civil Service but are not identified in the Code, despite PIDA 1998 allowing such disclosures in certain circumstances.[115]

III EXTERNAL DISCLOSURES

Disclosures to Members of Parliament

The Public Interest Disclosure Act (Prescribed Persons) (Amendment) Order 2014, SI 2014/2418 came into force on 6 April 2014. The effect of the order was to add Members of Parliament to the list of persons prescribed for the purposes of PIDA1998, section 43F. A civil servant who makes a disclosure to a Member of Parliament would be protected if the matter complained of fits within 'any matters specified in the column'. In practice, it means that a worker will receive protection under PIDA 1998, section 43F if they raise a concern about a matter which would already come within the remit of another prescribed person. Whilst this provides another option to individuals, it does not provide section 43F protection for a number of matters which may be relevant to MPs, for example, information regarding a criminal offence would have to come within the remit of another prescribed person to be protected under this section. Whilst it is acknowledged that disclosures not covered by PIDA 1998, section 43F could come within the protection of section 43G, this requires more stringent evidential requirements. A person without legal training is likely to encounter difficulty in working out whether or not he/she would be protected by section 43F. At the time of writing, neither Parliament nor the individual Members of Parliament themselves have provided specific guidance to identify when and how civil servants may raise concerns.

Disclosures to MPs may be particularly problematic for civil servants.[116] Civil servants have a contractual obligation[117] to be politically impartial.[118] Any disclosures to Members of Parliament are likely to be in conflict with this obligation because their work is more likely to be

---

[115] Applying either PIDA 1998, ss.43F, 43G or 43H. Note that this section does not consider the role of local and national regulators for reasons of emphasis. For discussion see further Chapter 4.

[116] For further discussion see also Chapter 3.

[117] *Civil Service Code* [20]: 'This Code is part of the contractual relationship between you and your employer'.

[118] *Civil Service Code* [14] and [15].

political in nature. Opposition Members of Parliament are primarily motivated by the desire to hold the executive to account; this motivation is at odds with the civil servant's duty of impartiality. MPs are most likely to benefit from disclosures relating to policy decisions and alleged ministerial misconduct, however PIDA 1998, section 43F is unlikely to protect such disclosures. Civil servants must make disclosures which would otherwise be covered by the remit of other prescribed persons. As there are no prescribed persons tasked with handling breaches of the Civil Service Code and no prescribed persons tasked with handling ministerial misconduct, this will be a very difficult task. Civil servants could still be protected by PIDA 1998, section 43G or 43H, however both sections require workers to prove a much higher evidential threshold.[119]

Whilst it is acknowledged that a civil servant may obtain protection under PIDA 1998, the Act provides protection post-detriment or dismissal. Therefore, the amendment provides the option for civil servants to raise concerns about matters within section 43F but provides no protection to deal with the breach of the Code. Any concerns raised to MPs will be reliant upon the goodwill of government departments not to impose detrimental treatment or dismiss civil servants. MPs do not receive any special training on handling whistleblowing concerns and Members of Parliament are not guided on whistleblowing disclosures. The handling of concerns by MPs is therefore likely to be inconsistent and may even be mishandled as a result. MPs may disclose allegations on the floor of the House of Commons which may identify a confidential whistleblower because of the unique nature of the allegations concerned.

Civil servants are placed under a heightened risk of prosecution if they disclose documents.[120] Members of Parliament are not authorised to receive disclosures under the Official Secrets Act 1989.[121] Ordinarily, individuals who receive and then disclose information entrusted in confidence would be guilty of an offence under the 1989 Act.[122] Members of Parliament are protected by parliamentary privilege which offers immunity from prosecution and suit where words are expressed in the House of Commons. The protection famously safeguarded Duncan

---

[119] For further discussion see Chapter 4.

[120] At the lowest level, the common law offence of misconduct in public office, at the highest level the Official Secrets Act 1989.

[121] This also includes the members of the Intelligence and Security Committee who, whilst being 'persons notified' for the purposes of Official Secrets Act 1989, s.1, are not authorised under s.8 or the relevant Prescription Orders to receive disclosures.

[122] Official Secrets Act 1989, s.5.

Sandys from threats of prosecution for offences under the Official Secrets Act 1920 after he reported concerns raised by officials regarding the nation's preparedness for war.[123] The protection did not, however, protect opposition MP Damian Green from arrest for misconduct in public office after receiving documents from Home Office civil servant, Christopher Galley. The police also conducted unprecedented searches of Mr Green's Westminster and constituency offices. The charges were later dropped, however Galley was sacked from his position at the Home Office.[124] The episode, whilst controversial, has paved the way for potential future searches to take place. It is submitted that privilege, in itself, is unlikely to protect individuals who make unauthorised disclosures to Members of Parliament. The political pressure that is likely to ensue where privilege is challenged by police officers or prosecuting authorities is likely to have more of an impact.[125] Discussion will now proceed to consider disclosures to Parliamentary Select Committees.

Select Committees

Parliamentary Select Committees provide a mechanism of parliamentary oversight which extends beyond the rowdy confines of the Commons chamber. Committees are staffed by backbench MPs and are headed by a chairperson. There are advantages to Select Committees in that they could investigate concerns raised regarding ministerial conduct and other matters which could not be investigated by the Civil Service Commission. They can effectively decide to investigate any matter which comes under the terms of their remit.[126] The clear disadvantage is that their investigatory work is limited to persons giving evidence before the Committees, unlike the Parliamentary Ombudsman and the Civil Service

---

[123] For discussion see David Hooper, *Official Secrets: The Use and Abuse of the Act* (Coronet Books, 1987) 11.

[124] Crown Prosecution Service, 'Decision on Prosecution: Mr Christopher Galley and Mr Damian Green MP', 16 April 2009.

[125] Former Assistant Commissioner, Bob Quick argued to the Leveson Inquiry that he had been placed under pressure by Conservative MPs and the media to drop the investigation. See further, Statement of Robert Quick, The Leveson Inquiry into the Culture, Practices and Ethics of the Press, available at http://webarchive.nationalarchives.gov.uk/20140122145147/http:/www.leveson inquiry.org.uk/wp-content/uploads/2012/03/Witness-Statement-of-Bob-Quick.pdf.

[126] Most Parliamentary Select Committees shadow the different government departments and agencies.

Commissioners who have the resources to investigate concerns.[127] This, in turn, impacts on the questions that the Committee will ask individuals and the outcome of any eventual report. Whilst Committees have the power to require the attendance of persons or the delivery of documents, these powers are arguably limited. Committees will be unable to request documents if they are unaware of their existence. The process is further constrained by issues with the general access to official information. The Freedom of Information Act 2000 contains numerous exemptions and government departments have a poor history at replying to requests within required timeframes.[128] During any evidence gathering process, a Committee and the civil servants appearing before them must grapple with the 'Osmotherly Rules'.[129] Officials are required to give evidence on behalf of Ministers who will ordinarily select which civil servants should appear. Where civil servants are summoned to appear, the Minster will determine what course of action to take. The rules were used as a screen to prevent former civil servants from testifying before the Treasury and Industry Committee, regarding the 'Supergun' affair. An inquiry was called after Customs and Excise officials alleged that the Matrix Church- ill Company had breached export regulations after exporting machine tools to Iraq for use in the construction of a 'supergun'.[130] Civil servants can provide valuable information to Committees and thus considerably enhance democratic accountability. To do so would identify loyalty to the extramural community, however such actions are likely to breach duties owed to the intramural community. The Civil Service Code requires civil servants to be impartial; disclosures to a parliamentary Committee place civil servants at risk of breaching the Civil Service Code as well running contrary to the spirit of the Osmotherly Rules.

---

[127] In contrast the Intelligence and Security Committee has access to investigators.

[128] For example, the Information Commissioner has had to monitor several central government departments to ensure compliance with the legislation; see further Information Commissioner, *Central Government Sector Monitoring Report* (2009), available at https://ico.org.uk/media/2795/central-government-sector-monitoring-report.pdf.

[129] For the latest guidance see Cabinet Office, *Giving Evidence to Select Committees: Guidance for Civil Servants* (2014), available at www.gov.uk/government/uploads/system/uploads/attachment_data/file/364600/Osmotherly_Rules_October_2014.pdf.

[130] Trade and Industry Select Committee, *Exports to Iraq: Project Babylon and Long-range Guns*, HC-86 (1991).

Select Committees and protection

Civil servants are be protected by parliamentary privilege if they provide oral evidence to a Committee. Civil servants may also be protected if they provide a written disclosure to a Committee, provided that it is accepted as evidence to an inquiry. Parliamentary privilege does not, however, prevent the mistreatment of civil servants by their departments or agencies. The Public Accounts Committee, for example, expressed their frustration at the treatment of whistleblowers Osita Mba and David Owen after they had raised concerns to that Committee. As identified above, Members of Parliament are now covered by PIDA 1998, section 43F. Therefore, civil servants could raise concerns to Select Committees and enjoy protection under section 43F, provided that the disclosure would be covered by the remit of other prescribed persons. Civil servants would not be able to raise matters regarding public policy and be protected by section 43F unless those matters fall within the prescribed remit of other prescribed persons. Public policy concerns may be raised if a civil servant can prove that they were the result of a breach of the Civil Service Code and could be protected by PIDA 1998, section 43G or 43H. However, the civil servant would breach the Code in making any disclosure. Parliamentary privilege does not protect civil servants from administrative action.

Scope for Reform

In order to afford civil servants the full opportunity to raise concerns to Members of Parliament and Select Committees, it is submitted that an additional prescribed remit entitled 'matters concerning the Civil Service Code' would need to be added to a new Public Interest Disclosure Act (Prescription) Order. An alternative, albeit more limited in scope, would be to prescribe 'a Chairman of a Select Committee of Parliament'. In written evidence to the PASC, Public Concern at Work suggested that the chairman of an appropriate Select Committee, such as the PASC, should be made a prescribed person under PIDA 1998, section 43F.[131] The PASC also recommended that a civil servant should be allowed to go directly to the PASC as a last resort.[132] In addition to the aforementioned recommendations, guidance should be issued and training provided to

---

[131] Public Concern at Work, Evidence to Inquiry on Leaks and Whistle-blowing in Whitehall, available at http://www.pcaw.co.uk/policy/policy_pdfs/PASCWBinWhitehallPCAWJan09.pdf.

[132] See www.publications.parliament.uk/pa/cm200809/cmselect/cmpubadm/83/83.pdf at [36].

MPs in order that they are fully aware of their role as a prescribed person. The Civil Service Management Code and Civil Service Code need to be updated to reflect that civil servants can now raise concerns to MPs. In turn, it is suggested that there should also be an update to the Osmotherly Rules guidance to allow for circumstances where in the course of giving evidence civil servants need to depart from the ministerial line in order to disclose instances of wrongdoing. Thought should also be given as to whether Parliament is suited to handing any disclosures of national security information. It is suggested that it is not. Consideration should therefore be given to the introduction of a security cleared Secretariat based in Parliament, or at least for a scoping exercise to ensure adequate liaison between Parliament and Whitehall where disclosures are received, which respects parliamentary privilege but also respects national security.[133] The next section of this chapter will consider public inquiries.

Public Inquiries

In the United Kingdom, some, if not all, of the most important investigations into executive malpractice over the last 25 years have involved either a leak of information or the involvement of a whistleblower.[134] The Government will decide whether or not to hold an inquiry, the terms of reference of the inquiry and whether it should be held under the Inquiries Act 2005 or on an 'ad hoc' basis, meaning that the Inquiry will not be subject to the legislative framework provided by the 2005 Act. Whether the Minister appoints a chairperson with a judicial background or a person of standing, for example, a privy counsellor, will often shape how the inquiry is set up and ultimately the protections afforded to Crown servants (in the Civil Service, security and intelligence services, Armed Forces or police) who provide evidence and appear as witnesses. The Public Administration Select Committee identified that ad hoc inquiries

---

[133] The Defence and Security Advisory Notice Committee provides an example whereby the media can seek advice on whether information, if published, could harm national security. See www.dsma.uk/.

[134] For example, Matrix Churchill employee in *Report of the Inquiry into the Export of Defence Equipment and Dual-Use Goods to Iraq and Related Prosecutions,* HC 1-15 (1996); Dr David Kelly (the subject of the inquiry); Dr Brian Jones, *Report of the Inquiry into the Circumstances of the Death of Dr David Kelly C.M.G.,* HC-247 (2004); Elizabeth Wilmshurst, Iraq Inquiry (ongoing at the time of writing), available at www.iraqinquiry.org.uk/media/44211/20100126pm-wilmshurst-final.pdf; Kay Sheldon, *Report of the Mid Staffordshire NHS Foundation Trust Public Inquiry,* HC 898-1 (2013).

had a tendency to be used 'mainly where Government or public bodies are under investigation'.[135]

In order to facilitate and encourage the giving of evidence at a public inquiry, several measures may be put in place. Inquiries Act 2005, section 37(1)(c), provides those engaged to provide assistance to the Committee with immunity from suit provided that such evidence is given in good faith. Further to this, an individual is protected from subsequent actions in defamation for 'any statement made in or for the purposes of proceedings before an inquiry and reports of proceedings before an inquiry' as would be 'the case if those proceedings were proceedings before a court in the relevant part of the United Kingdom'. Other measures available are not part of the Inquiries Act 2005, and in keeping with the nature of the inquiry process have been implemented on an ad hoc basis. Undertakings have been provided to safeguard against prosecution for unauthorised disclosures as well as for disciplinary action.

In the Scott Inquiry, the Government gave its 'lawful authority' to witnesses to disclose 'official information' to the Inquiry meaning that the 'normal constraints' imposed by the Official Secrets Acts were 'effectively suspended'. Such disclosure was dealt with by allowing hearings to go into closed session if the disclosure of information posed a risk to national security. Furthermore, in the 'interest of securing full and honest testimony' evidence given by witnesses would not be used in evidence in any subsequent prosecutions, this provision was afforded by the use of an undertaking given by the Attorney General.[136] The Cabinet Secretary also gave an assurance that any 'admissions made during testimony' before the Scott Inquiry would not be used in subsequent disciplinary proceedings against them. This assurance was facilitated by the sending of a letter to the heads of the Civil Service departments. The assurance contained two limitations. First, the Civil Service reserved the right to take disciplinary action against a civil servant if the evidence given before the inquiry 'turned out to be false' or 'incomplete'. Secondly, the exemption did not extend to information already available to the Government from sources other than witness testimony at the inquiry.

The question of whether a public inquiry should be provided with an undertaking to encourage witnesses to give full and frank testimony raises several considerations. It may be argued that an undertaking from

---

[135] Public Administration Select Committee, *Government by Inquiry,* HC 51-1 (2005) [185].

[136] Note that these arrangements are not superseded by the Inquiries Act 2005.

the Attorney General to give an assurance that evidence given before an inquiry will not be used in a subsequent prosecution is necessary in situations whereby the Crown servant as witness may disclose information protected by the Official Secrets Acts. The Government during the time of the Scott Inquiry dealt with the Official Secrets Act issue well by giving 'lawful authority', thereby authorising any disclosures of material normally protected by the Acts to the Inquiry.

The Hutton Inquiry provided a degree of protection for witnesses to speak freely. According to the Inquiry website, the inquiry was 'protected from any legal proceedings coming from information disclosed during the Inquiry, e.g. slander and libel, so long as publication of that material is consistent with the needs of the Inquiry'.[137] However, there is no information from either the Inquiry report or the available evidence on the Inquiry website that the Attorney General gave an undertaking that evidence given before the inquiry would not be used in any subsequent prosecutions. The Inquiry did state that witnesses should seek their own legal advice on legal protections required. In a similar way to the undertaking given to the Scott Inquiry, the Cabinet Secretary did provide Lord Hutton with an undertaking that civil servants would not be disciplined for information given in evidence before the inquiry.[138] An undertaking to safeguard against disciplinary action was considered at length by the Baha Mousa Inquiry, where the Inquiry Chairman drew a clear distinction between an undertaking to protect someone from disciplinary action if he gives evidence of his own misconduct and a person who gives evidence of someone else's misconduct.[139] Immunity for disciplinary action has also been afforded to serving officials and Armed Forces personnel by the Iraq Inquiry.[140]

---

[137] Hutton Inquiry, 'Frequently Asked Questions', available at www.the-hutton-inquiry.org.uk/content/faq.htm.

[138] Note also that the Cabinet Secretary provided a letter for disciplinary immunity in the Butler Review; interestingly, because the hearings were conducted in private this limited the potential risks of actions taken against witnesses; for a link to the letter see www.cabinetoffice.gov.uk/publications/reports/secletter/indem_let.pdf.

[139] See further Rt Hon. Sir William Gage, Rulings (First Direction Hearing) [4], available at www.bahamousainquiry.org/linkedfiles/baha_mousa/key_documents/rulings1.pdf.

[140] See further Iraq Inquiry, 'Frequently Asked Questions', available at www.iraqinquiry.org.uk/faq.aspx#H12.

Scope for Reform

The aforementioned discussion identifies that the piecemeal nature of ad hoc inquiries, in particular, has resulted in different approaches being taken by Inquiry chairpersons. It is submitted that regardless of whether a public inquiry is ad hoc or conducted under the Inquiries Act 2005, there should be a consistent approach to ensure that civil servants who provide evidence and appear before inquiries are protected. Inquiries conducted under the Inquiries Act 2005 allow for immunity from suit but do not provide protection from prosecution for offences under the Official Secrets Acts. There is no provision under the 2005 Act to protect individuals from detrimental treatment or dismissal for providing evidence or appearing as witnesses before an inquiry. Ad hoc inquiries are reliant upon the Inquiry chairperson to seek undertakings from the government to ensure that protections are put in place. This is problematical as, first, the background of chairpersons has varied; some but not all Inquiry chairpersons have come from judicial backgrounds and so the way in which inquiry protocols have been handled has also varied. Second is the issue of time: the Independent Inquiry into Child Sexual Abuse did not receive a written undertaking to protect against prosecution for the Official Secrets Act 1989 until a number of former officials and police officers had expressed concerns to the media that they felt at risk of prosecution if they spoke out. Members of Parliament then lobbied the government to provide immunity.[141] Although it is acknowledged that the Inquiry had difficulties due to the appointment of the chairperson, the Inquiry had begun its preparatory work over a number of months before the new chairperson was put in place and before the undertaking was received. At the time of writing, the Inquiry was yet to state that it had received an undertaking with regard to immunity from disciplinary action.

It is submitted that protections against prosecution and detriment and/or dismissal should be implemented from the outset. One option could be to add a new section in the Inquiries Act 2005 to protect civil servants and other Crown servants from disciplinary action or prosecution for unauthorised disclosures if made to an inquiry and to make the section applicable to all inquiries whether conducted on an ad hoc basis

---

[141]   Child Abuse and the Official Secrets Act 1989, Early Day Motion 38, 27 May 2015, available at www.parliament.uk/edm/2015-16/38.

or under the Act. Another option could be to deal with the disciplinary/dismissal protection by amending the Civil Service Management Code to include a protection for civil servants. Immunity from prosecution under the Official Secrets Act 1989 could be dealt with by making any disclosures to a public inquiry 'authorised' under section 7 of the Act. This authorisation would need a new Official Secrets Act (Prescription) Order and could be worded as authorising disclosures to 'a person appointed by a Secretary of State for the purposes of conducting a public inquiry'.

IV CONCLUSION

This chapter has identified that the treatment of authorised whistleblowing in the Civil Service needs to improve. The Civil Service Code currently places a disproportionate restriction on freedom of expression rights because it requires civil servants to seek authorisation before going to the media and because an individual could still breach the Code and be disciplined and dismissed even if disclosures would be protected by Article 10 ECHR and by PIDA 1998. Most notably, the empirical analysis in this chapter has identified that the majority of whistleblowing concerns raised are 'ordinary' watchdog-type concerns. Yet, the drafting of the Civil Service Code, aimed at maintaining impartiality and thus restricting protest speech, is likely to act as an inhibitor to the expression of these concerns where disclosures are raised to Members of Parliament or Select Committees. The Civil Service Code also needs to be more explicit to be fully in line with PIDA 1998.

There is a considerable variation in how Civil Service departments and agencies deal with concerns raised under the Code. As a consequence, a civil servant working in one department could experience a very different outcome to one working within another. It is also difficult to fully gauge the effectiveness of line management in handling whistleblowing concerns when many departments and agencies are not actively tracking and monitoring concerns across their organisation. Central co-ordination together with agreed baseline standards for handling, tracking and monitoring concerns should be applicable to all organisations regardless of size. The Civil Service Code and procedures place too much emphasis on official mechanisms working effectively. A civil servant has little option but to utilise the official channels; if those mechanisms are ineffective and if a civil servant is unable to obtain the support of the Civil Service Commission to investigate they will be forced to resign. In this context, some individuals may find the making of an unauthorised disclosure to a newspaper or online disclosure outlet a more effective method to obtain accountability, placing themselves at risk of prosecution and/or dismissal in the process.

6. Whistleblowing in the security and intelligence services

The Snowden revelations identified the extent to which the security and intelligence services are actively engaged in the interception of communications to counter a multitude of threats against the United Kingdom.[1] They also appear to identify that the agencies are operating on the very edges of what is necessary and proportionate to achieve this aim. Following the disclosures, Snowden was accused of causing significant damage to the capability of intelligence agencies to counter the threat posed by terrorism.[2] However, findings of subsequent inquiries by the Intelligence and Security Committee, the Interception of Communications Commissioner and the Independent Reviewer on Counter-terrorism Legislation have contributed to the drafting of a comprehensive new Investigatory Powers Bill.[3] Executive control of the security and intelligence services must rest with the executive and therefore it is essential that these services are under democratic control by elected politicians, who are the 'viable custodians of public office in a democracy'.[4] Ministers cannot be held to account without an effective oversight

---

[1] For background, see generally Luke Harding, *The Snowden Files: The Inside Story of the World's Most Wanted Man* (Guardian Books, 2014) and Glenn Greenwald, *No Place to Hide: The NSA and the Surveillance State* (Hamish Hamilton, 2014).

[2] See e.g., comments by Sir John Sawyers, Chief of SIS, to the Intelligence and Security Committee: 'the leaks from Snowden have been very damaging. They have put our operations at risk. It is clear that our adversaries are rubbing their hands with glee'. (Uncorrected transcript of evidence, 7 November 2013).

[3] Intelligence and Security Committee, *Privacy and Security: A Modern and Transparent Legal Framework*, HC-1075 (2015); Interception of Communications Commissioner, *Annual Report*, HC-1184 (2013). David Anderson QC, *A Question of Trust: Report of the Investigatory Powers Review*, ID 20051503 (2015).

[4] Hans Born and Ian Leigh, *Making Intelligence Accountable: Legal Standards and Best Practice for Oversight of the Intelligence Agencies* (Publishing House of the Parliament of Norway, 2005) 55.

regime. Whistleblowers can play a valuable role in supporting oversight bodies in this work.

Another consequence of the Snowden disclosures is that the directors of the agencies are now increasingly required to justify their activities in an open media forum and are more actively drawn into the political sphere.[5] Whilst the increase in externally facing activities can be seen as beneficial, contributing to a new era of openness, it can also lead to negative consequences. An agency which is required to constantly justify the value of its work to support executive policies will arguably lose independence.[6] It also identifies that the Directors of agencies and 'Whitehall sources' are afforded a platform whilst individuals working in those agencies are denied a voice.[7] Members of the public are denied the

---

[5] For example, Andrew Parker, the head of MI5 gave the first live radio interview of a serving Director General to justify electronic surveillance. See further 'MI5 boss warns of technology terror risk', BBC News, 17 December 2015, available at http://www.bbc.co.uk/news/uk-34276525. Following the Snowden revelations Parker was summoned to appear before a closed session of the Home Affairs Committee. See further, Patrick Wintour 'MPs ask MI5 boss to justify claim that NSA leaks endangered national security', *Guardian*, 3 December 2013.

[6] Justification of value is distinct from being accountable for activities. Leigh argues that 'with exposure comes the significant risk of politicising security and the presentation of intelligence'; see Ian Leigh, 'Changing the Rules of the Game: Some Necessary Reforms to United Kingdom Intelligence' (2009) 35(4) *Review of International Studies* 952. Glees and Davies also consider the impact of politicisation in Anthony Glees and Philip H.J. Davies, *Spinning the Spies: Intelligence, Open Government and the Hutton Inquiry* (Social Affairs Unit, 2004).

[7] The Director of the Security Service, Andrew Parker appeared on Radio 4: see www.mi5.gov.uk/home/news/news-by-category/speeches-and-statements/mi5-today-and-our-challenges-tomorrow.html. He later delivered the Lord Mayor's Defence and Security Lecture which was well timed to coincide with the Government's publication of the Investigatory Powers Bill, available at www.mi5.gov.uk/home/about-us/who-we-are/staff-and-management/director-general/speeches-by-the-director-general/a-modern-mi5.html. The UK government suspended flights to and from Britain following allegations that the downing of a Russian passenger plane had been a terrorist act; reports emerged in the UK press that the assessment had been made based upon intelligence obtained by analysis of communications data. In the same week the government introduced the Investigatory Powers Bill. See e.g., Tom Whiteford *et al.*, '"Chatter" led to Cameron's conclusion on jet disaster', *Telegraph*, 6 November 2015. Hastedt discusses the concept of 'voice' in Glenn Hastedt, 'An INS Special Forum: Implications of the Snowden Leaks' (2014) 29(6) *Intelligence and National Security* 798.

opportunity to test the veracity of these messages, further compounding the need for an effective oversight regime.[8] Despite the apparent value of whistleblowers in assisting oversight, the United Kingdom appears reluctant to provide employment protection for national security whistleblowers and to offer a controlled route to disclose concerns to the oversight bodies.[9] The United Kingdom is also currently lagging behind other jurisdictions where there are laws to protect whistleblowers working for intelligence agencies.[10] It is not suggested that authorised disclosure routes can prevent unauthorised leaking but there is an argument to suggest that they can contribute to their reduction. However, the authorised mechanisms must be considered a viable alternative.[11]

The purpose of this chapter is to provide an insight into the accountability mechanism provided to employees of the security and intelligence services to raise concerns. It will consider whether the oversight bodies, namely, the Commissioners that oversee the work of the agencies and the Intelligence and Security Committee (ISC), can receive whistleblowing concerns. It will consider whether employment protection for whistleblowing could be provided to employees, and will propose reforms.

I AUTHORISED MECHANISMS TO RAISE CONCERNS

Currently, there is limited publically available information on the authorised disclosure mechanisms available to employees of the agencies.[12] The

---

[8] As Neocleous identifies, society lacks its own 'spying machine', see Mark Neocleous, 'Privacy, Secrecy, Idiocy' (2002) 69 *Social Research* 86. The agencies and the executive are further able to apply the 'neither confirm or deny' policy.

[9] Whistleblowers are exempt from the PIDA 1998. The Intelligence and Security Committee considered the recommendations of whistleblowers raising concerns to them but did not take this further, see ISC, above n. 3, 80.

[10] See e.g., Public Interest Disclosure Act 2013 (Australia).

[11] Following *Bucur and Toma* v. *Romania*, Application No. 40238/02 (ECtHR, 2008), the ECtHR is likely to consider whether the alternative means of raising the concern were effective. For a comparative example see NSA employee Thomas Drake. Drake attempted to raise concerns using official channels and then took his concerns to a newspaper. For discussion, see Ashley Savage, 'Wikileaks and Whistleblowers: The Need for a New Legal Focus', *JURIST—Forum*, 28 June 2011, available at http://jurist.org/forum/2011/06/ashley-savage-whistleblowing.php.

[12] This should be contrasted to the position in Australia where information on the Public Interest Disclosure scheme is accessible. Moreover, in the United States, the Executive Director of Intelligence Community Whistleblowing and

Court of Appeal and House of Lords judgments in *Shayler* arguably provide the best source of information.[13] Lord Bingham identified that concerns relating to the work of the service could be reported to the independent staff counsellor. Concerns about the legality of what the service had done could be disclosed to the Attorney General, the Director of Public Prosecutions or the Commissioner of the Metropolitan Police. He emphasised that all three officers were 'subject to a clear duty, in the public interest, to uphold the law, investigate alleged infractions and prosecute where offences appear to have been committed, irrespective of any party affiliation or service loyalty'.[14]

The Attorney General and the Commissioner of the Metropolitan Police are both expressly mentioned as authorised persons to receive disclosures in the Official Secrets Act 1989.[15] It also makes sense to include the Attorney General on the list because his consent is required for prosecutions under the Official Secrets Act 1989.[16] Concerns about misbehaviour, irregularity, maladministration, waste of resources or incompetence could be referred to the Home Secretary, the Foreign Secretary, the Secretaries of State for Northern Ireland or Scotland, the Prime Minister, the Secretary to the Cabinet or the Joint Intelligence Committee, staff of the comptroller and Auditor General, the National Audit Office and the Parliamentary Commissioner for Administration.[17] The Parliamentary Commissioner for Administration, or Ombudsman as she is better known, has an extensive remit to investigate government departments but one which expressly excludes investigations relating to national security matters.[18] With regard to the Joint Intelligence Committee, several members of the security and intelligence services raised concerns as to the intelligence dossier used to justify invasion into Iraq, yet these concerns were not dealt with.[19]

Source Protection of the Office of Inspector General of the Intelligence Community, Dan Mayer, published a lengthy academic article detailing the scheme: Dan Meyer and David Berenbaum, 'The Wasp's Nest: Intelligence Community Whistleblowing and Source Protection' (2015) 8(1) *Journal of National Security Law and Policy* 1, available at http://jnslp.com/wp-content/uploads/2015/05/The-Wasp's-Nest.pdf.

[13] *R* v. *Shayler* [2001] EWCA Crim 1977; *R* v. *Shayler* [2002] UKHL 11.
[14] *R* v. *Shayler* [2002] UKHL 11, [27].
[15] Official Secrets Act 1989, s.7; Official Secrets Act (Prescription Order) 1990, SI 1990/200.
[16] Official Secrets Act 1989, s.9.
[17] *Shayler*, above n. 14, [36].
[18] Parliamentary Commissioner for Administration Act 1967, Sch. 3.
[19] Considered further below.

Lord Bingham refers to the Official Secrets Act 1989 (Prescription) Order 1990, SI 1990/200. This identifies that disclosures to the aforementioned persons and organisations would be authorised. What is most unclear is whether or not any of the above persons would have dealt with Shayler's concerns if he had approached them. Reports did suggest that Shayler's claims regarding the alleged plot to assassinate Colonel Gaddafi were being investigated, however, it would appear that no further action was taken.[20] Two distinctions can be made between Shayler, who had left the security service at the time he made the allegations, and a serving officer. Shayler's allegations drew the attention of the police following his unauthorised disclosures, rather than because he had attempted to raise concerns to the police or one of the aforementioned bodies.[21]

There appears to be no publically available information to suggest that the agencies support disclosures by staff to the above suggested routes. Thus a distinction should be made between the viability to raise concerns using one of the suggested routes whilst employed and whether the individual will be subjected to employment detriment or dismissal for doing so, and concerns raised once the individual has left. Current agency personnel do not have access to the Public Interest Disclosure Act (PIDA) 1998, therefore, whilst they may not be prosecuted for raising concerns staff may be dissuaded from doing so because of the lack of employment protection. Shayler was arguably less constrained as he had already left the organisation. Discussion will now proceed to consider the role of the Staff Counsellor.

Staff Counsellor

The role of an independent staff counsellor was established in 1987. Margaret Thatcher, then Prime Minister, described the role to the Commons:

> He will be available to be consulted by any member of the security and intelligence services who has anxieties relating to the work of his or her service which it has not been possible to allay through the ordinary processes of management-staff relations. He will have access to all relevant documents

---

[20]   Richard Norton Taylor, 'Shayler returns as Yard investigates Gaddafi claims', *Guardian*, 21 August 2000, available at www.theguardian.com/uk/2000/aug/21/davidshayler.richardnortontaylor.

[21]   Based on the determination of the facts by the House of Lords in the *Shayler* judgment, above n. 14, [3].

and to any level of management in each service. He will be able to make recommendations to the head of the service concerned. He will also have access to the Secretary of the Cabinet if he wishes and will have the right to make recommendations to him. He will report as appropriate to the heads of the services and will report not less frequently than once a year to me and to my Right Hon. friends the Foreign and Commonwealth Secretary and the Home Secretary as appropriate on his activities and on the working of the system.[22]

Historically there have been difficulties in assessing the precise role of the Staff Counsellor. The Staff Counsellor was originally introduced following the case of Michael Bettaney a former MI5 operative, who was arrested whilst attempting to offer secrets to Russian agents. Bettaney had been reportedly suffering from a drinking problem which was known to his superiors. The *Independent* reported that operatives of the security and intelligence services who were found to be spying for the other side often suffered from emotional problems.[23] The resulting appointee as Counsellor, Sir Philip Woodfield, was described by some newspapers as an 'agony uncle'[24] and by others as an 'ombudsman'.[25] It soon became clear that the role and jurisdiction of the Staff Counsellor had extended beyond the remit outlined by Thatcher. In the first few months of Sir Philip Woodfield's new role he was asked by a former MI6 officer, Anthony Cavendish, to appeal on his behalf after the Secret Intelligence Service blocked the publication of his memoirs – Sir Philip refused.[26] In 1991, the Staff Counsellor was asked to conduct a review into the detention of 91 Iraqi and Palestinian nationals during the Gulf War, and after exonerating the involvement of MI5 received criticism as a result.[27] In 1998, following the Shayler revelations, the ISC took evidence from Sir Christopher France, the Staff Counsellor at the time. Sir Christopher and his predecessors had handled approximately 149 cases since 1987.[28] The ISC also identified that the Counsellor's role had been widened to

---

[22]   Hansard, HC Debs, vol. 121, col. 512, 2 November 1987, written answers.

[23]   *Report of the Security Commission on the Case of Michael John Bettaney*, Cmnd 9514 (1985).

[24]   See 'Sir Philip Woodfield: Obituary', *The Times*, 19 October 2000.

[25]   Anon, 'Spies set to reveal own secrets to Ombudsman', *Sunday Times*, 1 November 1987.

[26]   Ben Penrose, 'How "Uncle" refused to help Cavendish', *Sunday Times*, 3 January 1988.

[27]   Nick Cohen, 'MI5 cleared over innocent Gulf War detainees', *Guardian*, 16 December 1991.

[28]   Intelligence and Security Committee, *Annual Report*, Cm 4073 (1997–98) [36].

deal with 'the whole range of management issues' as well as grievances from former employees.[29]

In 2002, the Staff Counsellor, then Sir John Chilcot, was asked to conduct a review into the theft of information relating to the identities and home addresses of police officers and informants from a Northern Ireland police station. The appointment of Sir John to review the matter was criticised by the Deputy Chairman of the Northern Ireland Policing Board who questioned his independence.[30]

In the book, *Spies, Lies and Whistleblowers*, Annie Machon, former MI5 officer and then girlfriend of David Shayler, justified why Shayler did not raise his concerns with the independent Staff Counsellor by suggesting that the Counsellor was 'seen as a joke amongst MI5 staff' and had 'no remit to investigate allegations of criminal activity'.[31] During the *Shayler* case another former employee of the security service chose to speak out. Jestyn Thirkell-White was reported to have backed many of Shayler's allegations and expressed that he had no confidence in the Staff Counsellor because he was 'required to inform the personnel department' if he had seen the counsellor and had 'little trust in the role'.[32] Former GCHQ employee Katherine Gun stated that she chose not to approach the Staff Counsellor before leaking documents to the *Guardian* because she felt that the matter was 'so urgent it needed direct action' and that she believed that the person would 'probably say "well, we appreciate your concerns, we'll take it into consideration and perhaps we should meet in a week or so" [which] was not going to be adequate'.[33] Without further information as to the work carried out by the Staff Counsellor it is impossible to carry out a thorough analysis of the role.[34] Where criticisms have been identified these have originated from individuals who have spoken out publicly to raise concerns and criticise the agencies. On some occasions, the Staff Counsellor has been required to conduct a

---

[29]   *Ibid.*

[30]   Anon, 'Cameras fail to catch raiders', *The People*, 24 March 2002. Sir John Chilcot had experience as former Permanent Secretary to Northern Ireland yet it was his role as Staff Counsellor which meant that he was considered 'too close to MI5'.

[31]   Annie Machon, *Spies, Lies and Whistleblowers* (Book Guild, 2005) 109.

[32]   Mark Hollingsworth, 'Opening the floodgates: when Jestyn Thirkell-White broke cover, he ruined MI5's strategy for dealing with David Shayler', *Guardian*, 25 July 2000.

[33]   Anon, 'GCHQ: it was full of people like me', *Gloucester Echo*, 27 October 2004.

[34]   Note that information relating to the security and intelligence services is exempt under Freedom of Information Act 2000, s.23.

role similar to an inspector general, on other occasions it would appear that the Counsellor is required to deal with personal grievance and management issues. It is not clear whether the agencies adopt separate policies for whistleblowing and grievance issues. However, to conflate the two would appear to be contrary to the British Standards Institute Code of Practice on Whistleblowing.[35] If the Counsellor is also performing an 'agony uncle' role, this may also dissuade individuals from raising concerns regarding wrongdoing on the basis that they may not be taken seriously. Conversely, it may be argued that the Staff Counsellor offers the opportunity for employees of the agencies to engage in acts of 'protest whistleblowing' which may otherwise not be considered within the scope of whistleblowing policies which contain explanations or definitions of wrongdoing which are based on PIDA 1998, section 43B.[36]

Ethical Counsellor

The Intelligence and Security Committee's Annual Report 2007–08 identified that the security service had established an 'Ethical Counsellor'.[37] The report explains that the post was established in 2006 to 'provide staff with an internal avenue to raise any ethical concerns they may have about the Service's work with someone who is outside their management line'.[38] The report details that around 12 individuals had approached the Ethical Counsellor since the post was established. Following the report, the ISC is yet to provide information on the current numbers of individuals approaching the Counsellor or to provide any form of audit and review. The report identified that the 'Ethical Counsellor' was a post held by 'a former Deputy Director General of the Service'.[39] It is not clear whether the individual concerned is still in post. However, it may be suggested that even though the person is outside of the management chain, individuals may be dissuaded from raising concerns for fear that the person is too close to management. In effect it would appear that the Ethical Counsellor is performing the role of a departmental nominated officer, the equivalent position in the Civil Service.

---

[35]   British Standards Institute, *Whistleblowing Arrangements: Code of Practice*, PAS 2008/1998, [0.5].
[36]   Considered further below.
[37]   Intelligence and Security Committee, *Annual Report*, Cm 7542 (2007–08) [66].
[38]   *Ibid.*
[39]   *Ibid.*

Defence Intelligence Staff

With regard to the Defence Intelligence Staff (DIS), the Personnel Director and the Director General Civilian Personnel act as counsellors for individuals to raise concerns. The Butler Report had recommended that the remit of the Independent Staff Counsellor should be extended to include DIS staff on the basis that a number of individuals had attempted to raise concerns regarding the intelligence assessments which led to the invasion in Iraq.[40] The Government justified provision of both Directors as counsellors on the basis that DIS is part of the Ministry of Defence.[41] The ISC welcomed the appointments; however in doing so, they failed to acknowledge that the Independent Staff Counsellor is independent of the three agencies and therefore has greater independence from the agencies than an internally appointed person.[42] This arguably places DIS staff at a disadvantage to staff in the intelligence agencies who have access to the Independent Staff Counsellor. The ISC made clear in its 1997–98 Annual Report that the Staff Counsellor had 'an important role in helping to resolve staff problems once internal procedures have been fully exhausted'.

It is impossible to provide detailed analysis as to how the arrangements are working based on the available information. Moreover, the ISC does not appear to take evidence on how the arrangements are working in practice.[43] In contrast to the UK Independent Staff Counsellor, the Inspector General for Intelligence and Security (IGIS) (Australia) is tasked to receive and investigate whistleblowing concerns under the Public Interest Disclosure Act 2013 (Australia) scheme. In addition, the IGIS has oversight of the agencies' internal PID schemes. The IGIS produces a publically available Annual Report. The 2014–15 Annual

---

[40] Committee of Privy Counsellors, *Review of Intelligence on Weapons of Mass Destruction*, HC-898 (2004) [566].

[41] HM Government, *Review of Intelligence of Weapons of Mass Destruction*, Cm 6492 (2005).

[42] Intelligence and Security Committee, *Annual Report*, Cm 6864 (2005–06) [21] and was discussed briefly in the following report a year later: Intelligence and Security Committee, *Annual Report*, Cm 7299 (2006–07) [84].

[43] Following debate on the Intelligence and Security Committee's Annual Report, Tom Brake MP suggested it would be useful for Parliament to be provided with more information as to the work of the Ethical Counsellor: Hansard, HC Debs, vol. 492, col. 408, 7 May 2009.

Report details the investigation of four PID concerns.[44] This section will now proceed to consider external oversight.

II EXTERNAL OVERSIGHT

Oversight of the agencies is carried out by the Interception of Communications Commissioner's Office (IOCCO), the Intelligence Services Commissioner (ISComm) and the ISC. The IOCCO has responsibility for Part I of the Regulation of Investigatory Powers Act (RIPA) 2000, which includes the mandate to review warrant authorisations and the agencies' acquiring and disclosure of communications data.[45] The ISComm reviews the warrants in relation to interference with property, electronic surveillance, covert human intelligence sources and the required disclosure of encrypted data. Complaints may also be made to the Interception of Communications Tribunal (IPT).

Whilst there would appear to be no publically available information as to whether agency staff could approach the Commissioners, the Official Secrets Act 1989 and the various Prescription Orders do not list the Commissioners as recipients where disclosures would be authorised.[46] Staff may technically be in breach of the Official Secrets Act 1989, in particular section 1 which relates to intelligence and security information, and section 4 which relates to criminal investigations and covers the issue of interception warrants. In addition, RIPA 2000, section 19 makes it an offence to disclose information concerning interception warrants. Both Acts contain possible defences which could be utilised by staff who raise concerns. Section 7(4) of the 1989 Act contains a defence where the individual can prove that at the time of the disclosure he/she 'had lawful authority to make the disclosure in question and no reasonable cause to believe otherwise'. Section 19(9) provides a defence for individuals where disclosure of information concerning the warrant is confined to the Interception of Communications Commissioner only. Therefore, staff

---

[44]   Inspector General Intelligence and Security, *Annual Report*, ISSN: 1030-4657 (2015) [16].

[45]   Responsibilities of the IOCCO principally concern RIPA 2000, ss.7–11 and ss.15–16. For discussion, see further Peter Gill, 'The Intelligence and Security Committee and the Challenge of Networks' (2009) 35(4) *Review of International Studies* 930, 931 and Anderson, above n. 3, [6.100].

[46]   Lord Justice Woolf suggested in the Court of Appeal judgment of *Shayler* that concerns could have been raised to the predecessors of the current Commissioners. The legality of this route was not tested: *R* v. *Shayler* [2001] EWCA Crim 1977, [38].

would need to ensure that in raising a concern they disclosed to the IOCCO only; a disclosure to the ISC would not be protected by section 54. However, it should also be noted that the Commissioners themselves are prevented from disclosing information concerning warrants under section 19. Therefore, whilst they could be informed of issues, they may be unable to publically report on matters concerning warrants.[47] In evidence to the Home Affairs Select Committee, Sir Anthony May, the Interception of Communications Commissioner appeared to confirm this position in stating that: 'Under the legislation, there is no clear indication that someone who was troubled should come to me'.[48] An individual could attempt to make a complaint to the Investigatory Powers Tribunal as a disclosure to the tribunal is authorised.[49] However, the complainant must be the person 'aggrieved by any conduct' done by the agencies and so cannot complain of wrongdoing which has affected others.[50] This section will now proceed to consider the Intelligence and Security Committee.

Intelligence and Security Committee

The ISC was established by the Intelligence and Security Act 1994.[51] The Committee's oversight powers were strengthened by the Justice and Security Act 2013 when it became a Committee of Parliament. It comprises of nine Parliamentarians drawn from both Houses of Parliament. The members are chosen by the Prime Minister with the agreement of the leaders of the two main opposition parties. Members of the ISC are notified under the Official Secrets Act 1989 and have access to highly classified material.[52] The ISC also has a small Secretariat staffed by civil servants.[53]

---

[47] The IOCCO identified the difficulties caused by this for oversight. See generally, IOCCO, 'Evidence for the Investigatory Powers Review', 5 December 2014, available at http://iocco-uk.info/docs/2014-12-5(2)%20IOCCO%20Evidence%20for%20the%20Investigatory%20Powers%20Review.pdf.

[48] Home Affairs Select Committee, *Counter-Terrorism*, HC-231 (2013–14) Q.682.

[49] Official Secrets Act 1989 (Prescription) (Amendment) Order 2003, SI 2003/1918, Sch. 2.

[50] RIPA 2000, s.65(4).

[51] Intelligence and Security Act 1994, s.10(1).

[52] Official Secrets Act 1989, s.1(1)(b) and (6).

[53] See generally Intelligence and Security Committee, *Annual Report*, HC-794 (2013–14) 5.

Prior to the 2013 reforms, the ISC was able to expand its remit beyond the scope of the Intelligence and Security Act 1994. This has been due, in part, to the development of trust between the agencies and the Committee.[54] The Committee's work, despite the lack of legal powers (prior to 2013) would suggest that it has been relatively effective.[55] As Phythian identifies, the Committee was able to look into operational matters concerning Kosovo, weapons of mass destruction (WMD) proliferation and the Mitrokhin affair.[56] The Committee has been the subject of criticism; writing in 2009, Gill noted that 'there was no substantial reference to human rights in any report of its first ten years'.[57]

The Committee did not look into the concerns raised by David Shayler, instead using the Annual Report as an opportunity to report on the internal arrangements for staff as well as to make recommendations for access to employment rights. The reluctance to engage in investigation of controversial matters may be due to the Committee's 'deliberate policy to adopt a sober, non-sensationalist approach to an issue which is often the subject of lurid speculation'.[58] The Committee took the same approach to Katherine Gun's allegations regarding the alleged interception of communications of UN member states voting on whether to take action against Iraq. The Committee expressed satisfaction, in a partially redacted paragraph, that the Attorney General's decision to drop criminal proceedings against Gun was not due to the illegality of the Iraq war.[59] However, it declined to investigate further. This analysis will now proceed to determine whether the ISC could receive concerns from agency staff.

Disclosures to the Intelligence and Security Committee
In the Court of Appeal and House of Lords judgments, it was suggested that Shayler could have raised his concerns with the ISC. However, the issue is one of authorisation. The disclosure must be authorised, at source, or by the recipient being prescribed as an authorised recipient

---

[54]   Gill, above n. 45, 931.
[55]   Ian Leigh, 'Accountability of Security and Intelligence in the United Kingdom' in Loch Johnson, Hans Born and Ian Leigh (eds), *Who's Watching the Spies?* (Potomac, 2005) 91–5.
[56]   Mark Phythian, 'The British Experience with Intelligence Accountability' (2007) 22(1) *Intelligence and National Security* 97.
[57]   Gill, above n. 45, 932.
[58]   Andrew Defty, 'Educating Parliamentarians about Intelligence: The Role of the British Intelligence and Security Committee' (2008) 61(4) *Parliamentary Affairs* 627.
[59]   Intelligence and Security Committee, *Annual Report*, Cm 6240 (2003–04).

under the Official Secrets Act 1989 or the various Prescription Orders. Despite its members and the Secretariat being notified and subject to Official Secrets Act 1989, section 1, the ISC is not prescribed for the purposes of authorisation. If an employee of the agencies made a disclosure to the Secretariat, members of the Secretariat would potentially be in breach of their own obligations under section 5 of the 1989 Act, by disclosing information entrusted in confidence to members of the Committee. The fact that both members of the Secretariat and the Committee have their own obligations under the 1989 Act is immaterial to the authorisation of disclosures made by a member of the security or intelligence services. Whilst it may appear highly unlikely that the Secretariat or members of the Committee would be charged under the Official Secrets Act 1989, this adds another limitation to the Committee as a route for the disclosure of concerns. In addition, the Committee would effectively need to receive the consent of the Prime Minister to publish the information in any reports or it would risk being in breach of section 1 of the 1989 Act. Further limitations may be identified with regard to the Committee's investigation of any concerns raised.

Investigatory capacity
Based on information from the ISC's Annual Reports it would appear that the ISC has lacked a consistent investigatory capacity and its use of an investigator has not been without difficulty. In 1999, the ISC appointed John Morrison who completed 14 reports before his contract was terminated in 2004 after he appeared on the BBC Panorama programme and criticised the 'misuse of intelligence' in the run up to the Iraq war. The agencies reportedly wrote to Sir David Omand, the Cabinet Office Security and Intelligence Coordinator, stating that they had 'lost trust' in Morrison and could 'no longer work with him'.[60] The 2013–14 Annual Report identifies that an investigator is currently in post.[61] However, despite the Committee's extended remit following the Justice and Security Act 2013, the ISC is still limited in what matters it can consider and investigate.

Section 2(3) of the 2013 Act identifies that the ISC may consider 'any particular operational matter' but the ISC and the Prime Minister must be satisfied that the matter is not part of any ongoing intelligence operation

---

[60] See 'No regrets for spy expert', BBC News, available at http://news.bbc.co.uk/1/hi/uk_politics/3965775.stm; see also Anthony Glees, Philip Davis and John Morrison, *The Open Side of Secrecy* (Social Affairs Unit, 2006) 45.
[61] See above, n. 54, 5.

and that it is 'of significant national interest'.[62] The Committee is therefore limited to a *post facto* review of events. This would possibly assist a former member of the agencies (the difficulties regarding the Official Secrets Acts aside) but would not assist a serving member of agency staff raising concerns about an operational matter. Further limitations concern access to information. Disclosure of requested documents can be refused by a Secretary of State on the basis that the information is sensitive; that it would not be in the interests of national security to disclose the information to the ISC; or if the information is such that if it were requested by a Departmental Select Committee the Secretary of State would not consider it proper to disclose the information.[63] Access to information concerning operational matters can only be provided in the circumstances described in section 2(3) above.[64] All of the above restrictions, if applied, can act as an inhibiter to oversight of the agencies.

More positively, Justice and Security Act 2013, schedule 1, 7(1) (which is given effect by section 1(7)) provides that evidence given by a person who is a witness before the ISC may not be used in any civil or disciplinary proceedings, unless the evidence was given in bad faith. Schedule 1, 7(2) provides that evidence given by a person who is a witness before the ISC may not be used against the person in any criminal proceedings, unless the evidence was given in bad faith. Therefore, if a member of staff from the agencies appeared as a witness as part of an inquiry before the ISC they could potentially obtain protection. They could also potentially use this avenue to raise concerns. By identifying to the Committee or its Secretariat that it had an issue of concern but without disclosing the substance of the concern, the Committee could arrange to take evidence from the individual, thus safeguarding the person from prosecution under the 2013 Act. However, as identified above, if the matter concerns an ongoing operational issue it is unlikely that the Committee, under the current framework, would be able to look into the matter further.

Schedule 1, 7 does open the possibility for a future whistleblowing mechanism. This is because, whilst being subject to the Justice and Security Act 2013, the Committee also has a memorandum of understanding with the agencies. The memorandum does not currently allow for the Committee to review ongoing operational matters. If this memorandum were to be reviewed and amended in the future, it would be possible for the Committee both to receive whistleblowing concerns and

---

[62] Justice and Security Act 2013, s.3(a)(i) and (ii).
[63] *Ibid.* s.4(4)(a).
[64] *Ibid.* s.4(1).

investigate, without significant amendment to the current legislative framework.[65] This recommendation would arguably offer whistleblowers in the security and intelligence services a better standard of protection against disciplinary action than that provided to individuals attempting to raise a concern with a Member of Parliament or Parliamentary Committee using PIDA 1998. This is because PIDA 1998 only offers protection to individuals post detriment or post dismissal. It would not, of course, safeguard against other detrimental treatment which may be encountered, such as the individual being side-lined for promotion or being demoted or re-assigned to punish the person for whistleblowing. The next section will consider employment protection for whistleblowing.

III EMPLOYMENT PROTECTION

Employment Rights Act (ERA) 1996, section 193, identifies that employees of the security service, the Secret Intelligence Service and Government Communications Headquarters do not have employment protection under PIDA 1998. Furthermore, the provisions under the Act do not have effect where there is a ministerial certificate in force which certifies that employment 'of a description specified in the certificate, or the employment of a particular person specified (or at a time specified in the certificate, was) required to be excepted from those provisions for the purpose of safeguarding national security'.[66] Effectively, this provision covers persons who may not work in the security and intelligence services but who are still involved in national security matters.

It should be noted that in any event PIDA 1998 is an employment law mechanism only. It provides no protection against prosecution for unauthorised disclosures, such as under the Official Secrets Act 1989 or the common law offence of misconduct in public office.[67] Moreover, if the worker commits a criminal offence in disclosing the information, the disclosure will not qualify for protection under the Act.[68] Therefore any prosecution for unauthorised disclosure brought under the Official

---

[65] It is suggested that the wording in *ibid.* s.2(3)(a)(i) 'is not part of any ongoing intelligence or security operation' could be repealed, together with the provision of improved access to documents.

[66] Employment Rights Act 1996, s.193.

[67] In contrast, Protected Disclosures Act 2014 (Ireland), ss. 14–15 and Protected Disclosures Act 2000 (New Zealand), s.18, both provide employment protection as well as protection from civil and criminal action.

[68] ERA 1996, s.43B(2).

Secrets Act 1989 would deny the Crown servant protection under PIDA 1998, and in any case it would be most likely that he would not have protection under the Act because of the exemptions in PIDA 1998, section 11 and ERA 1996, section 193.[69]

With regard to the offence of misconduct in public office, the provisions of PIDA 1998, section 43B(3) would preclude the Crown servant from protection under PIDA 1998 if they were prosecuted for such an offence. This situation is indicative of the particularly draconian nature of the offence. It is likely that a prosecution for misconduct in public office would be brought where the information leaked did not fall within the remit of the Official Secrets Act 1989. This means that any Crown servant not involved in national security matters (and thus not already exempted from PIDA 1998 protection) could still be prosecuted and would lose any protections under PIDA 1998 despite any public benefit arising from the disclosure. If a prosecution is brought for an offence committed under the Official Secrets Act 1989 or misconduct in public office, the employment tribunal would postpone the proceedings until the outcome of the trial. If the person is acquitted of the criminal charge, tribunal proceedings could then begin. If no proceedings have taken place, the employment tribunal may wish to consider whether the employee's conduct in making the disclosure amounted to a criminal offence. The employment tribunal should then assess the conduct against the same standard of proof as that used in criminal cases. This is again deeply problematic because of the 'catch all' nature of the misconduct offence.[70]

In the above paragraphs on PIDA 1998, it was stated that national security employees have no access to PIDA 1998 protection. Employees in the security and intelligence services were given the right to have

---

[69]   It should be noted here that if such a prosecution were unsuccessful the Crown servant would then be able to bring a PIDA 1998 claim provided that he was not subject to the exemptions listed in ERA 1996, s.193. Derek Pasquill is one such example. He was found not guilty of an offence under the Official Secrets Act 1989 and then chose to make a claim under PIDA 1998.

[70]   According to the view of Lord Nolan, Hansard, HL Debs, vol. 590, col. 614, 5 June 1998: 'If he has been prosecuted in a criminal court, questions of proof will proceed on ordinary lines. If the question arises in, say, an industrial tribunal, I believe the law to be that the offence would still have to be proved according to the standard appropriate for crime. That was certainly the view expressed by my noble and learned friend Lord Lane when he was Lord Chief Justice, and on a number of occasions by my noble and learned friend Lord Denning. It would be a rare and rash judge who would take a different view'.

employment disputes decided by an employment tribunal in 2001.[71] Despite this change, the exemption from PIDA 1998 remained. Currently, the tribunal procedures for national security employees are contained in Employment Tribunals (Constitution and Rules of Procedure) Regulations 2004, SI 2004/1861, Rule 54, Schedule 2. Rule 54 provides for a system of closed hearings whereby special advocates are used for parts of the hearing where evidence pertinent to national security is considered. Special advocates are chosen from a pool of advocates cleared for national security matters and have been most often used in proceedings of the Special Immigration Appeals Commission (SIAC). Because the employment tribunal register is not readily accessible to the public, there is little information as to how many times employment disputes regarding the security and intelligence services have gone to the employment tribunal.

The most readily accessible information on the relevant procedures comes from the Employment Appeals Tribunal judgment in *Farooq* v. *Commissioner of Police of the Metropolis*.[72] The case concerned a claim under the Race Relations Act 1976. The applicant was a police officer who was involved in diplomatic protection of the Prime Minister. The applicant failed security vetting and, as he was therefore not authorised to carry a firearm, he was required to transfer to other duties. The case was the first of its kind to involve the use of the new Rule 54 provisions. In *Home Office* v. *Tariq*, the applicant, an employee in the immigration department at the Home Office, lost his security clearance when members of his family were arrested after an alleged terrorist plot.[73] The claimant brought a claim for racial and religious discrimination before the employment tribunal and challenged the special advocate procedure. The Supreme Court held that the procedural safeguards were sufficient to achieve fairness in the instant case and were not in breach of European Convention on Human Rights (ECHR), Article 6. Chamberlin identifies that Article 6 rights may be waived provided that the waiver is voluntary.[74] On this basis, by voluntarily agreeing to a security vetting procedure he should have waived his right to sufficient disclosure in any

---

[71] ERA 1996, ss.191 and 193 (as amended).
[72] [2007] Appeal No. UKEAT/0542/07/DM. See also *Kiani* which concerned the alleged withdrawal of security clearance on discrimination grounds, *Kiani* v. *Home Office* [2014] Appeal No. UKEAT/0009/14/DM.
[73] *Home Office* v. *Tariq* [2011] UKSC 35.
[74] '*Al Rawi* v. *Security Service* and *Home Office* v. *Tariq*' (2011) 30(4) *Civil Justice Quarterly* 360.

proceedings to challenge the outcome of the process.[75] At a practical level, those employees who choose to undertake employment with the security and intelligence services must appreciate that the nature of their work requires careful handling if discussed before a tribunal, because employment tribunal judgments most often provide lengthy analysis of both working relationships and practices. Provided that there are sufficient procedural safeguards to support the claimant, the employment tribunal provides an adequate forum for agency staff to bring claims against the agencies and could be extended to allow for determination of whistleblowing claims.

IV SECURITY CLEARANCES

Staff in the intelligence agencies may lose their security clearance as a result of raising a whistleblowing concern. There is a high likelihood that the clearance will be lost if an individual makes an unauthorised disclosure and is arrested as a result. Revocation of security clearances can be used to punish whistleblowers, even if they don't make unauthorised disclosures.[76] In the United Kingdom, according to government guidelines, individuals may appeal any revocation of the clearance using an internal agency process.[77] If an existing employee is unable to overturn a clearance refusal using the internal process, they may appeal to the Security Vetting Appeals Panel. The Panel is independent of the agency and comprises of a chairman and a two members. The chairman and deputy chairmen are senior members of the judiciary. The Panel will seek representations from the appellant and the organisation. It can make recommendations to the head of the department identifying that the refusal should either stand or that the clearance should be given or restored. However, the Panel can only make recommendations to the agency. It cannot force an agency to re-establish the clearance and it cannot review any subsequent action or inaction taken by the organisation. Whereas Crown servants working in other government departments may apply to judicially review the decision before an ordinary

---

[75]   *Ibid.*
[76]   Robert G. Vaughn, *The Success and Failures of Whistleblower Laws* (Edward Elgar, 2012) 218.
[77]   Her Majesty's Government, Personnel Security Controls, Version 2.0 (2014), available at www.gov.uk/government/uploads/system/uploads/attachment_data/file/299547/HMG_Personnel_Security_Controls.pdf.

court, employees of the agencies must make a complaint to the Investigatory Powers Tribunal (IPT) unless their complaint concerns discrimination as per the Equality Act 2010.[78] This places the staff in the intelligence agencies at a considerable disadvantage. Decisions of the IPT cannot be appealed in domestic courts meaning that an individual would have to apply to the European Court of Human Rights (ECtHR). To date, the IPT has only found in favour of an applicant on one occasion. The IPT can decide what judgments may or may not be published meaning that the applicant cannot use the judgment to draw attention to their concern.[79] Ultimately, the IPT is unable to order reinstatement of the clearance. The current system is unsatisfactory. Arguably, all cases involving clearance revocation can and should be brought before an employment tribunal, using the special procedures outlined above.

V *SHAYLER* AND IMPACT OF THE ECTHR WHISTLEBLOWING CASES

Arguably, the House of Lords in *Shayler* failed to conduct sufficient analysis of the information disclosed. Whilst the court correctly identified that domestic authorities are provided with a margin of appreciation with regard to national security matters, by failing to accurately assess the information the court could not determine whether the information was capable of being harmful to national security. In keeping with existing values determined in a number of decided cases, the court should have determined whether the public interest in the disclosure outweighed the public interest in non-disclosure. Following the *Shayler* decision, the ECtHR has ruled on cases involving whistleblowing.[80] Whilst it is recognised that the Court is not required to follow precedent, it is submitted that in cases involving whistleblowing, the *Guja* v. *Moldova* framework should be used. The framework most closely aligns with Article 10 ECHR values by allowing for a determination of the public interest in the information disclosed. It is only after making this

---

[78] For two cases concerning GCHQ and complaints on security clearances see *Government Communications Headquarters* v. *Bacchus* [2012] Appeal No. UKEAT/0373/12/LA and *Storey* v. *Government Communications Headquarters* [2015] Appeal No. UKEAT/0269/14/LA.

[79] *Kennedy and others (Preliminary Ruling)* [2003] Application Nos IPT/01/62 and IPT/01/77.

[80] See further, Chapter 4.

determination that the court can hold whether or not the domestic authority has overstepped its margin of appreciation.

The ECtHR has since considered a case involving an employee in the intelligence services, applying the framework used in *Guja* v. *Moldova*. In *Bucur and Toma* v. *Romania*, the applicant worked for the Romanian Intelligence Service (RIS) tasked with the interception of telephone communications and raised concerns that the telephones of a large number of politicians, journalists and businessmen were being tapped.[81] Bucur had attempted to raise his concerns internally without success. He then approached a Member of Parliament on the parliamentary oversight Committee. He was advised to disclose the information to the media because members of the Committee had ties to the head of the intelligence service. The ECtHR determined that there was a lack of internal procedures for the raising of concerns,[82] and that the oversight Committee were likely to be ineffective in handling the concern.[83] The Court held that the disclosure was justified in the public interest. Moreover, the Court noted that the Romanian government had not supplied justifications as to why the information disclosed required a 'top secret' classification. In considering the applicant's good faith, the ECtHR identified that Bucur had approached the parliamentary Committee responsible for oversight of the RIS rather than make unauthorised disclosures directly to the press.[84]

In applying the *Guja* v. *Moldova* framework, the Court will be required to make a determination as to whether alternative channels for raising the concerns were available and whether those channels where effective. The ECtHR drew upon materials from both the United Nations and the Council of Europe in order to determine that the state of Moldova should have provided procedures and protection for whistleblowers. It is therefore submitted that the following recommendation by the United Nations Special Rapporteur on the Promotion and Protection of Human Rights while Countering Terrorism is relevant to this analysis:

> Practice 18. There are internal procedures in place for members of intelligence services to report wrongdoing. These are complemented by an independent body that has a mandate and access to the necessary information to fully investigate and take action to address wrongdoing when internal procedures have proved inadequate. Members of intelligence services who, acting in good faith, report wrongdoing are legally protected from any form of reprisal. These protections extend to disclosures made to the media or the

---

[81]   Application No. 40238/02 (ECtHR, 2008).
[82]   *Ibid.* [96].
[83]   *Ibid.* [98].
[84]   *Ibid.* [118].

public at large if they are made as a last resort and pertain to matters of significant public concern.[85]

It is further identified that the Council of Europe Resolution 1729 requires that whistleblowing provisions should be comprehensive and should extend to the security and intelligence services.[86] If the ECtHR were to consider a case involving an employee from the agencies in the United Kingdom, and that individual had made a public interest disclosure of information which was deemed of a high value to the public interest (for example, a disclosure concerning illegal activities or iniquity), there is a strong argument to suggest that the Court would find a breach of Article 10 ECHR. This is because, as the aforementioned analysis has identified, the available whistleblowing and oversight mechanisms appear to fall short of the recommended good practice. The consequences of making an unauthorised disclosure are severe because the drafting of the Official Secrets Act 1989 does not allow for determination of the public interest benefit of any disclosures raised and because it does not include a public interest defence. The ECtHR is also likely to find the United Kingdom in breach of Article 13 ECHR because the intelligence services do not have legal protection under PIDA 1998 for raising whistleblowing concerns. The next section will consider possible reforms.

VI SUGGESTED REFORMS

One of the key arguments against the inclusion of a public interest defence in the Official Secrets Act 1989 was that the services had introduced a Staff Counsellor to hear concerns; the role of the Staff Counsellor is therefore most important as he is meant to provide the clear alternative to making an unauthorised disclosure. The Staff Counsellor was meant to act as a conduit between agency staff and the respective agency head, or the Prime Minister, in dealing with any alleged malpractice. Despite the important contribution that the role can make to

---

[85]   Special Rapporteur on the Promotion and Protection of Human Rights and Fundamental Freedoms While Countering Terrorism, *Compilation of Good Practices on Legal and Institutional Frameworks and Measures that Ensure Respect for Human Rights by Intelligence Agencies While Countering Terrorism, Including on Their Oversight* (2010), available at http://daccess-dds-ny.un.org/doc/UNDOC/GEN/G10/134/10/PDF/G1013410.pdf?OpenElement.

[86]   Available at http://assembly.coe.int/Main.asp?link=/Documents/Adopted Text/ta10/ERES1729.htm.

accountability and oversight of the agencies, the ISC has not followed or actively reported on the work of the Staff Counsellor for many years. The following suggestions provide recommendations to strengthen the current processes available to agency staff.

Range of Controlled Disclosure Options

It would make sense to provide agency staff with a range of options to raise concerns whilst recognising the strictly controlled nature of their work. This is because the staff member may feel unable to approach the person designated to receive concerns. According to publically available information, DIS staff do not have access to the Independent Staff Counsellor. If this is the case then there is a strong argument to suggest that access should be made available. The Staff Counsellor is outside of the DIS organisation and has access to the Prime Minister and other high level officials. This would help to meet the recommendation made by the UN Special Rapporteur in Practice 18 (above).

The United Kingdom is arguably at a disadvantage because it lacks an inspector general with powers to conduct inquiries into operational matters. The Australian Inspector General for Intelligence and Security has the power to conduct inquiries into operational matters, although he cannot conduct inquiries into operational matters abroad without the consent of the Prime Minister. Consideration should be given as to whether the IOCCO and the ISComm should be made available for agency staff to raise concerns regarding matters falling under their remit. In addition, both Commissioners would support the oversight process by appearing before Parliament. The Home Affairs Select Committee, for example, expressed its dissatisfaction at having to summon the Intelligence Services Commissioner in order to take evidence from him.[87] The Committee was highly critical of the current oversight regime, suggesting that following the Snowden revelations it had become clear that the agencies needed a 'scrutiny system for the 21st century, to ensure that sophisticated security and intelligence agencies can get on with the job with the full confidence of the public'.[88]

In the light of the above statement it should also be considered whether the Intelligence and Security Committee should be designated to receive concerns. As identified above, this would require an extension of the Committee's current investigatory remit. The Committee and Secretariat

---

[87]   See above n. 49, [146].
[88]   *Ibid.* [170].

are well-equipped to handle secret official information. Disclosures to the Committee could be considered as a 'safety valve' mechanism to allow individuals to make disclosures where the other options have failed. The Security Intelligence Review Committee (SIRC) (Canada), for example, is able to receive disclosures.[89] The ISC do not appear, currently, to want to receive concerns from whistleblower.[90] It is therefore suggested that the ISC could, as a minimum recommendation, review how the whistleblowing procedures are working in practice. The ISC are currently prevented from reviewing ongoing operational matters but are not prevented from reviewing the effectiveness of the internal whistleblowing procedures available to agency staff.

At the time of writing, the UK Government had introduced the Investigatory Powers Bill. The proposals in the Bill suggest replacing the Commissioners with one single Investigatory Powers Commission (IPC). The Investigatory Powers Commissioner is intended to be a 'serving or former High Court judge' supported by a team of Judicial Commissioners (also current or former High Court judges) and a team of 'expert inspectors'. The Commission will conduct inspections and will report its findings to Parliament. Whilst the proposals are a welcome improvement on the current arrangements there are no plans to allow whistleblowers to raise concerns to the new Commission. The following paragraphs will now proceed to recommend legal protections for employees of the intelligence agencies.

Legal Protection

There are two possible options to provide whistleblower protection to staff in the security and intelligence agencies. Because of the flexible drafting of PIDA 1998, the exemption from the provision could be removed. Therefore, any disclosures to an employer or nominated officer would be covered under PIDA 1998, section 43C. Disclosures to the Staff Counsellor would be covered under section 43C(2) provided that the

---

[89] Security of Information Act 2001, s.15(5)(i), provides a defence where individuals have raised concerns to the SIRC or to the Communications Security Establishment Commissioner.

[90] See the Committee's report where they identified that they had received evidence on this point but did not subsequently make any recommendations to improve procedures for whistleblowers: Intelligence and Security Committee, *Privacy and Security: A Modern and Transparent Legal Framework*, HC-1075 (2015) [218]. For the author's evidence to the Committee, see http://isc.independent.gov.uk/public-evidence.

Staff Counsellor was designated under the policy to receive concerns. Any further disclosures to prescribed persons under section 43F must then be authorised disclosures for the purposes of the Official Secrets Act 1989. The National Audit Office, who are prescribed, could therefore be accessed. Disclosures to the Commissioner of the Metropolitan Police could be made under PIDA 1998, section 34G or 43H as the Commissioner is an authorised recipient. Wider disclosures to the media would then be protected unless the individual was successfully prosecuted. Any prosecutions for unauthorised disclosures would mean that the individual would lose protection. If the Official Secrets Act 1989 were reformed the legislation could offer protection against prosecution. Protected Disclosures Act 2000 (New Zealand), section 18, provides immunity from civil and criminal proceedings for an employee who makes a protected disclosure. This prevents individuals from being prosecuted under Crimes Act 1961 (NZ), section 78. Disclosures are strictly limited as a result of Protected Disclosures Act 2000 (NZ), section 12, to the Inspector General for Intelligence and Security, to the Minister responsible for intelligence and security, and to the Prime Minister. Section 18 provides immunity for disciplinary proceedings resulting from the disclosure.

The second option is to provide a specific whistleblowing law for members of the intelligence agencies. This could support disclosures made under the current official arrangements and/or support disclosures to Parliament. The Intelligence Community Whistleblower Protection Act (US) provides an example where members of the intelligence community are authorised to report an 'urgent concern' to Congress.[91] However, before raising a concern to Congress the staff member is required to inform the Inspector General. Upon receiving the complaint, the Inspector General has 14 days to decide whether or not the complaint appears credible. If he decides it is, the Inspector General is then required to inform the Director of the respective agency, who then has seven days to forward the matter to the Congressional Intelligence Committees. If the complainant is dissatisfied that the information has not been given correctly to the Committees, he may then approach one of the Committees directly. Whilst this allows the agencies to be in control of the information, it is clear why the Act has been subject to criticism. The requirement to approach the Inspector General followed by a tip off to the head of the agency at fault places an unnecessary administrative burden on the scheme and increases the potential for matters of wrongdoing to be covered up. The mechanism provided in the Protected

---

[91]   112 Stat. 2413-14 SS 701 (1998).

Disclosures Act 2014 (Ireland) allows for disclosures to be made to a 'Disclosures Recipient' who is a serving or retired judge of the High Court.[92] Upon determining that the information disclosed is national security sensitive (under section 18 of the Act), the Recipient will make a report to the holder of public office or a public body the he/she considers to be the most appropriate to consider the relevant information and may make recommendations on the information. The Act does not limit the scope of which public bodies or holders of public office may be subject to the referral of information. Moreover, the Recipient is required to make an annual report to Parliament.[93]

In addition to the above considerations, The ISC's Annual Report of 2007–08 revealed that protest whistleblowing concerns are being raised; for example, one concern related to 'whether it was ethical for the Government to seek to alter the ideological views of its citizens (as part of its counter-radicalisation strategy'.[94] In view of the limited capability for agency staff to engage in protest whistleblowing, it may be appropriate to adopt a wider protective remit than currently allowed by the categories provided in PIDA 1998, section 43B. It is unlikely that the aforementioned concern would be protected by PIDA 1998. Another concern identified related to the compliance of international standards for the treatment of individuals in detention.[95] Whilst this could technically be covered by 'health and safety' or a 'breach of a legal obligation' it identifies that the intelligence agencies are involved in work which concerns the legality of operations outside of the jurisdiction, as well as compliance with international standards. These matters are far from legally certain and would be open to challenge by the agency defending a claim under PIDA 1998 or a similar framework.

VII CONCLUSION

Regardless of whether Edward Snowden is considered a 'hero' or a 'traitor', this analysis has identified that there is a strong policy argument to support whistleblowing in the security and intelligence agencies

---

[92] Protected Disclosures Act 2014 (Ireland), Sch. 3.
[93] *Ibid.* Sch. 3 para. 6.
[94] See above n. 38.
[95] *Ibid.*

through robust authorised channels. The provision of authorised alternatives cannot prevent unauthorised disclosures.[96] However, the United Kingdom should at the very least consider the viability of the current mechanisms available. From a governmental perspective, controlled authorised disclosures can safeguard national security and should be seen as a better alternative to unauthorised leaking. If the United Kingdom were to encounter disclosures on the scale of those of Snowden or Manning, the Crown would face considerable difficulties in prosecuting the individuals. Following the decisions in *Guja* and *Bucur*, the ECtHR has made clear that disclosures of official information can be afforded the protection of Article 10 ECHR, particularly where the mechanisms available to raise concerns are not considered viable. This chapter has also identified that there are gaps in the oversight regime. Whilst this has not been the main focus of the chapter, oversight has an impact on whistleblowing. Failures in oversight can prompt individuals into making unauthorised disclosures but whistleblowers can also support the overseers in their role. As the state demands enhanced capabilities to counter the threat of terrorism and increased destabilisation in the Middle East and elsewhere, it is important that the oversight mechanisms also gain enhanced capabilities, including the ability to receive and investigate whistleblowing concerns.

---

[96] For example, it was alleged, that Snowden did not attempt to raise his concerns using the official mechanisms available to him.

7. Whistleblowing in the Armed Forces

Service personnel in the Armed Forces face considerable challenges if they witness wrongdoing or malpractice. They must observe a rigid command structure and risk breaching those rules if they disregard or disobey orders. Based upon rank, the structure requires subordinates to obey the orders of a superior officer. The structure also allows for 'administrative action' or punishments to be considered by superior officers for matters relating to discipline.[1] Therefore, whereas a civil servant would be subject to obligations prescribed by the criminal law and by the Civil Service Code, the military justice system is structured to deal with both matters of criminal law and discipline, by way of court martial or by administrative action. Whilst it is clear that discipline is a necessary feature of life in the Armed Forces, the command structure has served as a barrier to the resolution of service complaints. The command structure has also acted as a barrier against much needed reform of complaint handling and oversight of the services.

Military personnel face a number of restrictions on their expression rights and are excluded from the whistleblowing protections provided by the Public Interest Disclosure Act (PIDA) 1998.[2] However, not all work undertaken by military personnel takes place during combat and not all military personnel are working on the front line. There is a distinction between combat operations and life 'back at the barracks'. The size and nature of the UK Armed Forces means that a number of military personnel work in positions as doctors and nurses, chefs and engineers, roles which if undertaken in civilian life would afford them protection under PIDA 1998 and a greater degree of latitude to engage in protest

---

[1] For discussion of this in relation to the human rights of Armed Forces personnel, see Peter Rowe, *The Impact of Human Rights Law on Armed Forces* (CUP, 2006) 7.

[2] Members of the Armed Forces are excluded from the employment rights afforded by PIDA 1998 by virtue of Employment Rights Act 1996, s.192. For a comprehensive overview of the position of Armed Forces personnel as Crown servants, see P. Rowe, 'Military Servants' in Maurice Sunkin and Sebastian Payne (eds), *The Nature of the Crown: A Legal and Political Analysis* (OUP, 1999) 297.

expression. The scope to engage in protest speech in the military is significantly curtailed, particularly in the subordinate ranks. As a consequence, senior military personnel are much more likely than subordinates to voice concerns regarding government proposals concerning the military or the adequacy of equipment.

Where military personnel in the subordinate ranks choose to speak up the consequences can be severe. In 2015, William McNeilly, a Royal Navy submariner, went on the run after publishing a 30 page report alleging 30 security and safety concerns regarding the Trident nuclear submarine fleet.[3] McNeilly had attempted to raise concerns through the chain of command but suggested that they had not been taken seriously. After handing himself in to the authorities, McNeilly escaped prosecution for breaching the Official Secrets Act 1989 but was forced to leave the Armed Forces. In other jurisdictions, military personnel have also suffered reprisals for raising concerns.

I ECTHR STANDARDS

Article 10(2) of the European Convention on Human Rights (ECHR) allows a particularly wide restriction of the right to freedom of expression 'in the interests of national security'. A contrast can therefore be drawn between a Crown servant as a member of the Armed Forces and Crown servants involved in other areas of work. Unless Crown servants are involved in the work of a department which is involved in national security matters, such as the Ministry of Defence or the intelligence services, for example, they are much less likely to have their speech restricted. In comparison, the very nature of a position as a member of Armed Forces personnel can be deemed as 'in the interests of national security' and thus the restriction on the freedom of expression of

---

[3] 'Trident whistleblower William McNeilly hands himself in', *BBC News*, 19 May 2015, available at www.bbc.co.uk/news/uk-scotland-32791755. Several US military whistleblowers have suffered reprisals. Chelsea Manning received 35 years' imprisonment for the Wikileaks disclosures. For analysis see Ashley Savage, '35 years for Manning, and time for better whistleblowing laws', *The Conversation*, 21 August 2013, available at http://theconversation.com/35-years-for-manning-and-time-for-better-whistleblowing-laws-17333. See also John-Paul Ford Rojas, 'Decorated Royal Marine officer claims he was sacked for whistleblowing over misuse of funds', *Telegraph*, 6 January 2013, available at www.telegraph.co.uk/news/uknews/defence/9784081/Decorated-Royal-Marine-officer-claims-he-was-sacked-for-whistleblowing-over-misuse-of-funds.html.

servicemen will be far greater. This stance has been reflected in a number of decided cases heard by the European Court of Human Rights (ECtHR).

In *Hadjianastassiou* v. *Greece*,[4] the applicant, an officer in the Greek Air Force, failed to convince the Court the information he disclosed did not risk national security. The Court rejected the claim on the basis that the state's interest in keeping information regarding the development of the missile secret was legitimate. The Court was influenced by the reasoning in *Engel and others* v. *The Netherlands*.[5] In *Engel*, the Court held that Article 10 ECHR applies to members of the Armed Forces just as it does to other persons 'within the jurisdiction of the Contracting States', yet it identified that 'The proper functioning of an army is hardly imaginable without legal rules designed to prevent servicemen from undermining military discipline, for example by writings'. The Court's determination may be identified as the 'citizens in uniform' approach. Therefore, if a citizen joins the Armed Forces, they will still retain the right to freedom of expression, but will be subject to certain limitations imposed by the requirements of being a member of the Armed Forces. In essence, this means that the limitations of certain Convention rights are therefore acceptable as the individual chose to surrender those rights as a condition of service. A pertinent example of the voluntary surrender of freedom of expression can be found in the 'signing' of the Official Secrets Acts. The act of signing the Acts is not a legal requirement but it is a symbolic formal recognition that the individual will conform to the duty not to release information pertaining to national security, thus voluntarily surrendering the right to freedom of expression in those circumstances.[6]

The approach taken in *Engel* has continued to set the benchmark for subsequent Article 10 ECHR challenges regarding the rights of military personnel.[7] In *Engel*, the Court also considered the question of Article 14 ECHR which advocates that the rights and freedoms contained in the

---

4   (1992) 16 ECHR 219.
5   (1976) 1 EHRR 647.
6   For further discussion see Chapter 2 of this text.
7   See e.g. *Le Cour Grandmaison and Fritz* v. *France*, Application No. 11567/85 (1987) 53 DR 150, where the Court found that the imprisonment of two conscripts who distributed information calling for the withdrawal of French troops from Germany did not violate Art. 10 ECHR. Similarly, in *E.S.* v. *Germany*, Application No. 23576/94 84 (ECtHR, 1995), the Court held that the dismissal of German military personnel for criticising government policy on television was an acceptable limitation of rights under Art. 10.

Convention are to be secured without limitation. This would clearly apply to Article 10 ECHR rights. However, in following its own interpretation of the 'Citizens in Uniform' approach it stated that:

> The hierarchical structure inherent in armies entails differentiation according to rank. Corresponding to the various ranks are differing responsibilities which in their turn justify certain inequalities of treatment in the disciplinary sphere. Such inequalities are traditionally encountered in the contracting states and are tolerated by international humanitarian law. … In this respect, the European Convention allows for the competent national authorities a considerable margin of appreciation.[8]

According to the approach taken in *Engel*, it may be observed that the right to freedom of expression is considerably more restricted in the lower ranks that it will be for the higher ranks of the command structure. This will impact on military personnel engaging in acts of 'protest whistleblowing' as well as the raising of concerns regarding wrongdoing. Because the ECtHR places considerable emphasis on the margin of appreciation afforded to member states in this case, arguably any concern raised must be of a sufficiently high value to outweigh the public interest in maintaining the well-established command structure. Therefore, it is suggested that Article 10 ECHR will only protect service personnel where the concerns raised identify serious wrongdoing and cases whereby an act of expression has resulted in a penalty so clearly disproportionate as to outweigh Article 10(2). The ECtHR is yet to consider a case on military whistleblowing. It is highly likely that the Court will consider the judgments in *Engel* and *Hadjianastassiou* along-side the more recent decisions taken in *Guja* v. *Moldova*, *Bucur and Toma* v. *Romania* and *Heinisch* v. *Germany*.[9] The ECtHR suggests that courts should determine the following:

- whether the applicant had alternative channels for making the disclosure;
- the public interest in the disclosed information;
- the authenticity of the disclosed information;
- the detriment to the employer;

---

8   [1976] 1 EHRR 647, [72].

9   *Guja* v. *Moldova*, Application No. 14277/04 (ECtHR, 2008); *Bucur and Toma* v. *Romania*, Application No. 40238/02 (ECtHR, 2013); *Heinisch* v. *Germany*, Application No. 28274/08 (ECtHR, 2011).

- whether the applicant acted in good faith;
- the severity of the sanction.[10]

It is submitted that in applying the aforementioned framework, courts are likely to consider any impact that an unauthorised disclosure had on Forces discipline as well as any harm caused by the disclosure itself under the detriment to the employer criterion. This analysis will now consider the various restrictions on expression in the military with reference to decided cases.

II RESTRICTIONS ON EXPRESSION

The Queen's Regulations for the Army state that:

> Every officer is responsible for ensuring that all persons under his command are acquainted with the provisions of the Official Secrets Act 1911–1989, and with the need for strict compliance with those provisions. All personnel are to be reminded annually of their responsibilities under the Acts. On joining and leaving the Regular Services all personnel will sign declarations regarding the Official Secrets Act on Ministry of Defence Forms 134 and 135 respectively.[11]

Armed Forces Act 2006, section 42, reaffirms this position by expressly incorporating the Official Secrets Acts by extending all acts 'punishable by the law of England and Wales' into the jurisdiction of the Armed Forces.[12] The Official Secrets Acts impose extensive restrictions on the communication of information obtained in an official capacity. Official Secrets Act 1911, section 1, gives a broad definition of the act of spying which includes the communication of information which is intended to be 'directly or indirectly useful to the enemy'.[13] Official Secrets Act 1989, section 2, contains specific provisions relating to the work of the Armed Forces. Official Secrets Act 1989, section 3, concerns foreign relations. With regard to joint operations, for example, those conducted by NATO, Official Secrets Act 1989, section 6, protects information entrusted in confidence to other states or international organisations.

---

[10] *Ibid.*
[11] See further 'Official Information and Public Relations', Chapter 12 in *The Queen's Regulations for the Army*, J12.001.
[12] Armed Forces Act 2006, s.42, see in particular s.42(1).
[13] *Ibid.* s.1 also contains a separate provision with regard to 'assisting an enemy'.

One unsuccessful attempt to proceed in a prosecution for breaching the Official Secrets Acts concerned an Army whistleblower. Using the pseudonym Martin Ingram, the soldier contributed to a series of articles in the *Sunday Times* which detailed the activities of the Force Research Unit, a covert army intelligence unit, during the late 1980s and early 1990s.[14] Ingram's allegations prompted a police investigation into the claims, headed by the then Commissioner of the Metropolitan Police, Sir John Stevens, which focused upon the alleged collusion between members of army intelligence and loyalist paramilitaries in the murder of a Belfast solicitor, Pat Finucane.[15]

Breach of Confidence

The following cases concern attempts by the UK government to take proceedings against former military personnel for breach of confidence. Both cases are of significance because the individuals had made allegations of wrongdoing. They also identify the government's attempts to use confidentiality agreements to re-inforce the secrecy of UK Special Forces operations.

After the 1991 Gulf War, some former members of the Special Air Services (SAS) chose to publish their own accounts of a failed mission whilst acting as a patrol with the call sign 'Bravo Two Zero'. In 1993, a former soldier using the pseudonym Andy McNabb, published a book entitled *Bravo Two Zero* which later resulted in a television film. In 1995, another soldier using the pseudonym Chris Ryan, published his version of the events in a book entitled *The One that Got Away* which was also made into a television film. It was alleged that the two accounts of the operation appeared to differ and contained factual inaccuracies; some members of the SAS who believed that the writers had made errors in their accounts urged the Ministry of Defence to correct the errors in the public domain.[16]

The disclosures made by McNabb and Ryan prompted the SAS Regimental Association to conduct a poll of its members as to whether

---

[14] See N. Hopkins and R. Norton-Taylor, 'Army Whistleblower will Not be Prosecuted', *Guardian*, 30 November 2000.

[15] Despite making reference to the information, the Stevens Enquiry did not interview Ingram and did not discuss the incidents arising from the disclosure of information. See further *The Stevens Enquiry Report* (17 April 2003).

[16] For a detailed account of this, see *R* v. *Her Majesty's Attorney-General for England and Wales Respondent from the Court of Appeal of New Zealand*, Appeal No. 61/2002, Privy Council, 17 March 2003.

binding contracts preventing unauthorised disclosure should be introduced: 96.8 per cent of the respondents favoured the contracts and, in 1996, the Ministry of Defence introduced them.[17] Failure to agree to sign the contracts would result in the soldier being 'returned to unit', meaning that he would become an ordinary soldier in the position he was in before joining the Special Forces regiment, thus returning to a lower rate of pay, and losing the prestige associated with the position.

'Coburn' was a serving SAS soldier from New Zealand who was also present on the Bravo Two Zero patrol. After signing the contract during active service, Coburn decided to leave the SAS and then write his own book entitled *Soldier Five: The Real Truth About the Bravo Two Zero Mission*. After the UK publisher sent a copy of the manuscript to the Ministry of Defence for approval, the Attorney General issued proceedings in the High Court of New Zealand for breach of confidence to restrain publication, to obtain damages and any available profits.[18] Coburn then pleaded that he had signed the contract under military orders and this had amounted to duress or undue influence. Following proceedings before the Court of Appeal (NZ), the Privy Council refused the injunction, instead awarding the Ministry of Defence all proceeds from the sale of the book.[19] This had the effect of allowing the publication of the material in the public domain, whilst recognising the importance and validity of the contract in question by not allowing Coburn to profit from the disclosures. The Privy Council made reference to Tipping J's comments in the Court of Appeal (NZ) judgment which identified that 'the particular and unusual circumstances' justified a decision not to allow the injunction. It can therefore be observed that there was a clear public interest in allowing the general public to hear an alternative and conflicting account of the events surrounding the Bravo Two Zero mission but that the court also recognised the importance of the confidentiality contracts in preventing former members of the SAS from profiting from their experiences.

---

[17] *Ibid.*

[18] *Ibid.*

[19] In contrast, see the US case of *Snepp* v. *United States* 444 US 507 (1980). The case concerned a former CIA employee who had written a book about the Agency's activities in Vietnam and failed to seek approval before publication, contrary to the confidentiality contract he had signed. The court denied Snepp the royalties from the book for not seeking prior approval. It was held that this did not amount to a breach of First Amendment rights due to the fact that Snepp had breached the constructive trust between himself and the government which had jeopardised the safety of CIA operatives.

Since their introduction, confidentiality contracts have failed to prevent a number of former personnel from going 'on the record' about their time in the Special Forces.[20] However, more recently the case of *Ministry of Defence* v. *Griffin*[21] suggests that the use of confidentiality contracts by the UK Special Forces is having an impact on the control of operational and national security information, at least in recognising the importance of seeking prior authorisation before disclosing the information in the public domain. The Ministry of Defence (MOD) commenced proceedings against a former soldier in the UK Special Forces after several unauthorised disclosures had been made. The MOD sought permanent injunction to prevent further disclosures from taking place. The main consideration for the court was whether or not it was acceptable for an individual serviceman to decide whether or not the information concerned could be disclosed, or whether they should seek prior authorisation in a process referred to as obtaining 'express prior authority in writing' (EPAW) in all circumstances. The court identified that serving members and former members of the UK Special Forces were reluctant to approach the MOD for prior authority.[22]

Griffin had made allegations of wrongdoing involving the actions of American soldiers in Iraq and suggested that he did not trust the MOD authorisation procedure. He believed that the MOD would allow only a very narrow 'scope of permitted disclosure' and that if he reported the wrongdoing to the authorities, the allegations would either not be investigated properly or would be out of the authorities' jurisdiction.[23] Eady J held that the injunction would continue to be in force and that if Griffin had any further disclosures to make he must first seek authorisation for disclosure.[24] If he was dissatisfied with the response from the MOD he could then consider making an application for judicial review.

Eady J considered the public interest argument made by Griffin's counsel of disclosing allegations of wrongdoing. He identified that

---

[20]   In January 2005, the High Court issued a writ to sue four former SAS soldiers, John MacAleese, Eddie Stone and two unnamed others, despite the fact that the BBC television programme that they had contributed to, *SAS Survival Secrets*, had been screened a year before and had been repeated several times without complaint from the Ministry of Defence. It was reported that the men in question went into hiding. See further C. Leake, 'Gagged … the SAS embassy siege hero who gave survival tips on the BBC', *Mail on Sunday*, 16 January 2005.

[21]   [2008] EWHC 1542 (QB).

[22]   *Ibid.* [20].

[23]   *Ibid.* [14].

[24]   *Ibid.* [35].

members of the Armed Forces are exempt from the whistleblower protections provided by PIDA 1998. He stated that to allow such an argument would nullify the exemption in the Act.[25] Eady J made reference to *R* v. *Shayler* and the statutory obligation of confidence provided in the criminal law by the Official Secrets Act 1989. He suggested that clauses (1) and (2) in the confidentiality contract 'echo' Official Secrets Act 1989, section 1, and that the use of confidentiality contracts are 'clearly intended' to achieve the same 'policy objectives' which are in the interests of national security but with the distinction that a breach of obligation will be enforced through 'remedies available in civil litigation rather than by way of criminal sanctions'.[26]

The aforementioned cases show the difficulty in maintaining secrecy. The provision of confidentiality agreements for Special Forces personnel is arguably unnecessary in law because personnel will be subject to an implied duty of confidence which is reinforced by the 'signing' of the Official Secrets Acts.[27] The written agreements are an additional safeguard which can be utilised if any unauthorised disclosures have been made. As occurred in the case of *Griffin*, because the individual had signed the contract the court effectively had to consider whether he had broken the contract's express terms. It is suggested that confidentiality contracts are there to reinforce existing duties of confidence and in doing so place an additional restriction on Special Forces personnel. In effect this represents a sub-grouping of the wider intramural community.

Comparisons may be drawn between the UK Special Forces, employees of the security and intelligence services and civil servants. Security and intelligence employees are subject to a lifelong duty due to their obligations under Official Secrets Act 1989, section 1. In contrast, Armed Forces personnel are not automatically subject to section 1 and would require notification by the Secretary of State to be so. Security and intelligence employees must also seek prior authorisation before making disclosures regarding their work. However, following the case of *A* v. *B*, the only route to challenge any refusal to disclose is before the Investigatory Powers Tribunal (IPT).[28] This arguably places security and intelligence officers and agents at a disadvantage over Special Forces

---

[25] *Ibid.* [29].
[26] *Ibid.* [16].
[27] See generally, *Attorney General* v. *Blake* [2000] UKHL 45.
[28] *A* v. *B* [2009] SC 12. For analysis see Ashley Savage and Paul David Mora, 'Security Service Memoirs and the Jurisdiction of the Investigatory Powers Tribunal: The Supreme Court's Decision in A v. B' (2010) 21(5) *Entertainment Law Review* 197. For further discussion see Chapter 2.

personnel even when they could seek authorisation to disclose material on the same topic. This is because the IPT uses 'special advocates' appointed by the Crown. Applicants to the IPT are much less likely to have the opportunity to hear the details of the respondent's arguments for non-disclosure. The IPT can also select whether or not to make a judgment accessible to the public, meaning that the opportunity to obtain any form of publicity surrounding the proceedings is diminished. In contrast to civil servants, provided that the civil servant does not breach the Official Secrets Act 1989 in making the disclosure and provided that they have not been made exempt from the provisions by a ministerial certificate, civil servants can obtain protection under PIDA 1998, where, in addition, section 43J can void any agreement preventing individuals from making protected disclosures.

Serving personnel are likely to encounter a very different experience to former personnel if they raise concerns by making an unauthorised disclosure. In practical terms, serving personnel are likely to be subject to disciplinary procedures whereas former personnel may or may not be subject to criminal or civil action depending on the information complained of and the motivation to take action in Whitehall. It may be argued that the confidentiality agreements place a considerable fetter on an individual's right to raise a concern about wrongdoing. By placing undue weight on the need to seek prior authorisation, courts will fail to have sufficient regard to both the well-established public interest jurisprudence in breach of confidence cases, as well as a strong body of Article 10 ECHR principles.

With regard to consideration by courts in breach of confidence cases, in applying the *Guja* v. *Moldova* framework, the conduct of the applicant will be highly relevant. If the individual has sought to profit from the disclosures this will weigh heavily against them. A distinction must be made between civil law action for breach of confidence in order to recover profits made from a book (arguably less severe) and a criminal prosecution. In considering the detriment to the employer, it is likely that the Ministry of Defence would seek to argue that the disclosed information has harmed national security and that it is likely to impact on the Armed Forces by encouraging others to make unauthorised disclosures and on discipline in the ranks. The reasoning in *Engel* can be more readily applied to cases involving serving personnel because to sanction a serving individual would ordinarily be considered as a proportionate restriction. In contrast, the need to maintain order and discipline is arguably reduced when an individual has left the Armed Forces because the question for the court will no longer be about whether the restriction on the individual can be justified to maintain discipline but rather the more general impact that the actions of the individual will have on serving personnel. On that basis, it is suggested that with regard to former personnel the Court is more likely to find actions taken by the Ministry of Defence as disproportionate provided that the information concerned is of a high value to the public interest. Again, the margin of appreciation afforded to member states is likely to result in a significant hurdle for applicants.

Unlawful Orders and Official Complaints

In the United Kingdom jurisdiction, Armed Forces personnel do not have a duty to obey an order if it is deemed unlawful; however, in contrast there is no recognised obligation that servicemen have a duty to disobey unlawful orders either. One can consider, however, that there is an implied duty to disobey in the doctrine of individual accountability. Therefore, for any acts committed by a member of Armed Forces personnel, he will be individually liable. This point has been reiterated in Armed Forces Act 2006, section 42, which has extended all acts 'punishable by the law of England and Wales' into the jurisdiction of the Armed Forces.[29] In contrast, the doctrine of command responsibility applies to commanding officers. Under this doctrine, a commanding officer will not only be responsible for his own actions but for the actions of his subordinates. The UK approach differs from that of Denmark, France and Italy, where soldiers in the respective jurisdictions have a duty to disobey illegal orders.[30]

---

[29]   Armed Forces Act 2006, s.42, see in particular s.42(1): 'A person subject to service law, or a civilian subject to service discipline, commits an offence under this section if he does any act that: (a) is punishable by the law of England and Wales; or (b) if done in England or Wales, would be so punishable'. See also s.44 which deals with attempting criminal conduct, s.45 (conspiring to commit criminal conduct), s.46 (inciting criminal conduct) and s.47 (aiding, abetting, counselling or procuring criminal conduct).

[30]   For analysis, see generally Georg Nolte (ed.), *European Military Law Systems* (De Gruyter Recht, 2003). In particular, Military Penal Code (Denmark) Act No. 530 of 24/06/2005, s.9 states: 'The fact that a criminal offence was committed according to order from a superior shall not release the offender from criminal liability, unless the person in question was under an obligation to obey orders from the superior in question and did not know that the order was illegal, and the order was not clearly illegal'.

In comparison, German military personnel conduct their duties in accordance with the concept of '*Innere Führung*'.[31] Established alongside the 'citizen in uniform' approach, the doctrine places emphasis on leadership and civic education. Moral and ethical considerations are therefore placed at the forefront of conduct in military life. It is stated specifically that the internal order of the Armed Forces should 'diverge from society's standards of behaviour only where this is necessary to fulfil their military mission'.[32] The method for implementing the doctrine resides in a responsibility on commanding officers to 'set an example' to their subordinates. This means that superiors are required to develop an environment of trust between themselves and their subordinates and be ready to talk to their servicemen. Individuals are given 'considerable latitude' in taking decisions and action and are able to actively develop their own opinions freely.[33]

UK military personnel take a risk by refusing to obey an order because they believe it to be unlawful when it could actually be lawful. The implied duty to disobey orders does not therefore account for the extent to which the individual has knowledge of the law. By incorporating all offences deemed criminal into the Armed Forces jurisdiction, the serving soldier may not be fully aware of the complexities of certain legal principles. The situation is further complicated by adding a myriad of uncertain legal obligations as well as compliance with the law in different jurisdictions where forces are not engaged in combat operations. Moreover, the way in which an individual objects to the order is particularly important. If they directly approach an officer, they could be accused of using 'threatening or insubordinate language'.[34] The risk of reprisal is therefore high and can only serve to act as a barrier to the raising of concerns.[35] This is further compounded by the lack of legal protections available for UK military personnel who speak up and the lack of clear advice for individuals in the UK Armed Forces. The discussion will now consider how personnel might raise concerns in the military.

---

[31] For analysis comparing the doctrine to the South African perspective, see Mark Malan, 'Leadership, Integration and Civic Consciousness: From *Innere Führung* to *Ubuntu*' (2005) 4 *African Security Review* 3, available at www.issafrica.org/Pubs/ASR/4No3/FromInnerFuhrung.html.

[32] Federal Ministry of Defense, *Joint Service Regulation*, Innere Führung ZDV 10/1 (updated 1993) [207].

[33] *Ibid.* [302].

[34] Army Act 1955, s.33, concerns insubordinate behaviour.

[35] For a comparison, see the US Uniform Code of Military Justice, art. 92, which makes it a crime to disobey a military order.

III RAISING CONCERNS IN THE MILITARY

The following section will first consider authorised options for raising concerns by discussing the whistleblowing policy which covers Armed Forces personnel, as well as other authorised routes to raise concerns. Consideration will be given to the Service Complaints procedures and the external oversight provided by the Service Complaints Commissioner.

Whistleblowing

From the outset it should be observed that very little public information is provided on whistleblowing in the UK Armed Forces.[36] In a response to a freedom of information request by the author, the Ministry of Defence confirmed that prior to 31 March 2014, there were no whistleblowing procedures available to military personnel.[37] The Whistleblowing: Raising a Concern policy now made available to both civil servants and Armed Forces personnel identifies that whilst military personnel are not subject to PIDA 1998:

> The Service authorities have agreed to honour the spirit of the Act in that they will recognise and adhere to the criteria for protected disclosures and follow the prescribed procedures whether dealing with or making a qualifying disclosure.[38]

When asked, the Ministry of Defence were unable to provide confirmation when the agreement had been made or the exact contents of it. It is therefore extremely difficult to determine how the Armed Forces authorities can follow the 'prescribed procedures'. There are several difficulties in using PIDA 1998 in this way. First, PIDA 1998 provides individuals with the opportunity to sue their employer if they have suffered a

---

[36] The whistleblower support organisation Whistleblowers UK does provide guidance to military whistleblowers: see www.wbuk.org/sectors/defence.html. For information relating to the alleged failure to investigate concerns, see 'Whistleblower says Army abuse not investigated', *BBC News*, 11 October 2009, available at http://news.bbc.co.uk/1/hi/uk/8300726.stm.

[37] Ministry of Defence, FOI response, received 29 February 2015. The response has been published online and is available at www.gov.uk/government/uploads/system/uploads/attachment_data/file/408160/20150226_Whistleblowing_001.pdf.

[38] The whistleblowing policy is available at www.gov.uk/government/uploads/system/uploads/attachment_data/file/408161/Whistleblowing_and_Raising_a_concern.pdf.

detriment or dismissal. Secondly, PIDA 1998 does not prescribe procedures for organisations to follow in dealing with whistleblowing concerns.
As observed in Chapter 4, this has led to a variety of different
mechanisms and responses by Civil Service departments and agencies
and by regulators. Thirdly, whilst it may be advantageous to support
whistleblowing in an environment where civil servants and military
personnel are working side-by-side, there are clear differences between
the employment status of civil servants and military personnel and clear
differences in the restrictions on expression rights of those individuals.
Fourthly, the Armed Forces authorities' failure to observe the 'spirit of
the Act' is unlikely to result in adverse consequences: military personnel
have no access to PIDA 1998 or equivalent legislation and are not legally
protected when raising concerns.

The whistleblowing policy does not provide express guidance for
military personnel in raising concerns. Where advice is provided this
appears primarily to relate to concerns raised by civil servants. This is
further compounded by the guidance advising as to when it is appropriate
for individuals to raise concerns to regulators and to the media. Armed
Forces personnel have no statutory protection when raising a concern
using either option and military personnel may find themselves in breach
of Armed Forces regulations or the Official Secrets Act 1989. For
example, 'honouring the spirit of PIDA' did not prevent the Royal Navy
from sacking submariner William McNeilly after he alleged a number of
safety and security concerns.[39] McNeilly was not prosecuted under the
Official Secrets Act 1989. Had McNeilly worked in the Civil Service he
would have been able to make a claim using PIDA 1998.

When asked, the Ministry of Defence identified that military personnel
can raise concerns with their Commanding Officer or Service Police and
allegations may be made using the Service Justice System.[40] The
whistleblowing policy does not provide guidance on these avenues.
Moreover, the MOD identified that the Service Justice System does not
record when allegations have been made by whistleblowers. Savage and
Hyde recommended that it is good practice to centrally track and monitor
whistleblowing concerns, because whistleblowing concerns require special handling compared with ordinary complaints, particularly where the
individuals are exempt from PIDA 1998 protection.

---

[39] 'Trident whistleblower leaves Royal Navy', BBC News, 17 June 2015,
available at www.bbc.co.uk/news/uk-scotland-33161226.
[40] Ministry of Defence, above n. 37.

The MOD identified that there are two PIDA 1998 Focal Points which have been in existence since 2006. The Focal Points record disclosures relating to 'fraud, theft or corruption'. The whistleblowing policy makes reference to 'Fraud Focal Points' and identifies that there is a Fraud Incident and Irregularity Reporting Unit. The MOD were unable to provide data on the number of military personnel who had raised concerns because the Focal Points do not identify whether the concern was received from someone in the Armed Forces, the Civil Service or a member of the public.[41] Savage and Hyde have previously identified that whistleblowing concerns should be kept separate from public concerns because any subsequent investigation must be conducted with care to ensure that, where requested, confidentiality is maintained and the investigation does not lead back to the whistleblower.[42] It is not clear whether Armed Forces personnel are being advised and supported differently to their civil servant counterparts, since clearly a different approach is needed because individuals in the Armed Forces do not have access to PIDA 1998 protection.

In contrast to the UK approach, in the United States, significant reforms have been made in relation to whistleblowing systems following the scandal surrounding the conduct of US soldiers at Abu Grahib prison.[43] A reserve soldier, Joe Darby, was lent a CD containing a number of photographs during his time serving in Iraq. The CD had photographs containing general shots around the region but also contained horrific images of the abuse of Iraqi prisoners by his colleagues. Darby chose to send the CD to the US Army Criminal Investigation Command. An investigation followed which led to several soldiers, including Private Lynndie England (who was featured posing in a number of the photographs) being convicted by an army court-martial. Darby had wished to remain anonymous, however, during a televised Senate hearing, the Secretary of Defense, Donald Rumsfeld, publically thanked him.

---

[41] *Ibid.* For a comparison, the Department of Defence (Australia) has a Defence Force Whistleblower Scheme and operates a 24-hour hotline. The hotline is available to Armed Forces personnel, public servants as well as government contractors: see www.defence.gov.au/mjs/organisations.asp#2.

[42] Ashley Savage and Richard Hyde, 'The Response to Whistleblowing by Regulators: A Practical Perspective' (2015) 25(3) *Legal Studies* 408.

[43] 'Iraq prison abuse scandal', *BBC News*, 11 January 2008, available at http://news.bbc.co.uk/1/hi/world/americas/3701941.stm.

As a consequence, Darby's home in Maryland was vandalised, he faced death threats and was forced to live in protective custody.[44]

United States Armed Forces personnel are able to make a complaint via the chain of command[45] but also have direct and confidential access either to their respective service Inspector General or directly to the Department of Defense Inspector General by using the 'Defense Hotline'. The Service Inspector Generals effectively act as 'an extension of the commander', working directly for him. The Inspector General has the power to conduct investigations but does not have the power to provide resolution, as this is dealt with by the commander. This means that there must be a close relationship between the commander and the Inspector General. It has been stated that for the role to be effective the Inspector General must be 'sufficiently independent' in order to continue to receive complaints from soldiers.[46] Whilst one may question the independence of a service Inspector General, there is a clear advantage in that the Inspector General is an officer within the respective service, and the Inspector General system is therefore in keeping with the traditional 'command structure' doctrine. The Department of Defense Inspector General, in contrast, is entirely separate from the command structure and instead reports directly to the Secretary of Defense and to Congress. The scheme has, however, been criticised by the organisation Human Rights Watch, who suggested that the Military Whistleblowers Protection Act (US) scheme has failed to protect individuals who raise allegations of sexual assault.[47] This analysis will now proceed to consider Service Complaints.

Service Complaints

Personnel in the UK Armed Forces can make Service Complaints where they have been 'wronged in any matter relating to their service'.[48] It can therefore be observed that the emphasis of the scheme is placed on grievance matters which would ordinarily be dealt with separately to

---

[44] See further H. Rosin, 'When Joseph comes marching home', *Washington Post*, 17 May 2004.

[45] The communication to the chain of command will be regarded as a 'protected communication' under Title 10 USC s.1034(2)(b).

[46] See further, Inspector General website:, www.first.army.mil/ig/igevolut. htm.

[47] 'US: military whistleblowers at risk', *Human Rights Watch*, 18 May 2015, available at www.hrw.org/news/2015/05/18/us-military-whistleblowers-risk.

[48] Armed Forces Act 2006, s.334.

whistleblowing.[49] Any concern raised will need to directly affect the individual in order to be covered by this section. There is no further definition of what constitutes being 'wronged', however the Secretary of State can exempt certain categories of complaints from the scheme. For example, the guidelines identify that individuals wishing to complain about discipline matters should seek legal advice to determine whether the matter would be considered. It is suggested that the Service Complaints System would be best used to complain about detrimental treatment following the raising of a whistleblowing concern, rather than as an avenue to raise concerns.

Individuals have several options: they may seek informal resolution through the chain of command, lodge a Service Complaint directly with the Commanding Officer, or submit an allegation to the Service Complaints Commissioner; if he/she is of an officer rank they may wish to petition the Crown. If the complaint is dealt with formally it may proceed at one of three levels.[50] Level one complaints are heard by the 'prescribed officer' who will essentially be the Commanding Officer.[51] If the Commanding Officer feels that they cannot deal with the complaint effectively, or that they lack the 'authority to grant redress', he/she will submit it to Level two.[52] Level two complaints are heard by the Senior Officer, who will be at least one rank above the Commanding Officer, and again, the Senior Officer will consider whether or not it is appropriate for them to deal with the complaint. If he/she does not have the authority to grant redress they will refer the complaint to level three. Level three complaints represent the most serious level and are heard by the Defence Council, which can form a 'Service Complaints Panel'.[53]

Direct Complaints to Commanding Officers

An individual may also submit a complaint directly to the Commanding Officer. There is the possibility that a Commanding Officer may be involved in the wrongdoing complained of. This factor has been considered by the appeals mechanism. If a Commanding Officer is involved, his superior officer should be approached; if he too is implicated in the

---

[49] As a personal grievance issue. Personal grievance issues are unlikely to be covered by PIDA1998, as qualifying disclosures are subject to s.43B.

[50] Ministry of Defence, *Redress of Individual Grievances: Service Complaints*, JSP 831 (2014).

[51] *Ibid.* [15].

[52] *Ibid.*

[53] *Ibid.*

alleged wrongdoing then an officer of equal rank to the superior officer will be nominated by the lead headquarters for the respective service.[54] The Commanding Officer who receives the complaint must also check to see whether or not he/she is implicated or is the subject of the complaint and, if so, is required to refer the matter to their immediate superior in the chain of command, or if that officer is implicated in or the subject of the complaint, an officer of equal or superior rank will be chosen by the lead headquarters of the respective service.[55]

Upon receiving a complaint, the Commanding Officer will decide either to investigate the complaint, or to refer it to levels two and three. If the Commanding Officer decides to investigate the complaint, he/she will then make a decision as to whether the complaint is valid and whether they have the appropriate means of granting redress. If the Commanding Officer chooses to decide the complaint, the complainant has the option of having the matter referred to levels two and three if they are unhappy with the outcome. The Senior Officer at level two therefore acts as a further check on the actions of the Commanding Officer. If they choose to investigate and decide upon the compliant, they must consider whether to uphold, reject or refer the complaint. When doing so, they must notify the outcome of their decision in writing to the complainant.

At level three, the Defence Council has the option of making a decision on the complaint; of delegating the complaint to a Service Complaints Panel for consideration and a decision; or delegating the complaint to a Panel for consideration and a recommendation, in which case the Defence Council would then make the decision based upon the recommendation of the Panel.[56]

Services Complaints Panel

The Service Complaints Panel is comprised of two serving military officers of a 1* rank.[57] An independent member of the Panel will be appointed in cases where the matter relates to instances of:

> a. discrimination; b. harassment; c. bullying; d. dishonest, improper or biased behaviour; e. failure of the Ministry of Defence to provide medical, dental or nursing care where the Ministry of Defence was responsible for providing that care; f. negligence in the provision by Ministry of Defence healthcare

---

[54] *Ibid.*
[55] *Ibid.*
[56] *Ibid.* ch. 5.
[57] Armed Forces Act 2006, s. 336.

professionals of medical, dental or nursing care; or g. concerning the exercise by a Service policeman of his statutory powers as a Service policeman.[58]

Armed Forces Act 2006, section 336(7), gives the Secretary of State the power to appoint an 'independent person' who must not be either a member of the Civil Service or a serving member of the Armed Forces. This scheme appears comprehensive, however, the scheme's effectiveness is reliant upon those in the command structure who, in turn, receive orders themselves from others in the hierarchy. It is suggested therefore that there is a danger that important concerns will not be dealt with appropriately. The scheme may also deter individuals who, because of the hierarchical structure, may be concerned that they will be subjected to retaliation. This situation is not assisted by the lack of an effective oversight mechanism.

IV EXTERNAL OVERSIGHT

Following the deaths of four army recruits at Deepcut Barracks in Surrey, an independent inquiry headed by Nicholas Blake QC investigated the circumstances surrounding the deaths and concluded that there were serious instances of bullying and harassment and that trainees who felt poorly treated were reluctant to complain against NCOs. Those who did complain were vulnerable to reprisals and received an 'ineffective response' by their 'immediate supervisors'.[59] Ultimately, Blake identified that the system of military complaints cannot depend on the efficiency of an individual Commanding Officer or the perception 'he or she creates that the chain of command is approachable and caring'.[60] He stated that the evidence had presented a 'substantial challenge to the present system', identifying that other personnel had not brought instances of unacceptable conduct to the attention of the Commanding Officer. He further noted that the confidentiality of complainants was an issue: the alleged abuser and other members of staff had been aware of visits made

---

[58] Armed Forces (Redress of Individual Grievances) Regulations 2007, SI 2007/3353, reg. 9.

[59] Nicholas Blake QC, *The Deepcut Review: A Review of the Circumstances Surrounding the Deaths of Four Soldiers at Princess Royal Barracks, Deepcut Between 1995 and 2002*, HC-795 (2006).

[60] *Ibid.* [12.83].

to the Army Welfare Service, which gave the potential for retaliation against the complainants.[61]

The report recommended that a 'military ombudsman' be established with a remit to investigate complaints from military personnel or their families about 'specific allegations of conduct prejudicial to their welfare'.[62] It was also suggested that the proposed ombudsman took a supervisory role in the investigation of complaints made to the authorities, for example, the Royal Military Police. If the ombudsman was not satisfied with the way in which the complaint was handled he would be able to 'instigate legal proceedings to set aside legally flawed decisions not to prosecute'.[63]

The Government published a response to the review which acknowledged the need for an independent complaints commissioner but with significant limitations on the proposed powers. It argued that the proposed commissioner would undermine the chain of command, would undermine the role of the prosecuting authorities, and that the independent prosecuting authorities make their decisions under the general superintendence of the Attorney General.[64]

Services Complaints Commissioner

The first Services Complaints Commissioner (SCC) was appointed as part of an independent complaint mechanism with substantial limitations, on the model proposed in the Deepcut Report. The Armed Forces Act 2006 affords both serving and former Armed Forces personnel the right to make a complaint if the individual believes that they have been wronged in any matter relating to their service.[65] The complaint is submitted in writing either by completion of a 'Service Complaint Form' or in the form of a letter in the first instance. There is a time limit which extends to three months from the time that the matter complained of

---

[61]   *Ibid.*

[62]   *Ibid.* [12.101].

[63]   *Ibid.*

[64]   'Response to Recommendation 26' in *The Government's Response to the Deepcut Review*, Cm 6851 (June 2006).

[65]   Armed Forces Act, s.334, provides: '(1) If—(a) a person subject to service law thinks himself wronged in any matter relating to his service, or (b) a person who has ceased to be subject to service law thinks himself wronged in any such matter which occurred while he was so subject, he may make a complaint about the matter under this section (a "service complaint")'.

occurred.[66] This can be extended if the Commanding Officer decides that it would be 'just and equitable to do so'.[67] Examples given are if the complainant is hospitalised or deployed on operations and thus is unable to have access to the materials necessary to make the complaint.[68] Complaints are excluded if they relate to pensions, discretionary awards, and discipline in relation to judgments made by court-martial and other criminal or disciplinary decisions, compensation and criminal injuries compensation, decisions relating to exemption from call out (applicable to reservists) and decisions made by the Security Vetting Appeals Panel.[69]

The Commissioner has no investigatory powers and has been the subject of criticism. The father of one of the soldiers who died at the Deepcut Barracks branded the role of the Commissioner as 'pointless' and a 'toothless tiger'.[70] In reality, the Commissioner was limited to the ability to contact Commanding Officers to chase up the progress of complaints. The outgoing Services Complaints Commissioner found systematic failings in the complaints system, in particular noting that there were considerable delays in the resolution of complaints.[71] The Service Complaints System is due to be reformed and a new Armed Forces Ombudsman will replace the Commissioner in early 2016. The Armed Forces (Service Complaints and Financial Assistance) Act 2015 contains new powers to review and overturn decisions made regarding complaints. The new Ombudsman will also have the power to investigate concerns, however this is limited to investigation into the alleged maladministration of the handling of a complaint rather than investigation of the complaint itself.[72]

In the Republic of Ireland, the Irish Ombudsman for the Defence Forces provides a close comparison to the UK Services Complaints Commissioner.[73] The position was established in 2005 and is independent

---

[66] *Ibid.* s.334(5), (6).

[67] Ministry of Defence, *Redress of Individual Grievances: Service Complaints*, Issue 1.0, JSP 831 (2007) [5].

[68] *Ibid.*

[69] There is a full list of exemptions contained in Armed Forces (Redress of Individual Grievances) Regulations 2007, SI 2007/3353, Sch.1.

[70] Geoff Gray, father of Private Geoff Gray, speaking on *BBC News*, 7 November 2007.

[71] Service Complaints Commissioner, *Annual Report* (2014), available at http://armedforcescomplaints.independent.gov.uk/linkedfiles/afcindependent/009 488annualreport2014bookaccessible.pdf.

[72] Armed Forces (Service Complaints and Financial Assistance) Act 2015, s.340H.

[73] See www.odf.ie.

of the Irish Defence Force and the command structure. The Ombudsman is statutorily defined by virtue of the Defence Forces Act 2004 (Eire) and is appointed by the President of the Republic of Ireland on recommendation of the government. The complainant is required to exhaust all internal procedures before making a complaint to the Ombudsman. If the Ombudsman investigates the complaint, she can make recommendations to the Minister of Defence which offers proposals for corrective action. If she is dissatisfied with the response she may voice her concerns by publishing a special report.

The Ombudsman for the Defence Forces (Eire) offers a compromise which respects the traditional command structure of the Armed Forces and which provides oversight where necessary. However, the Ombudsman is excluded from investigating concerns raised about security or operational matters.[74] This imposes a substantial limitation on the investigatory remit of the office, suggesting that the Ombudsman, like the UK Service Complaints Commissioner, is best suited for investigating matters of person to person employment grievances (e.g. discrimination or allegations of personal malpractice, what is known in the US Public Service jurisdiction as 'prohibited personnel practices'), rather than major allegations of malpractice involving service personnel on operations. However, it should be noted that personnel in the Irish Defence Force can obtain protection under the Protected Disclosures Act 2014 (Ireland). Section 20 extends the remit of the Ombudsman by removing any inhibitor to the investigation of reprisal complaints in the Ombudsman Defence Forces Act 2004. Therefore, whilst the Ombudsman might not be suited to investigating whistleblowing concerns, they can investigate reprisals where individuals have raised concerns.

V SUGGESTED REFORMS

It is clear from the aforementioned analysis that substantial reform is needed to the way whistleblowing concerns are dealt with in the UK Armed Forces. Suggesting that the services will 'honour the spirit' of PIDA 1998 provides inadequate protection and reassurance to potential whistleblowers and fails to identify that PIDA 1998 does not prescribe complaint handling procedures.

First, new guidance on raising concerns is needed which is separate from the guidance issued to civil servants, in order to recognise the

---

74   See further Ombudsman (Defence Forces) Act 2004, s.5.

different employment status and more stringent restrictions on expression placed on military personnel. The Canadian Armed Forces provide detailed explanatory guidance which includes both public servants and military personnel but provides different sections for the different persons, as well as entirely separate schemes for military and civil personnel.[75] Secondly, it should be considered whether the Armed Forces should provide access to a person independent of the command structure for the purposes of investigating concerns. Whilst senior members of the Armed Forces may argue that this would weaken the chain of command, the Australian approach (the Australian Defence Force shares historical ties with the UK Armed Forces) includes an Inspector General for the Defence Force who can investigate whistleblowing concerns. The provision of a new Inspector General or Commissioner for dealing with whistleblowing concerns would arguably be preferable to expanding the remit of the current Services Complaints Commissioner/Ombudsman because the new Ombudsman will have limited investigatory powers and effectively be restricted to considering grievance issues. This should not preclude the SCC/ Ombudsman from investigating reprisals against whistleblowers. However, it is suggested that provision should be made to ensure that the new Ombudsman would be able to investigate whistleblower reprisals without the need to raise complaints using the Service Complaints procedures. A new section is needed to amend the Armed Forces Act 2015, to expand the powers of the Ombudsman in a similar way to the approach taken in Ireland. Finally, there should be statutory protection for whistleblowers in the UK Armed Forces. Amendment to PIDA 1998 could be one possible option, however, Armed Forces personnel currently only have access to the employment tribunal for the purposes of making discrimination claims. The Protected Disclosures Act 2014 (Ireland) proves that it is possible to include Armed Forces personnel as part of non-sector specific legislation. The Protected Disclosures Act 2013 (Australia) also provides a workable model.[76]

---

[75] Chief Review Services, *Disclosure of Wrongdoing*, (2014), available at www.forces.gc.ca/assets/FORCES_Internet/docs/en/contact/2014-guidelines-whistleblowing.pdf.

[76] Members of the Australian Defence Force are also able to raise concerns to the Commonwealth Ombudsman under the Public Interest Disclosure Scheme, see www.ombudsman.gov.au/pages/pid/information-for-disclosers/. For analysis of the Act see A.J. Brown, 'Towards "Ideal" Whistleblowing Legislation? Some Lessons from Recent Australian Experience' (2013) 2(3) *E-Journal of Comparative Labour Studies*, www.adapt.it/EJCLS/index.php/ejcls_adapt/article/view/134.

VI CONCLUSION

The European Court of Human Rights has repeatedly identified that 'freedom of expression constitutes one of the essential foundations of a democratic society and for each individual's self-fulfilment'.[77] However, members of the Armed Forces are subject to a proportionate restriction on their expression rights. This modification of the rights afforded means that individuals are unlikely to obtain protection for acts of protest whistleblowing. However, because of the wide margin of appreciation the ECtHR has placed on member states regarding security matters and the need to maintain forces discipline, it is suggested that individuals face a considerable struggle to argue that their whistleblowing disclosures should be protected unless the information is of a considerably high value. Armed Forces personnel are more likely to encounter administrative and legal sanctions even if they raise concerns internally; this is because in the Armed Forces individuals may be punished for insubordination, misconduct to superior officers and disobeying a lawful command. Therefore, the sanctions for raising whistleblowing concerns could be severe. A UK Armed Forces whistleblowing law is therefore needed to ensure that individuals are protected from reprisals.[78] The above analysis suggests that the current complaints procedures may be ineffective to deal with cases involving whistleblower reprisals. Without significant improvements to the scheme as a whole, it is likely that the United Kingdom will be in breach of their requirements to provide an effective remedy under Article 14 ECHR.

This analysis has identified that the whistleblowing mechanisms discussed above have been the subject of concerns expressed by both Armed Forces personnel and civil servants. There is a benefit in ensuring that whistleblowing is actively encouraged by both civilian and military personnel. The review by Charles Haddon-Cave QC into the crash of a Nimrod aircraft in Afghanistan which caused the death of 14 servicemen identified that safety concerns had been ignored.[79] Furthermore, the report highlighted failings involving the Air Force, the Ministry of

---

[77] See e.g. *Lingens v. Austria* (1996) 8 EHRR 103, [41].
[78] Council of Europe Resolution 1429 supports this proposition, suggesting that whistleblower protection should extend to personnel in the Armed Forces.
[79] Charles Haddon-Cave QC, *The Nimrod Review*, HC-1025 (2009); Alan E. Deihl, *Silent Knights: Blowing the Whistle on Military Accidents and their Cover-ups* (Brassy, 2003).

Defence and private contractors BAE Systems and Quintex. However, if whistleblowers from the military are to be encouraged it is essential that they receive an adequate level of protection when raising concerns. Extensive reform to the UK system is therefore required.

8. Final observations

This book has identified that public interest disclosures can take many forms, from internal authorised disclosures to line managers or nominated officers, to external disclosures to oversight bodies and Members of Parliament, and unauthorised disclosures to journalists or via a blog or disclosure outlet. In all of the possible routes to disclosure, this book has identified deficiencies in both the mechanisms and legal protections available. It would appear that considerable work still needs to be done, first, to appreciate the value of Crown servant whistleblowers, and secondly, to acknowledge that the provision of authorised whistleblowing mechanisms can act as an alternative to the making of unauthorised disclosures. The purpose of this final chapter is to outline the key findings made in the preceding chapters and to identify the main suggestions for reform. Section I will focus on recommendations. Section II will provide a public interest framework based on UK common law jurisprudence.

I RECOMMENDATIONS

Protection of Official Information

Chapter 2 identified that very few individuals are successfully prosecuted for offences under the Official Secrets Act 1989. This would appear to be similar to the position in the United States, where despite an increased effort to punish public servants for unauthorised disclosures the number of individuals being prosecuted remains relatively small. This chapter also suggested that the Official Secrets Act 1989 can serve as a barrier to individuals raising concerns about wrongdoing and malpractice. This is because several sections of the Act contain 'damaging disclosure tests' which are easily satisfied. There is no opportunity for the court to consider the public interest benefit of the disclosure. The Act does not contain an express public interest test. Whilst it is argued that there is still scope to claim a defence of necessity, this is a very limited and uncertain option. The emphasis that the Court of Appeal and House of Lords placed on authorised alternatives to raise concerns does not mitigate against the restrictions imposed by the Act. The effectiveness of those alternatives was questioned, particularly with regard to employees in the security and intelligence services, in Chapter 6. Even if a concern does not contain information which could breach the 1989 Act, there is a danger that individuals will be dissuaded from raising it. Empirical analysis of the UK government departments and agencies found that there are different approaches to how official secrecy and confidentiality are handled. There is a danger that individuals will be dissuaded from raising important concerns for fear that they will breach the 1989 Act because of a lack of clarity in the legislation as to what constitutes an official secret, and because many are required to sign the Official Secrets Acts without ever being likely to be exposed to secret material.

Considerable reforms are needed in this area. A new Official Information Act is required to more closely align the law with the classification of official documents. Courts and juries should be able to be provided with an indication of the level of classification of the document, as well as being able to consider the public interest benefit of the disclosure. Ultimately, it is suggested that a defence of necessity is provided based upon the Security of Information Act 2001 (Canada). Beyond this, a detailed review is required of the way government departments and agencies handle official information, and it should be questioned whether all Crown servants should still sign the Official Secrets Acts. Further clarity is also needed with regard to obligations in the Civil Service Code.

Legal Protection for Journalistic Sources

Chapter 3 considered the protection of journalistic sources. In doing so it identified the evolving nature of the journalist and source relationship and discussed the risks posed by mass surveillance by the United Kingdom, the United States and other intelligence partners. This chapter identified that post Human Rights Act 1998, domestic courts have failed to afford sufficient weight to the protection of journalistic sources. Part of the problem stems from the quality of the legal protections available. Contempt of Court Act 1981, section 10, was enacted prior to the Human Rights Act 1998 and does not sufficiently accord with the values enshrined in European Convention on Human Rights (ECHR), Article 10 and the strong degree of protection the European Court of Human Rights (ECtHR) provides to sources. This chapter provided several examples where the police have been able to circumvent the protections afforded in section 10 and also the special procedures contained in the Police and Criminal Evidence Act 1984 to obtain information related to sources.

Suggested reforms to the Regulation of Investigatory Powers Act (RIPA) 2000 aim to address some of the surveillance concerns, however, this analysis suggested that the reforms will not be sufficient to mitigate against the potential chilling effect on journalistic sources. The protection that the ECtHR affords to sources is strong but it is not absolute. There are very narrow exceptions under which the harmful nature of the content of information or the conduct of the source or journalist outweigh the requirement to protect the rights of individuals. It is therefore argued that a new Freedom of the Press Act is needed, similar to the model adopted in Sweden, to safeguard the protection of journalistic sources and to appropriately balance these safeguards against national security.

Legal Protection for Whistleblowers

Chapter 4 identified that there are gaps in the scope of protection available to whistleblowers. Whilst it should be acknowledged that introduction of the Public Interest Disclosure Act (PIDA) 1998 (UK) ensured that workers in the United Kingdom were some of the first in the world to receive protection for raising whistleblowing concerns, reforms enacted to cure deficiencies in the legislation have caused uncertainty and have potentially weakened the legislation as a result. The analyses identified that Article 10 ECHR protects expression more widely than PIDA 1998. Whilst 'watchdog whistleblowing' concerns may be pro-tected under PIDA 1998, it is unlikely that 'protest whistleblowing' concerns will be protected. However, protest concerns can still be protected under Article 10. It is therefore important that employment tribunals considering whistleblowing cases take full account of the Article 10 jurisprudence to ensure compliance with their obligations under Human Rights Act 1998, section 6.

Chapter 4 made a number of recommendations for reform. It was identified that the inclusion of an overarching public interest test in PIDA 1998 creates an unnecessary barrier for individuals to obtain employment protection and that it should be removed. The chapter suggested that the categories of protected disclosure contained in section 43B could be expanded to include the 'misuse of public funds' and 'gross maladministration'. A new 'gross maladministration' provision would support Crown servants wanting to raise concerns regarding decisions made by Ministers of the Crown or the Chief Executive of a government agency.

Improved Arrangements for Civil Servants and a New Civil Service Code

Chapter 5 focussed upon the arrangements available to civil servants. Section I of the chapter reported on data provided by departments and agencies which identified that the majority of whistleblowing concerns raised are 'ordinary' watchdog-type concerns. However, the Civil Service Code is likely to act as an inhibitor to the expression of these concerns where disclosures are raised to Members of Parliament or Select Committees because of the limits placed on political expression. Analysis in this chapter found that the Civil Service Code should be made clearer with regard to whistleblowing disclosures, with more explanation of the interaction of the Code with PIDA 1998. The Civil Service Code and Civil Service Management Code could be amended to include protections from disciplinary action for individuals who raise concerns, as well as making the mistreatment of individuals who raise concerns a breach of the Code.

The chapter identified that there are variations in how Civil Service departments and agencies deal with concerns under the Code, and that a civil servant working in one department could therefore experience a different outcome to one working within another. The chapter identified that despite recommendations made by Public Concern at Work and the Public Administration Select Committee to spread nominated officers across pay grades, many are still placed in senior roles. Based on the information provided as a result of the freedom of information requests, many departments and agencies are not centrally recording or monitoring whistleblowing concerns. The chapter recommended the central tracking and monitoring of all concerns in a manner which is consistent across the Civil Service. The chapter identified concerns regarding the effectiveness of the Civil Service Commission in investigating concerns to initiate action for wrongdoing. The chapter concluded by identifying the value of Crown servant whistleblowers who appear before public inquiries, but noted that legislative reform is required to ensure that individuals who do so are protected.

Legal Protections and Improved Arrangements for Employees of the Security and Intelligence Agencies

Chapter 6 focussed upon the security and intelligence agencies. The chapter questioned the effectiveness of the routes to raise concerns which were identified in the Court of Appeal and House of Lords judgments in *R* v. *Shayler*. The chapter identified that the Intelligence and Security

Committee has not actively reported on the work of the Independent Staff Counsellor and also appears reluctant to receive whistleblowing concerns from agency staff. The chapter identified that the Defence Intelligence Staff are placed at a considerable disadvantage because, based on publically available information, they do not appear to have access to the Independent Staff Counsellor. The analysis suggested that the current oversight regime in the United Kingdom requires reform. The Interception of Communications Commissioner, the Intelligence Services Commissioner or the Intelligence and Security Committee have limited powers to investigate operational matters, particularly where a concern is ongoing. This limits the viability of oversight mechanisms to receive whistleblowing concerns and to investigate them effectively. Proposals in the Investigatory Powers Bill suggest replacing the Commissioners with one single Investigatory Powers Commission (IPC). The proposals are unlikely to enhance the position of whistleblowers, as there are no plans to allow individuals to raise concerns to the new Commission.

The chapter suggested a number of reforms. If the Commissioners and the Intelligence and Security Committee will receive whistleblowing concerns, then it is important, at the very least, that there is oversight of the internal whistleblowing arrangements and the Staff Counsellor. This could easily be conducted by the Intelligence and Security Committee under the current arrangements. The chapter identified that the arrangements in place in the United Kingdom appear weak in comparison with other jurisdictions, such as Australia and Ireland, which provide authorised and secure mechanisms and legal protections for those who raise concerns. The chapter identified that PIDA 1998 (UK) was sufficiently flexible to allow individuals to obtain protection for raising concerns under the current framework provided that the disclosures did not breach the Official Secrets Acts. Chapter 2 provided recommendations to replace the Act with a new Official Information Act which would allow for disclosures to the media or wider public to be protected on duress of circumstances grounds, following the approach taken by Security of Information Act 1985 (Canada), section 15.

Legal Protections and New Arrangements for the Armed Forces

Chapter 7 identified that members of the UK Armed Forces, like their counterparts in the UK security and intelligence services, do not have access to PIDA 1998. Jurisprudence from the ECtHR makes it clear that persons who sign up to the Armed Forces agree to a restriction of freedom of speech under Article 10 ECHR. Members of the UK Armed Forces also have an obligation to adhere to a rigid command structure, whereby the failure to carry out the instructions of a superior officer may result in criminal sanction. As a consequence, the Armed Forces restrict the autonomy rights of the individual. The aforementioned obligations are likely to weigh heavily against a military whistleblower in a proportionality analysis. However, it is recognised that whilst soldiers act as citizens in uniform, the restrictions on speech may be outweighed where the information disclosed is of a high value to the public interest. The framework adopted in *Guja* v. *Moldova* is sufficiently flexible to include members of the Armed Forces, however whistleblowers face a significant hurdle to obtain protection. The ECtHR will be prepared to award a wide margin of appreciation to member states on issues concerning the Armed Forces. Article 10 ECHR cannot, therefore, be relied upon in the absence of domestic whistleblowing protections.

This chapter provided empirical analysis based on information obtained by a freedom of information request to the Ministry of Defence. The information identified that the Armed Forces have 'agreed to honour the spirit' of PIDA 1998, however, analysis in this chapter questioned how effective this could be in practice. PIDA 1998 does not provide steps for organisations to follow in handling concerns, nor does it provide protection pre-detriment or dismissal. The chapter also identified that the whistleblowing policy made available to military personnel does not differentiate between civilian and military staff. In addition, the 'PIDA Focal Points' where personnel can raise concerns do not currently record whether disclosures have been received by a civilian or military person or by a member of the public. The chapter identified that the current status of whistleblowing in the UK Armed Forces needs to be reviewed and should be reformed.

The chapter questioned the effectiveness of the Service Complaints mechanism and the Service Complaints Commissioner. Despite the implementation of a new complaints scheme and an Ombudsman, these reforms are unlikely to support whistleblowing concerns. The new Ombudsman will effectively handle grievance complaints where individuals have been 'wronged in matters relating to their service'.

The chapter argued for a new whistleblowing policy and guidance to be made available to Armed Forces personnel which is separate to the guidance issued to civil servants. This is needed to reflect the different nature of the employment status of civil servants and Armed Forces personnel, the command structure and the enhanced limitations on public interest expression. It questioned whether a whistleblowing mechanism, independent of the command structure, should be made available to military personnel. This should provide an avenue to raise concerns and to have those concerns investigated effectively. Whilst it is identified that the command structure places a barrier on external oversight, it should be recognised that jurisdictions such as Australia and the United States have adopted an Inspector General model.

In terms of protecting those who raise concerns, the chapter argued that the limited investigatory remit of the Services Complaints Commissioner or the new Ombudsman should not prevent her from investigating reprisals against whistleblowers. This should not, however, be considered as a substitute for legal protection for Armed Forces whistleblowers. PIDA Act 1998 could be amended, however; Armed Forces personnel currently only have access to the employment tribunal for the purposes of making discrimination claims. Both the Protected Disclosures Act 2014 (Ireland) and the Protected Disclosures Act 2013 (Australia) identify that it is possible to include Armed Forces personnel in a general whistle-blowing law available to all sectors.

II A PUBLIC INTEREST FRAMEWORK

The purpose of this section of the chapter is to outline domestic common law principles considering the public interest. At the time of writing it was suggested that the Human Rights Act 1998 could be repealed and replaced by a UK-centric 'Bill of Rights'. This is likely to mean that courts would increasingly make reference to principles developed in domestic case law rather than focussing on Strasbourg jurisprudence. This was evident in the *Miranda* case.[1] It is likely that the United Kingdom would remain a signatory to the European Convention on Human Rights. Therefore, it would still be necessary for courts to determine cases in line with the Convention. The following case principles are more likely to be used as an aid to this determination, rather than to replace wholesale longstanding Strasbourg jurisprudence.

Prior to the enactment of the Human Rights Act 1998, defining what constituted the public interest proved difficult for the courts. In *B and C v. A*, the Court of Appeal stated that it was impossible to provide a uniform definition as the '[c]ircumstances in any particular case under consideration can vary so much that a judgment in one case is unlikely to be decisive in another case'.[2]

The case of *Gartside* v. *Outram* established that there is no confidence in the disclosure of iniquity.[3] This reasoning was further extended in *Lion*

---

[1] Discussed in Chapter 3.
[2] [2002] EWCA Civ 337.
[3] (1856) 26 LJ Ch. 114.

Laboratories v. *Evans and others* to provide that publication of confidential information would be acceptable in situations where it could be proved that there was a serious and legitimate interest in the information being disclosed to the public domain.[4] In *Bellof* v. *Pressdram*, the Court further attempted to define a defence of public interest in breach of confidence cases, suggesting that disclosure:

> Must be disclosure justified in the public interest, of matters carried out or contemplated, in breach of the country's security, or in breach of the law, including statutory duty, fraud or otherwise destructive of the country or its people, including matters medically dangerous to the public; and doubtless other misdeeds of similar gravity.[5]

In *Initial Services* v. *Putterill*, Lord Denning focussed upon the disclosure of information, noting the significance of the recipient of the information. He opined that the disclosure should be to a person who has a 'proper interest to receive the information'. He suggested that it would be appropriate to disclose a crime to the police and that there may also be 'some cases where the misdeed is of such a character that the public interest may demand, or at least excuse, publication on a broader field, even to the press'.[6] In *D* v. *National Society for the Prevention of Cruelty to Children*,[7] the plaintiff was subject to an inaccurate complaint and sought disclosure of the identity of the complainant. Lord Diplock indicated that the private confidentiality agreement made between individuals must give way to:

> the general public interest that in the administration of justice truth will out, unless by reason of the character of the informant, a more important public interest is served by protecting the information or the identity of the informant from disclosure in a court of law.[8]

In *Marks* v. *Beyfus*, it was indicated that if the identities of police informants were able to be disclosed in a prosecution, the number of persons assisting the police with information on criminal activity would

---

4 [1985] QB 526, [534].
5 *Beloff* v. *Pressdram Ltd* [1973] 1 All ER 241, [260].
6 *Initial Services Ltd* v. *Putterill* [1968] 1 QB 396, [405]–[406].
7 *Ibid.*
8 *Ibid.* [218].

be dramatically reduced, preventing the police from effectively performing their duties, contrary to the public interest.[9] However, it was later
confirmed in *R* v. *Agar* that disclosure of a police informant's identity
could be necessary in order to enable the defendant to argue that he had
been set up by both the police and the informant. This was dependent on
the nature of the defendant's defence in each case.[10] Mustill LJ placed
emphasis on the fact that whilst there was a strong public interest in not
revealing the identities of informants, there was a greater requirement in
ensuring that the accused could put forward his defence, although he did
concede that the position might alter if the defence put forward was
'doomed to failure'.[11]

Private Information and the Public Interest

An individual's right to freedom of expression becomes more difficult to
justify when the information concerned does not appear to be in the
public interest, but is rather of interest to the public. A conflict between
the individual's Article 10 ECHR rights and the Article 8 rights of the
subject of the information communicated is likely to arise where an
individual chooses to criticise the private conduct of an individual in a
position of authority, as opposed to criticising the conduct of an
organisation as a whole. The Article 8 rights of individuals may also be
engaged as a consequence of the unauthorised disclosure of official
documents. For example, the Manning disclosures included documents
concerning private information.[12] In the United Kingdom, rigorous
analysis of the conflicting rights has been a necessary consequence of the
developing misuse of private information case law. The domestic courts
have arguably gone further in this area than the ECtHR, creating a 'new
methodology' to balance these rights.

Domestic principles relating to the private conduct of public figures
were established prior to the Human Rights Act 1998 coming into force.

---

[9]   (1890) 25 QBD 494, *Ibid* [498] per Lord Escher MR. See also Yvonne
Cripps, *The Legal Implications of Disclosure in the Public Interest* (2nd edn,
Sweet & Maxwell, 1994).

[10]   [1990] 2 All ER 442.

[11]   *Ibid.*

[12]   For example, the disclosure of unredacted diplomatic cables by Wikileaks
allegedly identified victims of sexual abuse: James Ball, 'Julian Assange could
face arrest in Australia over unredacted cables', *Guardian*, 2 September 2011,
available at www.theguardian.com/media/2011/sep/02/julian-assange-arrest-
australia-wikileaks.

For example, in *Woodward* v. *Hutchins*, the case involved alleged sexual activities concerning a pop star travelling on a passenger plane. An employee who was subject to a confidentiality agreement sought to disclose the information to a newspaper.[13] Lord Denning identified that if a group of people aimed to seek publicity which is to their advantage, they then 'cannot complain if a servant or employee of theirs afterwards discloses the truth about them, if the image which they fostered was not a true image, it is in the public interest that it should be corrected'.[14] Bridge LJ further supported this position by suggesting that 'those who seek and welcome publicity of every kind so long as it shows them in a favourable light are in no position to complain of an invasion of their privacy by publicity which shows them in an unfavourable light'.[15]

The following cases post Human Rights Act 1998, identify that the courts will be willing to favour Article 10 ECHR over Article 8 in cases where the information concerned is evidence to correct the public's impression of a public figure. In *Theakston* v. *MGN Ltd*,[16] a well known television personality had been photographed, without his consent, whilst attending a brothel. Lord Justice Ousley identified that there was a real element of public interest in publishing the details of Theakston's activities. Theakston's role on television suggested that his life was 'harmless if followed' whereas the claimant's activities were likely to make the public feel differently towards him.[17]

In *Campbell* v. *MGN*, the model Naomi Campbell brought proceedings against a newspaper after it published photographs of her leaving a Narcotics Anonymous meeting. The court identified that Campbell was a public figure who had made 'very public false statements' that she had not taken drugs; it was these falsehoods which the newspaper argued had made it justifiable for a newspaper to report the fact that she was addicted to drugs.[18] Lord Hoffman identified that had Campbell been an 'ordinary citizen' with a drug addiction the case would have been different. Campbell had sought publicity about various aspects of her private life.[19] Baroness Hale identified that political speech could include revealing information about 'public figures – especially those in elected office – which would otherwise be private but is relevant to their

---

13 [1997] 1 WLR 760.
14 *Ibid.* 763.
15 *Ibid.* [765].
16 [2002] EWHC 137 (QB).
17 *Ibid.* [69].
18 [2004] UKHL 22, [36].
19 *Ibid.* [54].

participation in public life'.[20] Campbell had presented herself to the public as a person who was not involved in drug taking and it was therefore in the public interest to correct this false impression. Despite this, the court found Article 8 ECHR to outweigh the public interest in publication of the photographs.[21] Publication of the photographs was therefore unnecessary.

In *Mosley* v. *News Group Newspapers*,[22] a newspaper had alleged that Max Mosley, the then president of the Fédération Internationale de l'Automobile, had been involved in a Nazi themed event and published a video of Mr Mosley engaged in sexual activity. Eady J identified that it had been recognised in *Campbell* that there could be a genuine public interest in the disclosure of the existence of a sexual relationship if such a relationship resulted in a situation giving rise to favouritism or corruption.[23] Yet the addition of 'salacious details' or 'intimate photographs' would be disproportionate and unacceptable and would be too intrusive even if they accompanied a legitimate disclosure of the relationship.[24] Public figures are entitled to a private and personal life, a notion of privacy which extends beyond sexual relationships to include personal relationships more generally.[25] People's sex lives are to be regarded as essentially their own business, provided at least that the participants are genuinely consenting adults and there is no question of exploiting the young or vulnerable.[26]

Information relating to a sexual relationship will more likely be considered as a matter for the public interest when balancing the competing rights. It is submitted that a politician who gives the impression of a family man or a man who claims family values when the reality is quite different is less likely to tip the balance in favour of the protection of privacy. Using the aforementioned privacy jurisprudence, it is submitted that a whistleblower may be justified in revealing information relating to a personal matter the disclosure of which is necessary to correct a false impression. It is submitted that such information may be of a lower value than information which highlights serious wrongdoing or illegality in government. The public interest in the disclosure may be heightened if the personal matter in question has an impact on the

---

[20]   *Ibid.* [54].
[21]   *Ibid.* [154].
[22]   *Mosley* v. *News Group Newspapers Ltd* [2008] EWHC 1777.
[23]   *Campbell* v. *Mirror Group Newspapers Ltd* [2004] 2 AC 457, [60].
[24]   *Ibid.* [20].
[25]   *Ibid.* [101].
[26]   *Ibid.* [100].

conduct of the individual in public life. An example of this conduct may include circumstances where a Minister engaged in an extra-marital affair with a member of his staff and then promoted the person, thus giving the individual an unfair advantage over colleagues, and bypassing procedures relating to fair recruitment and promotion.

In whistleblowing cases involving information considered to be of a private or personal nature, it is submitted that it may be necessary for the court to engage in a parallel analysis of the competing rights to private and family life afforded by Article 8 ECHR and the right to freedom of expression afforded by Article 10. The court must first consider whether the applicant enjoys a reasonable expectation of privacy in respect of the information which is intended to be published. If this is determined, the courts must then, secondly, balance the competing Convention rights against each other in the parallel analysis. Guidance on the parallel analysis was provided by Lord Steyn in *Re S*:

> First, neither article has as such precedence over the other. Secondly, where the values under the two articles are in conflict, an intense focus on the comparative importance of the specific rights being claimed in the individual case is necessary. Thirdly, the justifications for interfering with or restricting each right must be taken into account. Finally, the proportionality test must be applied to each.[27]

This approach clearly identifies that domestic courts will not grant presumptive priority to either Convention right, and the value of both privacy and free speech will be equally scrutinised when they are structurally balanced against each other. Therefore, it is suggested that in cases applying the *Guja* v. *Moldova* framework for assessing proportionality, domestic courts will need to adapt the test to take into account the competing privacy interest afforded by Article 8.[28] It is submitted that the correct approach in such a case would be for the court first to apply the 'new methodology' test established in *Re S*. Secondly, the court should apply the *Guja* v. *Moldova* framework. However, in considering whether it would be in the public interest to disclose the information, an 'intense focus' will be required to balance Article 10 against Article 8. Therefore, it would not be sufficient just to consider the detriment to the employer in cases where privacy rights are engaged. In cases where Article 8 is engaged, it is suggested that a new category should be included to consider the 'detriment caused to individuals' as a result of

---

[27] *Re S (A Child)* [2004] UKHL 47, [17].
[28] Application No. 1427704 (ECtHR, 12 February 2008).

the disclosure. The next section will consider matters specific to the operation of government.

Matters Specific to the Operation of Government

Government departments may decide to withhold the release of information relating to the formulation of government policy or other aspects of the decision-making process. The justification for doing so stems from the need to maintain the longstanding doctrine of collective responsibility and to allow for 'candour' – the frank and open discussion of ideas without fear of inhibition. According to the convention of Cabinet collective responsibility, members of Cabinet must:

> Publically support all Government decisions made in Cabinet, even if they do not privately agree with them and may have argued in Cabinet against their adoption. They must also preserve the confidentiality of the Cabinet debate that led to the decision.[29]

The purpose of the doctrine is essentially to allow 'Ministers to consider and test policy in robust debate' without fear that their decisions would be 'criticised by political opponents or a hostile media'.[30]

In *Attorney General* v. *Jonathan Cape Ltd*,[31] an attempt was made to prevent the publication of Richard Crossman's diaries on the ground that they contained confidential information of Cabinet discussions. Lord Widgery considered the public interest in disclosing the information to the public domain against the public interest in maintaining the doctrine of collective responsibility, which entails the ability of Ministers to speak frankly and receive and make decisions on the advice of civil servants without the possibility of the details of such discussions from reaching the public domain.[32] It was argued that, in allowing such information to reach the public domain, Ministers would not feel free to discuss matters frankly, and that this would therefore be harmful to the public interest.[33]

Lord Widgery focussed upon the amount of time which had passed since the discussions were first documented; in this case 11 years had passed. He then stated that the Attorney General must show '(a) that such

---

[29]   See further, *Cabinet Office* v. *Information Commissioner* [2009] Information Tribunal Appeal No. EA/2008/0024 and EA/2008/0029, [38].

[30]   *Ibid*. [39].

[31]   [1976] 1 QB 752.

[32]   *Ibid*. [765].

[33]   *Ibid*. [761].

publication would be a breach of confidence; (b) that the public interest requires that the publication be restrained; and (c) that there are no other facets of the public interest contradictory of and more compelling than that relied upon'[34] and that the court must then 'closely examine which relief is necessary to ensure that restrictions are not imposed beyond the strict requirement of public need'.[35] There was a clear breach of confidence in this case; however, the fact that the information was 11 years old meant that the confidential character of the information had lapsed.[36] Perhaps most importantly, Lord Widgery was unconvinced that the Attorney General had made out a case that the public interest required such a Draconian remedy when due regard was had to other public interests, such as freedom of speech.[37] Lord Widgery clearly distinguished between different types of information discussed in Cabinet meetings. He identified that:

> Secrets relating to national security may require to be preserved indefinitely. Secrets relating to new taxation proposals may be of the highest importance until Budget day, but public knowledge thereafter. To leak a Cabinet decision a day or so before it is officially announced is an accepted exercise in public relations, but to identify the Ministers who voted one way or another is objectionable because it undermines the doctrine of joint responsibility.[38]

Judicial arguments for justifying candour in official decision-making were considered at length in *Burmah Oil Co. Ltd v. Bank of England*.[39] Lord Wilberforce considered the public interest in keeping the information private; in particular he focussed upon the need for candour in communications between those concerned with the business of policy-making. He identified that:

> To remove protection from revelation in court in this case at least could well deter frank and full expression in similar cases in the future … another such ground is to protect from inspection by possible critics the inner workings of government while forming important government policy.[40]

---

34   *Ibid.* [770].
35   *Ibid.* [770].
36   *Ibid.* [771].
37   *Ibid.* [767].
38   *Ibid.* [770].
39   [1980] AC 1090.
40   *Ibid.* [707].

Later, in *Air Canada and others* v. *Secretary of State for Trade and another*,[41] Lord Wilberforce again opined that familiar contentions were put forward as to the need to protect Cabinet decisions against disclosure in the interest of the confidentiality of the inner workings of government and of the free and candid expressions of views.[42]

In order to balance the competing interests between the need to maintain candour and open government, concerns raised by whistle-blowers regarding the identities of decision-makers and civil servant advisers should only be justified where the information concerned is of a high value to the advancement of the public interest and debate and truth. The disclosure of information which identifies that a Cabinet Minister who decided to vote in favour of a policy in private and then later vehemently opposes it in public would therefore be justifiable as evidence to correct a false impression. The disclosure of information regarding wrongdoing or illegality would also be justified. In contrast, the disclosure of information relating to routine policy decision-making should not be justified. Such information, if disclosed, would make a limited contribution to public debate.

Whilst the disclosure of such information may be beneficial to a minority of individuals whom may be affected by the decision, it may be outweighed by a countervailing argument that candour is required to allow the free and frank exchange of views and uninhibited decision-making. Routine disclosure would inevitably lead to the 'panopticized' extreme identified by Bentham, resulting in an inevitable breakdown of the machinery of government. As Shauer identifies, public citizens are sovereign but confer power to elected representatives to carry out actions in their name.[43] It is therefore necessary, in a democratic society, to allow those representatives when making decisions beneficial to society, to do so without inhibition. The next section will consider national security as a justification for restricting the disclosure of information and whether the disclosure of national security information by a whistleblower may be justified.

National Security

In *The Zamora*, Lord Parker suggested that 'Those who are responsible for the national security must be the sole judges of what the national

---

[41]   [1983] 1 All ER 910.
[42]   *Ibid.* [919].
[43]   Frederick Shauer, *Free Speech: A Philosophical Enquiry* (CUP, 1982) 10.

security requires'.[44] Later in *Council for Civil Service Unions* v. *Minister for the Civil Service*, Lord Roskill identified that it was for the government, not the courts, to determine whether the requirements of national security outweigh the duty of fairness in any particular case. The 'government alone' had access to the necessary information, and he suggested that the judicial process was unsuitable for reaching decisions on national security.[45] The question of whether information pertaining to national security may be disclosed by a whistleblower was considered in *Attorney General* v. *Guardian (No. 2)*, where the House of Lords engaged in a lengthy balancing exercise in order to determine what constitutes the public interest. The case concerned the government's attempt to suppress publication of *Spycatcher*, the memoirs of a former MI5 employee, Peter Wright. Lord Goff highlighted that in a free society there was 'a continuing public interest that the workings of government should be open to scrutiny and criticism'.[46] Lord Griffiths conceded that if an employee of the security service discovered malpractice 'detrimental to the national interest', and he was unable to 'persuade any senior members of his service or any members of the establishment, or the police, to do anything about it', then he should be 'relieved of his duty of confidence so that he could alert his fellow citizens to the impending danger'.[47]

Lord Bingham, in the *Shayler* case, justified his position by suggesting that 'however well intentioned' the employee or former employee may be, he may not be 'equipped with sufficient information to understand the potential impact of the disclosure' which may cause 'far more damage than the person making the disclosure was ever in a position to anticipate'.[48] It is submitted that the consequences of the disclosure of national security material may be harmful to the safety and public security of citizens. However, it has been identified that the widely drafted Official Secrets Act 1989 carries the potential to protect information not only harmful to the public interest but also information which may be more harmful to government or ministerial interests than national security.

Disclosures relating to genuine national security information may be justified where the information ordinarily protected by the Official

---

[44] [1916] 2 AC 77, [107].
[45] [1984] 3 All ER 935, [28].
[46] *Attorney General* v. *Guardian Newspapers Ltd (No. 2)* [1998] 3 WLR 776, [807]; Lord Griffiths found that no such considerations arose in the instant case.
[47] *Ibid.* [795].
[48] [2000] UKHL 45, [84].

Secrets Act 1989 is of a high value to the public interest. Such high value information could include a situation where a confidential diplomatic initiative includes an agreement to conduct illegal extraordinary rendition between nation states. The disclosure of bureaucratic secrecy may be less easy to justify. Routine leaks of routine bureaucratic secret information may damage the ability of the security and intelligence services to remain 'secret'. The consequences of leaked material which is of a low value contribution to public debate may lead to a loss of confidence in the services. Lord Nicholls argued in *Attorney General* v. *Blake and another* that it was 'of paramount importance' that members of the security and intelligence services and those recruited as informers should 'have complete confidence' in their dealings with each other. Breaching that confidence, he suggested would, undermine 'the willingness of prospective informers to co-operate with the services', and the 'trust between members of the services when engaged on secret and dangerous operations' which would 'jeopardise the effectiveness of the services'.[49]

III CONCLUSION

The Introduction to this book identified that upon entering employment, Crown servants enter an intramural community. Entrance to this community requires Crown servants to agree to a voluntary restriction of their expression rights. However, Crown servants do not lose the values or political views which have been developed as citizens of the state. Therefore, they maintain a connection to the wider extramural community of which they continue to be a part. This creates an inevitable conflict between the obligations owed to both communities. Unauthorised disclosures concerning national security information arguably present the most risk to both communities because of the potential to cause harm. Leaks of national security information require the Crown servant, and later the journalist or disclosure outlet, to make an assessment of whether or not the disclosure will cause harm, effectively requiring them to judge without knowing the true extent or impact of the information concerned. Conversely, information classified to safeguard national security can be used as a shield to mask wrongdoing or malpractice. Whilst circumstances may arise where public disclosure is the only suitable option to address the concern, it may be argued that authorised disclosures using available mechanisms provide the safest route to disclosure and a way to

---

[49]   *Ibid.* [12].

reconcile these conflicting tensions. If governments across the globe are to address the issue of leaking, they must recognise that it is the individuals working in public organisations who will ultimately decide whether or not to disclose information. Efforts must therefore be re-focused from the *post facto* punishment of leakers to the support and encouragement of whistleblowing through viable authorised channels from the outset.

Select bibliography

Aitken, J., *Officially Secret* (Weidenfield and Nicolson, 1971)

Anderson, D., *A Question of Trust: Report of the Investigatory Powers Review* (2015)

Andrew, C., *Secret Service* (Hienmann, 1985)

Andrews, J., 'Public Interest and Criminal Proceedings' (1988) 104 *Law Quarterly Review* 413

Bailin, A., *The Last Cold War Statute* (2008) 8 *Criminal Law Review* 625

Barendt, B., *Freedom of Speech* (OUP, 2005)

Beatson, J. and Cripps, Y. (eds.), *Freedom of Expression and Freedom of Information, Essays in Honour of Sir David Williams* (OUP, 2000)

Birkinshaw, P., *Freedom of Information: The Law the Practice the Ideal* (Butterworths, 2001)

Blake, N., *The Deepcut Review: A Review of the Circumstances Surrounding the Deaths of Four Soldiers at Princess Royal Barracks, Deepcut between 1995 and 2002*, HC-795 (2006)

Bok, S., *Secrets: On the Ethics of Concealment and Revelation* (Vintage, 1989)

Born, H. and Leigh, I., *Making Intelligence Accountable: Legal Standards and Best Practice for Oversight of the Intelligence Agencies* (Publishing House of the Parliament of Norway, 2005)

Born, H., Leigh, I. and Wills, A., *International Intelligence Cooperation and Accountability* (Routledge, 2011)

Brabyn, J., 'Protecton Against Judicially Compelled Disclosure of the Identity of News Gathers' Confidential Sources in Common Law Jurisdictions' (2006) 69(6) *Modern Law Review* 895

British Standards Institute, *Whistleblowing Arrangements: Code of Practice* (PAS 2008/1998)

Brooke, H., The *Revolution will be Digitised: Dispatches from the Information War* (William Heinemann, 2011)

Brown, A.J., 'Towards "Ideal" Whistleblowing Legislation? Some Lessons from Recent Australian Experience' (2013) 2(3) *E-Journal of Comparative Labour Studies* available at www.adapt.it/EJCLS/index.php/ejcls_adapt/article/view/134

Brown, S.D., *Combating International Crime: The Longer Arm of the Law* (Routledge Cavendish, 2008)

Brudner, A., 'A Theory of Necessity' (1987) 7(3) *Oxford Journal of Legal Studies* 340

Calland, R. and Dehn, G., *Whistleblowing Around the World: Law, Culture and Practice* (ODAC, 2004)

Carney, D., 'The Theoretical Underpinnings of the Protection of Journalists' Confidential Sources' (2009) 1 *Journal of Media Law* 97

Chamberlain, M., 'Al Rawi v Security Service and Home Office v Tariq' (2011) 30(4) *Civil Justice Quarterly* 360

Chapman Pincher, H., *Chapman Pincher: Dangerous to Know* (Biteback Publishing, 2014)

Chief Review Services, *Disclosure of Wrongdoing* (2014), available at www.forces.gc.ca/assets/FORCES_Internet/docs/en/contact/2014-guide lines-whistleblowing.pdf

Colaresi, M.P., *Democracy Declassified: The Secrecy Dilemma in National Security* (OUP, 2014)

Committee of Privy Counsellors, *Review of Intelligence on Weapons of Mass Destruction*, HC-898 (2004)

Constitutional Affairs Committee, *Constitutional Role of the Attorney General*, HC-306 (2006–07)

Crawford, M., 'Regimes of Tolerance: A Communitarian Approach to Freedom of Expression and its Limits' (1998) 48 *University of Toronto Faculty of Law Review* 4

Cripps, Y., *The Legal implications of Disclosure in the Public Interest* (Sweet & Maxwell, 1994)

Dean, J., 'Publicity's Secret' (2001) 29(5) *Political Theory* 624

Defty, A., 'Educating Parliamentarians about Intelligence: The Role of the British Intelligence and Security Committee' (2008) 61(4) *Parliamentary Affairs* 627

Deihl, A.E., *Silent Knights: Blowing the Whistle on Military Accidents and their Cover-ups* (Brassy, 2003)

Dennis, I.H., 'On Necessity as a Defence to a Crime: Possiblities, Problems and Limitations of Justification and Excuse' (2009) 3(1) *Criminal Law and Philosophy* 29

Dworkin, R., *Taking Rights Seriously* (Harvard University Press, 1978)

Dworkin, R., *A Matter of Principle* (Harvard University Press, 1985)

Edwards, J.L.J., *The Law Officers of the Crown* (Sweet & Maxwell, 1964)

Ellison, J., *Whistleblowing Research: Methodological and Moral Issues* (Praeger, 1985)

Etzioni, A., *The New Normal: Finding a Balance Between Individual Rights and the Common Good* (Transaction, 2015)

Feldman, D., *Civil Liberties and Human Rights in England and Wales* (2nd edn, OUP, 2002)

Fenster, M., 'Seeing the State: Transparancy as Metaphor' (2010) 63 *Administrative Law Review* 669

Fenwick, H. and Phillipson, G., *Media Freedom under the Human Rights Act* (OUP, 2007)

Finnis, J., *Natural Law and Natural Rights* (Clarendon, 2011)

Fowler-Watt, K. and Allen, S. (eds.), *Journalism: New Challenges* (Centre for Journalism and Communication Research, 2013)

Geneva Centre for the Democratic Oversight of Armed Forces (DCAF), *Making Intelligence Accountable* (2015)

Glees, A. and Davies, P.H.J., *Spinning the Spies: Intelligence, Open Government and the Hutton Inquiry* (Social Affairs Unit, 2004)

Glees, A., Davis, P. and Morrison, J., *The Open Side of Secrecy* (Social Affairs Unit, 2006)

Goldfarb, R., *The Contempt Power* (Columbia University Press, 1963)

Greenwald, G., *No Place to Hide: The NSA and the Surveillance State* (Hamish Hamilton, 2014)

Griffith, J., 'The Official Secrets Act 1989' (1989) 16(2) *Journal of Law and Society* 280

Gutiérrez Zarza, A., *Exchange of Information and Data Protection in Cross-border Criminal Proceedings in Europe* (Springer, 2015)

Haddon-Cave, C., *Nimrod Review*, HC-1025 (2009)

Harding, L., *The Snowden Files: The Inside Story of the World's Most Wanted Man* (Guardian Books, 2014)

Hastedt, G., 'An INS Special Forum: Implications of the Snowden Leaks' (2014) 29(6) *Intelligence and National Security* 798

Headley, J.H., *Secrets, Free Speech and Fig Leaves* (Centre for the Study of Intelligence, 2007)

HM Government, *Review of Intelligence of Weapons of Mass Destruction*, Cm 6492 (2005)

HM Government, *The Government's Response to the Deepcut Review*, Cm 6851 (2006)

Hobbes, T., *Leviathan* (OUP, 2008, first published 1651)

Home Affairs Select Committee, *Counter-Terrorism*, HC-231 (2013–14)

Hooper, D., *Official Secrets: The Use and Abuse of the Act* (Coronet Books, 1987)

Inspector General Intelligence and Security (Australia), *Annual Report*, ISSN 1030-4657 (2015)

Intelligence and Security Committee, *Annual Report*, Cm 4073 (1997–98)

Intelligence and Security Committee, *Annual Report*, Cm 6240 (2003–04)

Intelligence and Security Committee, *Annual Report*, Cm 68-64 (2005–06)

Intelligence and Security Committee, *Annual Report*, Cm 7299 (2006–07)

Intelligence and Security Committee, *Annual Report*, Cm 7542 (2007–08)

Intelligence and Security Committee, *Annual Report*, HC-794 (2013–14)

Intelligence and Security Committee, *Report on the Intelligence Relating to the Murder of Lee Rigby*, HC-795 (2014)

Intelligence and Security Committee, *Privacy and Security: A Modern and Transparent Legal Framework*, HC-1075 (2015)

Interception of Communications Commissioner, *Annual Report*, HC-1184 (2013)

Interception of Communications Commissioner, *Inquiry into the Use of Chapter 2 of Part 1 of the Regulation of Investigatory Powers Act (RIPA) to Identify Journalistic Sources* (4 February 2015)

Jones, N., *Trading Information* (Politicos, 2006)

Jubb, P.B., 'Whistleblowing: A Restrictive Definition and Interpretation' (1999) 21 *Journal of Business Ethics* 77

Lee, Y., 'The Defence of Necessity and Powers of the Government' (2009) 3 *Criminal Law and Philosophy* 133

Leigh, D. and Harding, L., *Inside Julian Assange's War on Secrecy* (Guardian Books, 2011)

Leigh, I., 'Accountability of Security and Intelligence in the United Kingdom' in L. Johnson, H. Born and I. Leigh (eds.), *Who's Watching the Spies?* (Potomac, 2005)

Leigh, I., 'Changing the Rules of the Game: Some Necessary Reforms to United Kingdom Intelligence' (2009) 35(4) *Review of International Studies* 952

Lewis, D., *Whistleblowing at Work* (Athlone Press, 2001)

Lowe, N. and Sufrin, B., *Borrie and Lowe, The Law of Contempt* (3rd edn, Butterworths, 1996)

Lustgarten, L. and Leigh, I., *In from the Cold: National Security and Parliamentary Democracy* (OUP, 1994)

Lyon, D., 'The Snowden Stakes: Challenges for Understanding Surveillance Today' (2015) 13(2) Surveillance and Society 139

Maer, L., *Misconduct in Public Office,* SN/PC/04909 (2008)

Maer, L. and Gay, O., *Official Secrecy*, SN/PC/02023 (Parliament and Constitution Centre, 30 December 2008)

Malan, M., 'Leadership, Integration and Civic Consciousness: From *Innere Führung* to *Ubuntu*' (2005) 4 *African Security Review* 3

Martin, B., 'Strategy for Public Interest Leaking' in G. Martin, R. Scott Bray and M. Kumar (eds.), *Secrecy, Law and Society* (Routledge, 2015)

Martin, G., Scott Bray, R. and Kumar, M. (eds.), *Secrecy, Law and Society* (Routledge, 2015)

Matthews, J., 'Journalists and their Sources: The Twin Challenges of Diversity and Verification' in K. Fowler-Watt and S. Allen (eds.), *Journalism: New Challenges* (Centre for Journalism and Communication Research, 2013)

Mcleod, I., *Legal Theory* (5th edn, Palgrave, 2010)

Meyer, D. and Berenbaum, D., 'The Wasp's Nest: Intelligence Community Whistleblowing and Source Protection' (2015) 8(1) *Journal of National Security Law and Policy* 1, available at http://jnslp.com/wp-content/uploads/2015/05/The-Wasp's-Nest.pdf

Mill, J.S., *On Liberty* (Cosimo, 2001, first published 1889)

Murphy, M.H., 'The Pendulum Effect: Comparisons between the Snowden Revelations and the Church Committee—What are the Potential Implications for Europe?' (2014) 23(2) *Information and Communications Technology Law* 192

Near, J. and Miceli, M., 'Organizational Dissidence: The Case of Whistle-blowing' (1985) 4 *Journal of Business Ethics* 1

Neocleous, M., 'Privacy, Secrecy, Idiocy' (2002) 69 *Social Research* 86

Nolte, G., *European Military Law Systems* (De Gruyter Recht, 2003)

Oliver, D. and Austin, R., 'Political and Constitutional Aspects of the Westland Affair' (1987) 40 *Parliamentary Affairs* 1

Patfield, F., 'Spycatcher Worldwide: An Overview' (1989) 11 *European Intellectual Property Review* 6

Perry, M.J., *Morality Politics and Law* (OUP, 1991)

Peter, G., 'The Intelligence and Security Committee and the Challenge of Networks' (2009) 35(4) *Review of International Studies* 931

Phythian, M., 'The British Experience with Intelligence Accountability' (2007) 22(1) *Intelligence and National Security* 97

Pilkington, C., *The Civil Service Today* (Manchester University Press, 1999)

Ponting, C., *The Right to Know: The Inside Story of the Belgrano Affair* (Sphere Books, 1985)

Pozen, D.E., 'The Mosaic Theory: National Security and the Freedom of Information Act' (2005) 115 *Yale Law Journal* 628

Pozen, D.E., 'The Leaky Leviathan: Why the Government Condemns and Condones Unlawful Disclosures of Information' (2013) 127 *Harvard Law Review* 512

Rains, S.A. and Scott, C.A., 'To Identify or Not to Identify: A Theoretical Model of Receiver Responses to Anonymous Communication' (2007) 1 *Communication Theory* 74

Rawls, J., *A Theory of Justice* (2nd edn, OUP, 1999)

Rodgers, D., *By Royal Appointment: Tales from the Privy Council, the Unknown Arm of Government* (Biteback, 2015)

Rowe, P., 'Military Servants' in M. Sunkin and S. Payne (eds.), *The Nature of the Crown: A Legal and Political Analysis* (OUP, 1999)

Rowe, P., *The Impact of Human Rights Law on Armed Forces* (CUP, 2006)

Royal United Services Institute, *A Democratic Licence to Operate: Report of the Independent Surveillance Review*, ISSN 1750-9432 (July 2015)

Sagar, R., *Secrets and Leaks: The Dilemma of State Secrecy* (Princeton University Press, 2013)

Savage, A., 'Whistleblowing in the Police Service: Developments and Challenges' (2016) 22(1) *European Journal of Current Legal Issues* (forthcoming)

Savage, A. and Hyde, R., 'The Response to Whistleblowing by Regulators: A Practical Perspective' (2015) 35(3) *Legal Studies* 408

Savage, A. and Mora, P.D., 'Security Service Memoirs and the Jurisdiction of the Investigatory Powers Tribunal: The Supreme Court's Decision in A v. B' (2010) 21(5) *Entertainment Law Review* 197

Savage, A. and Mora, P.D., 'Independent Judicial Oversight to Guarantee Proportionate Revelations of Journalistic Sources: The Grand Chamber's Decision in Sanoma Uitgevers B.V. v. The Netherlands' (2011) 22 *Entertainment Law Review* 1

Security Commission, *Report on the Case of Michael John Bettaney*, Cmnd 9514 (1985)

Senate Select Committee on Public Interest Whistleblowing, *In the Public Interest* (AGPS, Canberra, 1994)

Shauer, F., *Free Speech: A Philosophical Enquiry* (CUP, 1982)

Simon, J.D., *Lone Wolf Terrorism: Understanding the Growing Threat* (Prometheus Books, 2013)

Szikinger, I., Privacy, 'Secrecy, Idiocy: A Response to Mark Neocleous' (2002) 69 *Social Research* 1

Thoreau, H.D., *Walden or Life in the Woods; and on the Duty of Civil Disobedience* (New American Library, 1960)

Tomkins, A., *The Constitution after Scott: Government Unwrapped* (OUP, 1998)

Vaughn, R.G., *The Success and Failures of Whistleblower Laws* (Edward Elgar, 2012)

Vickers, L., *Freedom of Speech and Employment* (OUP, 2002)

Walsh, J.I., *The International Politics of Intelligence Sharing* (Columbia University Press, 2010)

Yihdego, Z. and Savage, A., 'The UK Arms Export Regime: Progress and Challenges' (2008) *Public Law* 546

Yong, B. and Hazel, R., *Special Advisers: Who They Are and Why They Matter* (Hart, 2014)

Index